Machine Learning Algorithms

Reference guide for popular algorithms for data science and machine learning

Giuseppe Bonaccorso

BIRMINGHAM - MUMBAI

Machine Learning Algorithms

First published: July 2017

Production reference: 1200717

Published by Packt Publishing Ltd.
Livery Place
35 Livery Street
Birmingham
B3 2PB, UK.
ISBN 978-1-78588-962-2

www.packtpub.com

Credits

Author
Giuseppe Bonaccorso

Reviewers
Manuel Amunategui
Doug Ortiz
Lukasz Tracewski

Commissioning Editor
Veena Pagare

Acquisition Editor
Divya Poojari

Content Development Editor
Mayur Pawanikar

Technical Editor
Prasad Ramesh

Copy Editors
Vikrant Phadkay
Alpha Singh

Project Coordinator
Nidhi Joshi

Proofreader
Safis Editing

Indexer
Tejal Daruwale Soni

Graphics
Tania Dutta

Production Coordinator
Arvindkumar Gupta

About the Author

Giuseppe Bonaccorso is a machine learning and big data consultant with more than 12 years of experience. He has an M.Eng. in electronics engineering from the University of Catania, Italy, and further postgraduate specialization from the University of Rome, Tor Vergata, Italy, and the University of Essex, UK. During his career, he has covered different IT roles in several business contexts, including public administration, military, utilities, healthcare, diagnostics, and advertising. He has developed and managed projects using many technologies, including Java, Python, Hadoop, Spark, Theano, and TensorFlow. His main interests on artificial intelligence, machine learning, data science, and philosophy of mind.

About the Reviewers

Manuel Amunategui is the VP of data science at SpringML, a start-up offering Google Cloud, TensorFlow, and Salesforce enterprise solutions. Prior to that, he worked as a quantitative developer on Wall Street for a large equity options market-making firm and as a software developer at Microsoft. He holds master's degrees in predictive analytics and international administration.

He is a data science advocate, blogger/vlogger (`http://amunategui.github.io`) and trainer on Udemy.com and O'Reilly Media, and technical reviewer at Packt.

Doug Ortiz is a senior big data architect at ByteCubed who has been architecting, developing, and integrating enterprise solutions throughout his career. Organizations that leverage his skill set have been able to rediscover and reuse their underutilized data via existing and emerging technologies such as Microsoft BI Stack, Hadoop, NoSQL databases, SharePoint, and related tool sets and technologies. He is also the founder of Illustris, LLC and can be reached at `ougortiz@illustris.org`.

Some interesting aspects of his profession are that he has experience in integrating multiple platforms and products, big data, data science certifications, R, and Python certifications. Doug also helps organizations gain a deeper understanding of and value their current investments in data and existing resources, turning them into useful sources of information. He has improved, salvaged, and architected projects by utilizing unique and innovative techniques. His hobbies include yoga and scuba diving.

Lukasz Tracewski is a software developer and a scientist, specializing in machine learning, digital signal processing, and cloud computing. Being an active member of open source community, he is also an author of numerous research publications. He has worked for 6 years as a software scientist in high-tech industry in the Netherlands, first in photolithography and later in electron microscopy, helping to build algorithms and machines that reach physical limits of throughput and precision. Currently, he leads a data science team in the financial industry.

For 4 years now, Lukasz has been using his skills pro bono in conservation science, involved in topics such as classification of bird species from audio recordings or satellite imagery analysis. He inhales carbon dioxide and exhales endangered species in his spare time.

www.PacktPub.com

For support files and downloads related to your book, please visit www.PacktPub.com.

Did you know that Packt offers eBook versions of every book published, with PDF and ePub files available? You can upgrade to the eBook version at www.PacktPub.com and as a print book customer, you are entitled to a discount on the eBook copy. Get in touch with us at service@packtpub.com for more details.

At www.PacktPub.com, you can also read a collection of free technical articles, sign up for a range of free newsletters and receive exclusive discounts and offers on Packt books and eBooks.

https://www.packtpub.com/mapt

Get the most in-demand software skills with Mapt. Mapt gives you full access to all Packt books and video courses, as well as industry-leading tools to help you plan your personal development and advance your career.

Why subscribe?

- Fully searchable across every book published by Packt
- Copy and paste, print, and bookmark content
- On demand and accessible via a web browser

Customer Feedback

Thanks for purchasing this Packt book. At Packt, quality is at the heart of our editorial process. To help us improve, please leave us an honest review on this book's Amazon page at https://www.amazon.com/dp/1785889621.

If you'd like to join our team of regular reviewers, you can e-mail us at customerreviews@packtpub.com. We award our regular reviewers with free eBooks and videos in exchange for their valuable feedback. Help us be relentless in improving our products!

Table of Contents

Preface

This book is an introduction to the world of machine learning, a topic that is becoming more and more important, not only for IT professionals and analysts but also for all those scientists and engineers who want to exploit the enormous power of techniques such as predictive analysis, classification, clustering and natural language processing. Of course, it's impossible to cover all the details with the appropriate precision; for this reason, some topics are only briefly described, giving the user the double opportunity to focus only on some fundamental concepts and, through the references, examine in depth all those elements that will generate much interest. I apologize in advance for any imprecision or mistakes, and I'd like to thank all Packt editors for their collaboration and constant attention.

I dedicate this book to my parents, who always believed in me and encouraged me to cultivate my passion for this extraordinary subject.

What this book covers

Chapter 1, *A Gentle Introduction to Machine Learning*, introduces the world of machine learning, explaining the fundamental concepts of the most important approaches to creating intelligent applications.

Chapter 2, *Important Elements in Machine Learning*, explains the mathematical concepts regarding the most common machine learning problems, including the concept of learnability and some elements of information theory.

Chapter 3, *Feature Selection and Feature Engineering*, describes the most important techniques used to preprocess a dataset, select the most informative features, and reduce the original dimensionality.

Chapter 4, *Linear Regression*, describes the structure of a continuous linear model, focusing on the linear regression algorithm. This chapter covers also Ridge, Lasso, and ElasticNet optimizations, and other advanced techniques.

Chapter 5, *Logistic Regression*, introduces the concept of linear classification, focusing on logistic regression and stochastic gradient descent algorithms. The second part covers the most important evaluation metrics.

Chapter 6, *Naive Bayes*, explains the Bayes probability theory and describes the structure of the most diffused naive Bayes classifiers.

Chapter 7, *Support Vector Machines*, introduces this family of algorithms, focusing on both linear and nonlinear classification problems.

Chapter 8, *Decision Trees and Ensemble Learning*, explains the concept of a hierarchical decision process and describes the concepts of decision tree classification, Bootstrap and bagged trees, and voting classifiers.

Chapter 9, *Clustering Fundamentals*, introduces the concept of clustering, describing the k-means algorithm and different approaches to determining the optimal number of clusters. In the second part, the chapter covers other clustering algorithms such as DBSCAN and spectral clustering.

Chapter 10, *Hierarchical Clustering*, continues the explanation started in the previous chapter and introduces the concept of agglomerative clustering.

Chapter 11, *Introduction to Recommendation Systems*, explains the most diffused algorithms employed in recommender systems: content- and user-based strategies, collaborative filtering, and alternating least square.

Chapter 12, *Introduction to Natural Language Processing*, explains the concept of bag-of-words and introduces the most important techniques required to efficiently process natural language datasets.

Chapter 13, *Topic Modeling and Sentiment Analysis in NLP*, introduces the concept of topic modeling and describes the most important algorithms, such as latent semantic analysis and latent Dirichlet allocation. In the second part, the chapter covers the problem of sentiment analysis, explaining the most diffused approaches to address it.

Chapter 14, *A Brief Introduction to Deep Learning and TensorFlow*, introduces the world of deep learning, explaining the concept of neural networks and computational graphs. The second part is dedicated to a brief exposition of the main concepts regarding the TensorFlow and Keras frameworks, with some practical examples.

Chapter 15, *Creating a Machine Learning Architecture*, explains how to define a complete machine learning pipeline, focusing on the peculiarities and drawbacks of each step.

What you need for this book

There are no particular mathematical prerequisites; however, to fully understand all the algorithms, it's important to have a basic knowledge of linear algebra, probability theory, and calculus.

All practical examples are written in Python and use the **scikit-learn** machine learning framework, **Natural Language Toolkit (NLTK)**, **Crab, langdetect, Spark, gensim**, and **TensorFlow** (deep learning framework). These are available for Linux, Mac OS X, and Windows, with Python 2.7 and 3.3+. When a particular framework is employed for a specific task, detailed instructions and references will be provided.

scikit-learn, NLTK, and TensorFlow can be installed by following the instructions provided on these websites: http://scikit-learn.org, http ://www.nltk.org, and https://www.tensorflow.org.

Who this book is for

This book is for IT professionals who want to enter the field of data science and are very new to machine learning. Familiarity with the Python language will be invaluable here. Moreover, basic mathematical knowledge (linear algebra, calculus, and probability theory) is required to fully comprehend the content of most of the chapters.

Conventions

In this book, you will find a number of text styles that distinguish between different kinds of information. Here are some examples of these styles and an explanation of their meaning. Code words in text, database table names, folder names, filenames, file extensions, pathnames, dummy URLs, user input, and Twitter handles are shown as follows: "We have created a configuration through the SparkConf class."

Any command-line input or output is written as follows:

```
>>> nn = NearestNeighbors(n_neighbors=10, radius=5.0, metric='hamming')
>>> nn.fit(items)
```

New terms and **important words** are shown in bold.

Warnings or important notes appear in a box like this.

Tips and tricks appear like this.

Reader feedback

Feedback from our readers is always welcome. Let us know what you think about this book-what you liked or disliked. Reader feedback is important for us as it helps us develop titles that you will really get the most out of. To send us general feedback, simply e-mail `feedback@packtpub.com`, and mention the book's title in the subject of your message. If there is a topic that you have expertise in and you are interested in either writing or contributing to a book, see our author guide at `www.packtpub.com/authors`.

Customer support

Now that you are the proud owner of a Packt book, we have a number of things to help you to get the most from your purchase.

Downloading the example code

You can download the example code files for this book from your account at `http://www.packtpub.com`. If you purchased this book elsewhere, you can visit `http://www.packtpub.com/support`, and register to have the files e-mailed directly to you. You can download the code files by following these steps:

1. Log in or register to our website using your e-mail address and password.
2. Hover the mouse pointer on the **SUPPORT** tab at the top.
3. Click on **Code Downloads & Errata**.
4. Enter the name of the book in the **Search** box.
5. Select the book for which you're looking to download the code files.
6. Choose from the drop-down menu where you purchased this book from.
7. Click on **Code Download**.

Once the file is downloaded, please make sure that you unzip or extract the folder using the latest version of:

- WinRAR / 7-Zip for Windows
- Zipeg / iZip / UnRarX for Mac
- 7-Zip / PeaZip for Linux

The code bundle for the book is also hosted on GitHub at `https://github.com/PacktPubl ishing/Machine-Learning-Algorithms`. We also have other code bundles from our rich catalog of books and videos available at `https://github.com/PacktPublishing/`. Check them out!

Downloading the color images of this book

We also provide you with a PDF file that has color images of the screenshots/diagrams used in this book. The color images will help you better understand the changes in the output. You can download this file from `https://www.packtpub.com/sites/default/files/down loads/MachineLearningAlgorithms_ColorImages.pdf`.

Errata

Although we have taken every care to ensure the accuracy of our content, mistakes do happen. If you find a mistake in one of our books-maybe a mistake in the text or the code-we would be grateful if you could report this to us. By doing so, you can save other readers from frustration and help us improve subsequent versions of this book. If you find any errata, please report them by visiting `http://www.packtpub.com/submit-errata`, selecting your book, clicking on the **Errata Submission Form** link, and entering the details of your errata. Once your errata are verified, your submission will be accepted and the errata will be uploaded to our website or added to any list of existing errata under the Errata section of that title. To view the previously submitted errata, go to `https://www.packtpub.com/book s/content/support`, and enter the name of the book in the search field. The required information will appear under the **Errata** section.

Piracy

Piracy of copyrighted material on the Internet is an ongoing problem across all media. At Packt, we take the protection of our copyright and licenses very seriously. If you come across any illegal copies of our works in any form on the Internet, please provide us with the location address or website name immediately so that we can pursue a remedy. Please contact us at `copyright@packtpub.com` with a link to the suspected pirated material. We appreciate your help in protecting our authors and our ability to bring you valuable content.

Questions

If you have a problem with any aspect of this book, you can contact us at `questions@packtpub.com`, and we will do our best to address the problem.

1
A Gentle Introduction to Machine Learning

In the last few years, machine learning has become one of the most important and prolific IT and artificial intelligence branches. It's not surprising that its applications are becoming more widespread day by day in every business sector, always with new and more powerful tools and results. Open source, production-ready frameworks, together with hundreds of papers published every month, are contributing to one of the most pervasive democratization processes in IT history. But why is machine learning so important and valuable?

Introduction - classic and adaptive machines

Since time immemorial, human beings have built tools and machines to simplify their work and reduce the overall effort needed to complete many different tasks. Even without knowing any physical law, they invented levers (formally described for the first time by Archimedes), instruments, and more complex machines to carry out longer and more sophisticated procedures. Hammering a nail became easier and more painless thanks to a simple trick, so did moving heavy stones or wood using a cart. But, what's the difference between these two examples? Even if the latter is still a simple machine, its complexity allows a person to carry out a composite task without thinking about each step. Some fundamental mechanical laws play a primary role in allowing a horizontal force to contrast gravity efficiently, but neither human beings nor horses or oxen knew anything about them. The primitive people simply observed how a genial trick (the wheel) could improve their lives.

The lesson we've learned is that a machine is never efficient or trendy without a concrete possibility to use it with pragmatism. A machine is immediately considered useful and destined to be continuously improved if its users can easily understand what tasks can be completed with less effort or completely automatically. In the latter case, some intelligence seems to appear next to cogs, wheels, or axles. So a further step can be added to our evolution list: automatic machines, built (nowadays we'd say programmed) to accomplish specific goals by transforming energy into work. Wind or watermills are some examples of elementary tools able to carry out complete tasks with minimal (compared to a direct activity) human control.

In the following figure, there's a generic representation of a classical system that receives some input values, processes them, and produces output results:

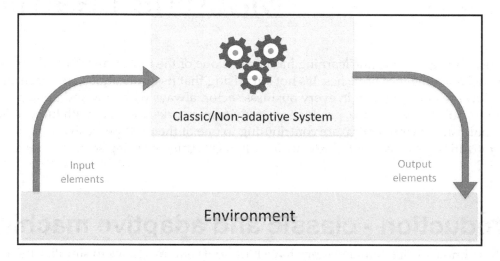

But again, what's the key to the success of a mill? It's not hasty at all to say that human beings have tried to transfer some intelligence into their tools since the dawn of technology. Both the water in a river and the wind show a behavior that we can simply call flowing. They have a lot of energy to give us free of any charge, but a machine should have some awareness to facilitate this process. A wheel can turn around a fixed axle millions of times, but the wind must find a suitable surface to push on. The answer seems obvious, but you should try to think about people without any knowledge or experience; even if implicitly, they started a brand new approach to technology. If you prefer to reserve the word intelligence to more recent results, it's possible to say that the path started with tools, moved first to simple machines and then to smarter ones.

Without further intermediate (but not less important) steps, we can jump into our epoch and change the scope of our discussion. Programmable computers are widespread, flexible, and more and more powerful instruments; moreover, the diffusion of the internet allowed us to share software applications and related information with minimal effort. The word-processing software that I'm using, my email client, a web browser, and many other common tools running on the same machine are all examples of such flexibility. It's undeniable that the IT revolution dramatically changed our lives and sometimes improved our daily jobs, but without **machine learning** (and all its applications), there are still many tasks that seem far out of computer domain. Spam filtering, Natural Language Processing, visual tracking with a webcam or a smartphone, and predictive analysis are only a few applications that revolutionized human-machine interaction and increased our expectations. In many cases, they transformed our electronic tools into actual cognitive extensions that are changing the way we interact with many daily situations. They achieved this goal by filling the gap between human perception, language, reasoning, and model and artificial instruments.

Here's a schematic representation of an adaptive system:

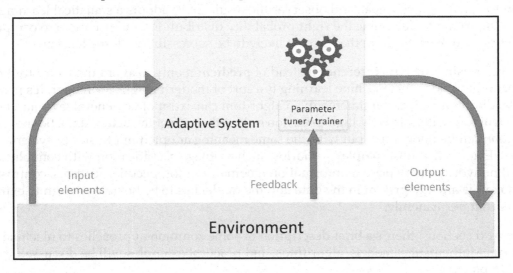

Such a system isn't based on static or permanent structures (model parameters and architectures) but rather on a continuous ability to adapt its behavior to external signals (datasets or real-time inputs) and, like a human being, to predict the future using uncertain and fragmentary pieces of information.

Only learning matters

What does learning exactly mean? Simply, we can say that learning is the ability to change according to external stimuli and remembering most of all previous experiences. So machine learning is an engineering approach that gives maximum importance to every technique that increases or improves the propensity for changing adaptively. A mechanical watch, for example, is an extraordinary artifact, but its structure obeys stationary laws and becomes useless if something external is changed. This ability is peculiar to animals and, in particular, to human beings; according to Darwin's theory, it's also a key success factor for the survival and evolution of all species. Machines, even if they don't evolve autonomously, seem to obey the same law.

Therefore, the main goal of machine learning is to study, engineer, and improve mathematical models which can be trained (once or continuously) with context-related data (provided by a generic environment), to infer the future and to make decisions without complete knowledge of all influencing elements (external factors). In other words, an agent (which is a software entity that receives information from an environment, picks the best action to reach a specific goal, and observes the results of it) adopts a statistical learning approach, trying to determine the right probability distributions and use them to compute the action (value or decision) that is most likely to be successful (with the least error).

I do prefer using the term **inference** instead of **prediction** only to avoid the weird (but not so uncommon) idea that machine learning is a sort of modern magic. Moreover, it's possible to introduce a fundamental statement: an algorithm can extrapolate general laws and learn their structure with relatively high precision only if they affect the actual data. So the term *prediction* can be freely used, but with the same meaning adopted in physics or system theory. Even in the most complex scenarios, such as image classification with convolutional neural networks, every piece of information (geometry, color, peculiar features, contrast, and so on) is already present in the data and the model has to be flexible enough to extract and learn it permanently.

In the next sections, there's a brief description of some common approaches to machine learning. Mathematical models, algorithms, and practical examples will be discussed in later chapters.

Supervised learning

A supervised scenario is characterized by the concept of a teacher or supervisor, whose main task is to provide the agent with a precise measure of its error (directly comparable with output values). With actual algorithms, this function is provided by a training set made up of couples (input and expected output). Starting from this information, the agent can correct its parameters so as to reduce the magnitude of a global loss function. After each iteration, if the algorithm is flexible enough and data elements are coherent, the overall accuracy increases and the difference between the predicted and expected value becomes close to zero. Of course, in a supervised scenario, the goal is training a system that must also work with samples never seen before. So, it's necessary to allow the model to develop a generalization ability and avoid a common problem called **overfitting**, which causes an *overlearning* due to an excessive capacity (we're going to discuss this in more detail in the next chapters, however we can say that one of the main effects of such a problem is the ability to predict correctly only the samples used for training, while the error for the remaining ones is always very high).

In the following figure, a few training points are marked with circles and the thin blue line represents a perfect generalization (in this case, the connection is a simple segment):

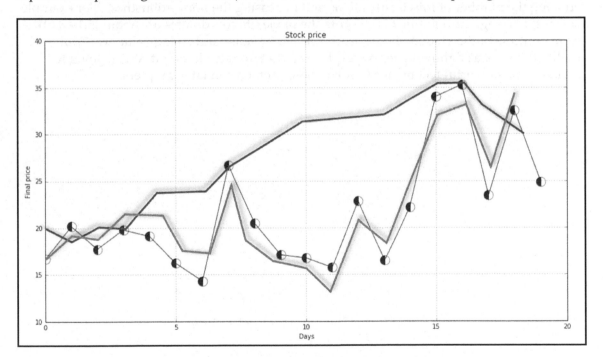

Two different models are trained with the same datasets (corresponding to the two larger lines). The former is unacceptable because it cannot generalize and capture the fastest dynamics (in terms of frequency), while the latter seems a very good compromise between the original trend and a residual ability to generalize correctly in a predictive analysis.

Formally, the previous example is called **regression** because it's based on continuous output values. Instead, if there is only a discrete number of possible outcomes (called **categories**), the process becomes a **classification.** Sometimes, instead of predicting the actual category, it's better to determine its probability distribution. For example, an algorithm can be trained to recognize a handwritten alphabetical letter, so its output is categorical (in English, there'll be 26 allowed symbols). On the other hand, even for human beings, such a process can lead to more than one probable outcome when the visual representation of a letter isn't clear enough to belong to a single category. That means that the actual output is better described by a discrete probability distribution (for example, with 26 continuous values normalized so that they always sum up to 1).

In the following figure, there's an example of classification of elements with two features. The majority of algorithms try to find the best separating hyperplane (in this case, it's a linear problem) by imposing different conditions. However, the goal is always the same: reducing the number of misclassifications and increasing the noise-robustness. For example, look at the triangular point that is closer to the plane (its coordinates are about [5.1 - 3.0]). If the magnitude of the second feature were affected by noise and so the value were quite smaller than 3.0, a slightly higher hyperplane could wrongly classify it. We're going to discuss some powerful techniques to solve these problems in later chapters.

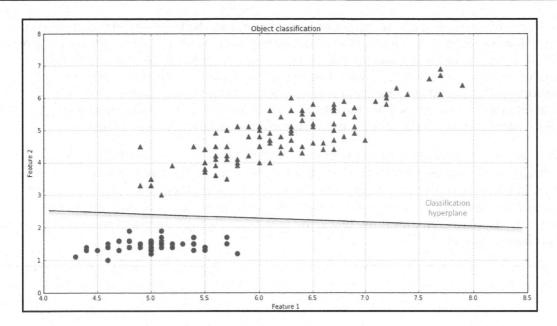

Common supervised learning applications include:

- Predictive analysis based on regression or categorical classification
- Spam detection
- Pattern detection
- Natural Language Processing
- Sentiment analysis
- Automatic image classification
- Automatic sequence processing (for example, music or speech)

Unsupervised learning

This approach is based on the absence of any supervisor and therefore of absolute error measures; it's useful when it's necessary to learn how a set of elements can be grouped (clustered) according to their similarity (or distance measure). For example, looking at the previous figure, a human being can immediately identify two sets without considering the colors or the shapes. In fact, the circular dots (as well as the triangular ones) determine a coherent set; it is separate from the other one much more than how its points are internally separated. Using a metaphor, an ideal scenario is a sea with a few islands that can be separated from each other considering only their mutual position and internal cohesion.

In the next figure, each ellipse represents a cluster and all the points inside its area can be labeled in the same way. There are also boundary points (such as the triangles overlapping the circle area) that need a specific criterion (normally a trade-off distance measure) to determine the corresponding cluster. Just as for classification with ambiguities (P and malformed R), a good clustering approach should consider the presence of outliers and treat them so as to increase both the internal coherence (visually, this means picking a subdivision that maximizes the local density) and the separation among clusters.

For example, it's possible to give priority to the distance between a single point and a centroid, or the average distance among points belonging to the same cluster and different ones. In this figure, all boundary triangles are close to each other, so the nearest neighbor is another triangle. However, in real-life problems, there are often boundary areas where there's a partial overlap, meaning that some points have a high degree of uncertainty due to their feature values.

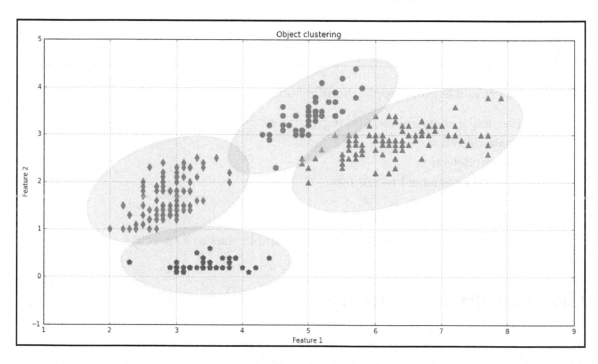

Another interpretation can be expressed using probability distributions. If you look at the ellipses, they represent the area of multivariate Gaussians bound between a minimum and maximum variance. Considering the whole domain, a point (for example, a blue star) could potentially belong to all clusters, but the probability given by the first one (lower-left corner) is the highest, and so this determines the membership. Once the variance and mean (in other words, the shape) of all Gaussians become stable, each boundary point is automatically captured by a single Gaussian distribution (except in the case of equal probabilities). Technically, we say that such an approach maximizes the likelihood of a Gaussian mixture given a certain dataset. This is a very important statistical learning concept that spans many different applications, so it will be examined in more depth in the next chapter. Moreover, we're going to discuss some common clustering methodologies, considering both strong and weak points and comparing their performances for various test distributions.

Other important techniques involve the usage of both labeled and unlabeled data. This approach is therefore called semi-supervised and can be adopted when it's necessary to categorize a large amount of data with a few complete (labeled) examples or when there's the need to impose some constraints to a clustering algorithm (for example, assigning some elements to a specific cluster or excluding others).

Commons unsupervised applications include:

- Object segmentation (for example, users, products, movies, songs, and so on)
- Similarity detection
- Automatic labeling

Reinforcement learning

Even if there are no actual supervisors, reinforcement learning is also based on feedback provided by the environment. However, in this case, the information is more qualitative and doesn't help the agent in determining a precise measure of its error. In reinforcement learning, this feedback is usually called **reward** (sometimes, a negative one is defined as a penalty) and it's useful to understand whether a certain action performed in a state is positive or not. The sequence of most useful actions is a policy that the agent has to learn, so to be able to make always the best decision in terms of the highest immediate and cumulative reward. In other words, an action can also be imperfect, but in terms of a global policy it has to offer the highest total reward. This concept is based on the idea that a rational agent always pursues the objectives that can increase his/her wealth. The ability to *see* over a distant horizon is a distinction mark for advanced agents, while short-sighted ones are often unable to correctly evaluate the consequences of their immediate actions and so their strategies are always sub-optimal.

Reinforcement learning is particularly efficient when the environment is not completely deterministic, when it's often very dynamic, and when it's impossible to have a precise error measure. During the last few years, many classical algorithms have been applied to deep neural networks to learn the best policy for playing Atari video games and to teach an agent how to associate the right action with an input representing the state (usually a screenshot or a memory dump).

In the following figure, there's a schematic representation of a deep neural network trained to play a famous Atari game. As input, there are one or more subsequent screenshots (this can often be enough to capture the temporal dynamics as well). They are processed using different layers (discussed briefly later) to produce an output that represents the policy for a specific state transition. After applying this policy, the game produces a feedback (as a reward-penalty), and this result is used to refine the output until it becomes stable (so the states are correctly recognized and the suggested action is always the best one) and the total reward overcomes a predefined threshold.

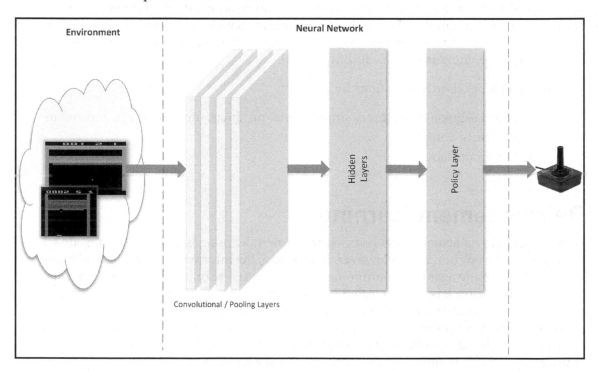

We're going to discuss some examples of reinforcement learning in the chapter dedicated to introducing deep learning and TensorFlow.

Beyond machine learning - deep learning and bio-inspired adaptive systems

During the last few years, thanks to more powerful and cheaper computers, many researchers started adopting complex (deep) neural architectures to achieve goals there were unimaginable only two decades ago. Since 1957, when Rosenblatt invented the first perceptron, interest in neural networks has grown more and more. However, many limitations (concerning memory and CPU speed) prevented massive research and hid lots of potential applications of these kinds of algorithms.

In the last decade, many researchers started training bigger and bigger models, built with several different layers (that's why this approach is called **deep learning**), to solve new challenging problems. The availability of cheap and fast computers allowed them to get results in acceptable timeframes and to use very large datasets (made up of images, texts, and animations). This effort led to impressive results, in particular for classification based on photo elements and real-time intelligent interaction using reinforcement learning.

The idea behind these techniques is to create algorithms that work like a brain and many important advancements in this field have been achieved thanks to the contribution of neurosciences and cognitive psychology. In particular, there's a growing interest in pattern recognition and associative memories whose structure and functioning are similar to what happens in the neocortex. Such an approach also allows simpler algorithms called **model-free**; these aren't based on any mathematical-physical formulation of a particular problem but rather on generic learning techniques and repeating experiences.

Of course, testing different architectures and optimization algorithms is quite simpler (and it can be done with parallel processing) than defining a complex model (which is also more difficult to adapt to different contexts). Moreover, deep learning showed better performance than other approaches, even without a context-based model. This suggests that in many cases, it's better to have a less precise decision made with uncertainty than a precise one determined by the output of a very complex model (often not so fast). For animals, this is often a matter of life and death, and if they succeed, it is thanks to an implicit renounce of some precision.

Common deep learning applications include:

- Image classification
- Real-time visual tracking
- Autonomous car driving
- Logistic optimization
- Bioinformatics
- Speech recognition

Many of these problems can also be solved using classic approaches, sometimes much more complex, but deep learning outperformed them all. Moreover, it allowed extending their application to contexts initially considered extremely complex, such as autonomous cars or real-time visual object identification.

This book covers in detail only some classical algorithms; however, there are many resources that can be read both as an introduction and for a more advanced insight.

 Many interesting results have been achieved by the Google DeepMind team (`https://deepmind.com`) and I suggest you visit their website to learn about their latest research and goals.

Machine learning and big data

Another area that can be exploited using machine learning is big data. After the first release of Apache Hadoop, which implemented an efficient MapReduce algorithm, the amount of information managed in different business contexts grew exponentially. At the same time, the opportunity to use it for machine learning purposes arose and several applications such as mass collaborative filtering became reality.

Imagine an online store with a million users and only one thousand products. Consider a matrix where each user is associated with every product by an implicit or explicit ranking. This matrix will contain 1,000,000 x 1,000 cells, and even if the number of products is very limited, any operation performed on it will be slow and memory-consuming. Instead, using a cluster, together with parallel algorithms, such a problem disappears and operations with higher dimensionality can be carried out in a very short time.

Think about training an image classifier with a million samples. A single instance needs to iterate several times, processing small batches of pictures. Even if this problem can be performed using a streaming approach (with a limited amount of memory), it's not surprising to wait even for a few days before the model begins to perform well. Adopting a big data approach instead, it's possible to asynchronously train several local models, periodically share the updates, and re-synchronize them all with a master model. This technique has also been exploited to solve some reinforcement learning problems, where many agents (often managed by different threads) played the same game, providing their periodical contribute to a *global* intelligence.

Not every machine learning problem is suitable for big data, and not all big datasets are really useful when training models. However, their conjunction in particular situations can drive to extraordinary results by removing many limitations that often affect smaller scenarios.

In the chapter dedicated to recommendation systems, we're going to discuss how to implement collaborative filtering using Apache Spark. The same framework will be also adopted for an example of Naive Bayes classification.

 If you want to know more about the whole Hadoop ecosystem, visit `http://hadoop.apache.org`. Apache Mahout (`http://mahout.apache.org`) is a dedicated machine learning framework and Spark (`http://spark.apache.org`), one the fastest computational engines, has a module called **MLib** that implements many common algorithms that benefit from parallel processing.

Further reading

An excellent introduction to artificial intelligence can be found in the first few chapters of Russel S., Norvig P., *Artificial Intelligence: A Modern Approach*, Pearson. In the second volume, there's also a very extensive discussion on statistical learning in many different contexts. A complete book on deep learning is Goodfellow I., Bengio Y., Courville A., *Deep Learning*, The MIT Press. If you would like to learn more about how the neocortex works, a simple but stunning introduction is present in Kurzweil R., *How to Create a Mind*, Duckworth Overlook. A comprehensive introduction to the Python programming language can be found in Lutz M., *Learning Python*, O'Reilly.

Summary

In this chapter, we introduced the concept of adaptive systems; they can learn from their experiences and modify their behavior in order to maximize the possibility of reaching a specific goal. Machine learning is the name given to a set of techniques that allow implementing adaptive algorithms to make predictions and to auto-organize input data according to their common features.

The three main learning strategies are supervised, unsupervised, and reinforcement. The first one assumes the presence of a teacher that provides a precise feedback on errors. The algorithm can hence compare its output with the right one and correct its parameters accordingly. In an unsupervised scenario, there are no external teachers, so everything is learned directly from the data. An algorithm will try to find out all features common to a group of elements to be able to associate new samples with the right cluster. Examples of the former type are provided by all the automatic classifications of objects into a specific category according to some known features, while common applications of unsupervised learning are the automatic groupings of items with a subsequent labeling or processing. The third kind of learning is similar to supervised, but it receives only an environmental feedback about the quality of its actions. It doesn't know exactly what is wrong or the magnitude of its error but receives generic information that helps it in deciding whether to continue to adopt a policy or to pick another one.

In the next chapter, we're going to discuss some fundamental elements of machine learning, with particular focus on the mathematical notation and the main definitions that we'll need in all the other chapters. We'll also discuss important statistical learning concepts and some theory about learnability and its limits.

2
Important Elements in Machine Learning

In this chapter, we're going to discuss some important elements and approaches which span through all machine learning topics and also create a philosophical foundation for many common techniques. First of all, it's useful to understand the mathematical foundation of data formats and prediction functions. In most algorithms, these concepts are treated in different ways, but the goal is always the same. More recent techniques, such as deep learning, extensively use energy/loss functions, just like the one described in this chapter, and even if there are slight differences, a good machine learning result is normally associated with the choice of the best loss function and the usage of the right algorithm to minimize it.

Data formats

In a supervised learning problem, there will always be a dataset, defined as a finite set of real vectors with m features each:

$$X = \{\bar{x}_1, \bar{x}_2, \dots, \bar{x}_n\} \ where \ \bar{x}_i \in \mathbb{R}^m$$

Considering that our approach is always probabilistic, we need to consider each X as drawn from a statistical multivariate distribution D. For our purposes, it's also useful to add a very important condition upon the whole dataset X: we expect all samples to be **independent and identically distributed (i.i.d)**. This means all variables belong to the same distribution D, and considering an arbitrary subset of m values, it happens that:

$$P(\bar{x}_1, \bar{x}_2, \ldots, \bar{x}_m) = \prod_{i=1}^{m} P(\bar{x}_i)$$

The corresponding output values can be both numerical-continuous or categorical. In the first case, the process is called **regression**, while in the second, it is called **classification**. Examples of numerical outputs are:

$$Y = \{y_1, y_2, \ldots, y_n\} \text{ where } y_n \in (0,1) \text{ or } y_i \in \mathbb{R}^+$$

Categorical examples are:

$$y_i \in \{red, black, white, green\} \text{ or } y_i \in \{0,1\}$$

We define generic **regressor**, a vector-valued function which associates an input value to a continuous output and generic **classifier**, a vector-values function whose predicted output is categorical (discrete). If they also depend on an internal parameter vector which determines the actual instance of a generic predictor, the approach is called **parametric learning**:

$$\hat{y} = r(\bar{x}, \bar{\theta})$$

$$\hat{y} = c(\bar{x}, \bar{\theta})$$

where $\bar{\theta}$ is the generic internal parameter vector

On the other hand, **non-parametric learning** doesn't make initial assumptions about the family of predictors (for example, defining a generic parameterized version of *r(...)* and *c(...)*). A very common non-parametric family is called **instance-based learning** and makes real-time predictions (without pre-computing parameter values) based on hypothesis determined only by the training samples (instance set). A simple and widespread approach adopts the concept of neighborhoods (with a fixed radius). In a classification problem, a new sample is automatically surrounded by classified training elements and the output class is determined considering the preponderant one in the neighborhood. In this book, we're going to talk about another very important algorithm family belonging to this class: **kernel-based support vector machines**. More examples can be found in Russel S., Norvig P., *Artificial Intelligence: A Modern Approach*, Pearson.

The internal dynamics and the interpretation of all elements are peculiar to each single algorithm, and for this reason, we prefer not to talk now about thresholds or probabilities and try to work with an abstract definition. A generic parametric training process must find the best parameter vector which minimizes the regression/classification error given a specific training dataset and it should also generate a predictor that can correctly generalize when unknown samples are provided.

Another interpretation can be expressed in terms of additive noise:

$$\hat{y} = r(\bar{x}, \bar{\theta}) + n(\mu; \sigma^2)$$

$$\hat{y} = c(\bar{x}, \bar{\theta}) + n(\mu; \sigma^2)$$

$$where \; E[n] = 0 \; and \; E[n^2] = \sigma^2 \ll 1$$

For our purposes, we can expect zero-mean and low-variance Gaussian noise added to a perfect prediction. A training task must increase the signal-noise ratio by optimizing the parameters. Of course, whenever such a term doesn't have zero mean (independently from the other X values), probably it means that there's a hidden trend that must be taken into account (maybe a feature that has been prematurely discarded). On the other hand, high noise variance means that X is dirty and its measures are not reliable.

Until now we've assumed that both regression and classification operate on m-length vectors but produce a single value or single label (in other words, an input vector is always associated with only one output element). However, there are many strategies to handle multi-label classification and multi-output regression.

In unsupervised learning, we normally only have an input set X with m-length vectors, and we define clustering function (with n target clusters) with the following expression:

$$k_t = C(\bar{x}, \bar{\theta}) \; where \; k_t \in (0,1,2,\dots,n)$$

In most scikit-learn models, there is an instance variable `coef_` which contains all trained parameters. For example, in a single parameter linear regression (we're going to widely discuss it in the next chapters), the output will be:

```
>>> model = LinearRegression()
>>> model.fit(X, Y)
>>> model.coef_
array([ 9.10210898])
```

Multiclass strategies

When the number of output classes is greater than one, there are two main possibilities to manage a classification problem:

- One-vs-all
- One-vs-one

In both cases, the choice is transparent and the output returned to the user will always be the final value or class. However, it's important to understand the different dynamics in order to optimize the model and to always pick the best alternative.

One-vs-all

This is probably the most common strategy and is widely adopted by scikit-learn for most of its algorithms. If there are n output classes, n classifiers will be trained in parallel considering there is always a separation between an actual class and the remaining ones. This approach is relatively lightweight (at most, *n-1* checks are needed to find the right class, so it has an $O(n)$ complexity) and, for this reason, it's normally the default choice and there's no need for further actions.

One-vs-one

The alternative to one-vs-all is training a model for each pair of classes. The complexity is no longer linear (it's $O(n^2)$ indeed) and the right class is determined by a majority vote. In general, this choice is more expensive and should be adopted only when a full dataset comparison is not preferable.

 If you want to learn more about multiclass strategies implemented by scikit-learn, visit
`http://scikit-learn.org/stable/modules/multiclass.html`.

Learnability

A parametric model can be split into two parts: a static structure and a dynamic set of parameters. The former is determined by choice of a specific algorithm and is normally immutable (except in the cases when the model provides some re-modeling functionalities), while the latter is the objective of our optimization. Considering n unbounded parameters, they generate an n-dimensional space (imposing bounds results in a sub-space without relevant changes in our discussion) where each point, together with the immutable part of the estimator function, represents a learning hypothesis H (associated with a specific set of parameters):

$$H = \{\theta_1, \theta_2, \dots, \theta_n\}$$

The goal of a parametric learning process is to find the best hypothesis whose corresponding prediction error is minimum and the residual generalization ability is enough to avoid overfitting. In the following figure, there's an example of a dataset whose points must be classified as red (**Class A**) or blue (**Class B**). Three hypotheses are shown: the first one (the middle line starting from left) misclassifies one sample, while the lower and upper ones misclassify 13 and 23 samples respectively:

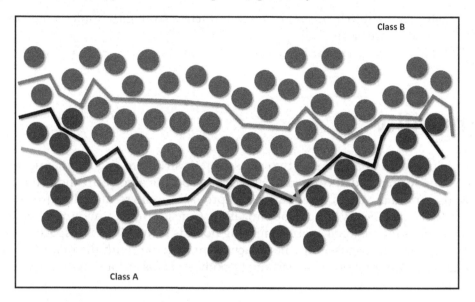

Of course, the first hypothesis is optimal and should be selected; however, it's important to understand an essential concept which can determine a potential overfitting. Think about an *n*-dimensional binary classification problem. We say that the dataset *X* is *linearly separable* (without transformations) if there exists a hyperplane which divides the space into two subspaces containing only elements belonging to the same class. Removing the constraint of linearity, we have infinite alternatives using generic hypersurfaces. However, a parametric model adopts only a family of non-periodic and approximate functions whose ability to oscillate and fit the dataset is determined (sometimes in a very complex way) by the number of parameters.

Consider the example shown in the following figure:

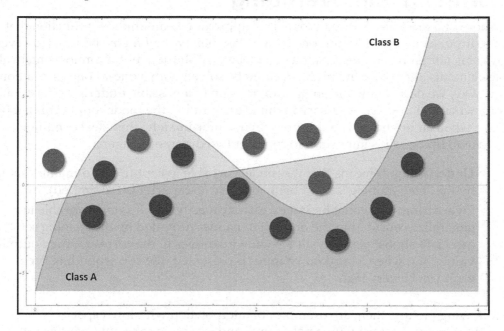

The blue classifier is linear while the red one is cubic. At a glance, non-linear strategy seems to perform better, because it can capture more expressivity, thanks to its concavities. However, if new samples are added following the trend defined by the last four ones (from the right), they'll be completely misclassified. In fact, while a linear function is globally better but cannot capture the initial oscillation between 0 and 4, a cubic approach can fit this data almost perfectly but, at the same time, loses its ability to keep a global linear trend. Therefore, there are two possibilities:

- If we expect future data to be exactly distributed as training samples, a more complex model can be a good choice, to capture small variations that a lower-level one will discard. In this case, a linear (or lower-level) model will drive to underfitting, because it won't be able to capture an appropriate level of expressivity.
- If we think that future data can be locally distributed differently but keeps a global trend, it's preferable to have a higher residual misclassification error as well as a more precise generalization ability. Using a bigger model focusing only on training data can drive to overfitting.

Underfitting and overfitting

The purpose of a machine learning model is to approximate an unknown function that associates input elements to output ones (for a classifier, we call them classes). However, a training set is normally a representation of a global distribution, but it cannot contain all possible elements; otherwise the problem could be solved with a one-to-one association. In the same way, we don't know the analytic expression of a possible underlying function, therefore, when training, it's necessary to think about fitting the model but keeping it free to generalize when an unknown input is presented. Unfortunately, this ideal condition is not always easy to find and it's important to consider two different dangers:

- **Underfitting**: It means that the model isn't able to capture the dynamics shown by the same training set (probably because its capacity is too limited).
- **Overfitting**: the model has an excessive capacity and it's not more able to generalize considering the original dynamics provided by the training set. It can associate almost perfectly all the known samples to the corresponding output values, but when an unknown input is presented, the corresponding prediction error can be very high.

In the following picture, there are examples of interpolation with low-capacity (underfitting), normal-capacity (normal fitting), and excessive capacity (overfitting):

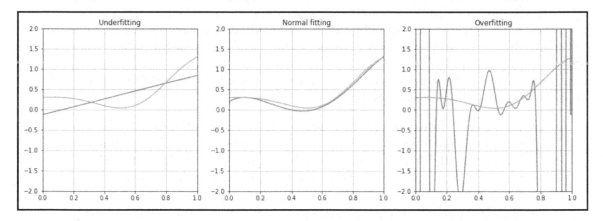

It's very important to avoid both underfitting and overfitting. Underfitting is easier to detect considering the prediction error, while overfitting may prove to be more difficult to discover as it could be initially considered the result of a perfect fitting.

Cross-validation and other techniques that we're going to discuss in the next chapters can easily show how our model works with test samples never seen during the training phase. That way, it would be possible to assess the generalization ability in a broader context (remember that we're not working with all possible values, but always with a subset that should reflect the original distribution).

However, a generic rule of thumb says that a residual error is always necessary to guarantee a good generalization ability, while a model that shows a validation accuracy of 99.999... percent on training samples is almost surely overfitted and will likely be unable to predict correctly when never-seen input samples are provided.

Error measures

In general, when working with a supervised scenario, we define a non-negative error measure e_m which takes two arguments (expected and predicted output) and allows us to compute a total error value over the whole dataset (made up of n samples):

$$Error_H = \sum_{i=1}^{n} e_m(\tilde{y}_i, y_i) \; where \; e_m \geq 0 \; \forall \tilde{y}_i, y_i$$

This value is also implicitly dependent on the specific hypothesis H through the parameter set, therefore optimizing the error implies finding an optimal hypothesis (considering the hardness of many optimization problems, this is not the absolute best one, but an acceptable approximation). In many cases, it's useful to consider the **mean square error** (**MSE**):

$$Error_H = \frac{1}{n} \sum_{i=1}^{n} (\tilde{y}_i - y_i)^2$$

Its initial value represents a starting point over the surface of a n-variables function. A generic training algorithm has to find the global minimum or a point quite close to it (there's always a tolerance to avoid an excessive number of iterations and a consequent risk of overfitting). This measure is also called **loss function** because its value must be minimized through an optimization problem. When it's easy to determine an element which must be maximized, the corresponding loss function will be its reciprocal.

Another useful loss function is called **zero-one-loss** and it's particularly efficient for binary classifications (also for one-vs-rest multiclass strategy):

$$L_{0/1H}(\tilde{y}_i, y_i) = \begin{cases} 0 & if \ \tilde{y}_i = y_i \\ 1 & if \ \tilde{y}_i \neq y_i \end{cases}$$

This function is implicitly an indicator and can be easily adopted in loss functions based on the probability of misclassification.

A helpful interpretation of a generic (and continuous) loss function can be expressed in terms of potential energy:

$$Energy_H = \frac{1}{2} \sum_{i=1}^{n} e_m(\tilde{y}_i, y_i)^2$$

The predictor is like a ball upon a rough surface: starting from a random point where energy (=error) is usually rather high, it must move until it reaches a stable equilibrium point where its energy (relative to the global minimum) is null. In the following figure, there's a schematic representation of some different situations:

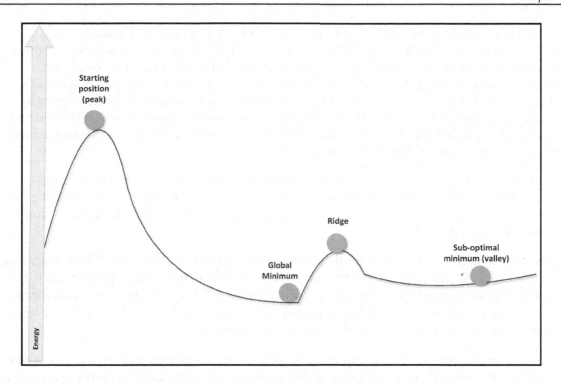

Just like in the physical situation, the starting point is stable without any external perturbation, so to start the process, it's needed to provide initial kinetic energy. However, if such an energy is strong enough, then after descending over the slope the ball cannot stop in the global minimum. The residual kinetic energy can be enough to overcome the ridge and reach the right valley. If there are not other energy sources, the ball gets trapped in the plain valley and cannot move anymore. There are many techniques that have been engineered to solve this problem and avoid local minima. However, every situation must always be carefully analyzed to understand what level of residual energy (or error) is acceptable, or whether it's better to adopt a different strategy. We're going to discuss some of them in the next chapters.

PAC learning

In many cases machine learning seems to work seamlessly, but is there any way to determine formally the learnability of a concept? In 1984, the computer scientist L. Valiant proposed a mathematical approach to determine whether a problem is learnable by a computer. The name of this technique is **PAC**, or **probably approximately correct**.

The original formulation (you can read it in Valiant L., *A Theory of the Learnable*, *Communications of the ACM*, Vol. 27, No. 11 , Nov. 1984) is based on a particular hypothesis, however, without a considerable loss of precision, we can think about a classification problem where an algorithm *A* has to learn a set of concepts. In particular, a concept is a subset of input patterns *X* which determine the same output element. Therefore, learning a concept (parametrically) means minimizing the corresponding loss function restricted to a specific class, while learning all possible concepts (belonging to the same universe), means finding the minimum of a global loss function.

However, given a problem, we have many possible (sometimes, theoretically infinite) hypotheses and a probabilistic trade-off is often necessary. For this reason, we accept good approximations with high probability based on a limited number of input elements and produced in polynomial time.

Therefore, an algorithm *A* can learn the class *C* of all concepts (making them PAC learnable) if it's able to find a hypothesis *H* with a procedure $O(n^k)$ so that *A*, with a probability *p*, can classify all patterns correctly with a maximum allowed error m_e. This must be valid for all statistical distributions on *X* and for a number of training samples which must be greater than or equal to a minimum value depending only on *p* and m_e.

The constraint to computation complexity is not a secondary matter, in fact, we expect our algorithms to learn efficiently in a reasonable time also when the problem is quite complex. An exponential time could lead to computational explosions when the datasets are too large or the optimization starting point is very far from an acceptable minimum. Moreover, it's important to remember the so-called **curse of dimensionality**, which is an effect that often happens in some models where training or prediction time is proportional (not always linearly) to the dimensions, so when the number of features increases, the performance of the models (that can be reasonable when the input dimensionality is small) gets dramatically reduced. Moreover, in many cases, in order to capture the full expressivity, it's necessary to have a very large dataset and without enough training data, the approximation can become problematic (this is called **Hughes phenomenon**). For these reasons, looking for polynomial-time algorithms is more than a simple effort, because it can determine the success or the failure of a machine learning problem. For these reasons, in the next chapters, we're going to introduce some techniques that can be used to efficiently reduce the dimensionality of a dataset without a problematic loss of information.

Statistical learning approaches

Imagine that you need to design a spam-filtering algorithm starting from this initial (over-simplistic) classification based on two parameters:

Parameter	Spam emails (X_1)	Regular emails $(X2)$
p_1 - Contains > 5 blacklisted words	80	20
p_2 - Message length < 20 characters	75	25

We have collected 200 email messages (X) (for simplicity, we consider p_1 and p_2 mutually exclusive) and we need to find a couple of probabilistic hypotheses (expressed in terms of p_1 and p_2), to determine:

$$P(spam|h_{p1}, h_{p2})$$

We also assume the conditional independence of both terms (it means that h_{p1} and h_{p2} contribute conjunctly to spam in the same way as they were alone).

For example, we could think about rules (hypotheses) like: "If there are more than five blacklisted words" or "If the message is less than 20 characters in length" then "the probability of spam is high" (for example, greater than 50 percent). However, without assigning probabilities, it's difficult to generalize when the dataset changes (like in a real world antispam filter). We also want to determine a partitioning threshold (such as green, yellow, and red signals) to help the user in deciding what to keep and what to trash.

As the hypotheses are determined through the dataset X, we can also write (in a discrete form):

$$P(spam|X) = \sum_i P(spam|h_{pi})P(h_{pi}|X)$$

In this example, it's quite easy to determine the value of each term. However, in general, it's necessary to introduce the Bayes formula (which will be discussed in `Chapter 6`, *Naive Bayes*):

$$P(h_{pi}|X) \propto P(X|h_{pi})P(h_{pi})$$

The proportionality is necessary to avoid the introduction of the marginal probability *P(X)*, which acts only as a normalization factor (remember that in a discrete random variable, the sum of all possible probability outcomes must be equal to 1).

In the previous equation, the first term is called **a posteriori** (which comes after) probability, because it's determined by a marginal **Apriori** (which comes first) probability multiplied by a factor which is called **likelihood**. To understand the philosophy of such an approach, it's useful to take a simple example: tossing a fair coin. Everybody knows that the marginal probability of each face is equal to 0.5, but who decided that? It's a theoretical consequence of logic and probability axioms (a good physicist would say that it's never 0.5 because of several factors that we simply discard). After tossing the coin 100 times, we observe the outcomes and, surprisingly, we discover that the ratio between heads and tails is slightly different (for example, 0.46). How can we correct our estimation? The term called **likelihood** measures how much our actual experiments confirm the Apriori hypothesis and determines another probability (**a posteriori**) which reflects the actual situation. The likelihood, therefore, helps us in correcting our estimation dynamically, overcoming the problem of a fixed probability.

In `Chapter 6`, *Naive Bayes*, dedicated to naive Bayes algorithms, we're going to discuss these topics deeply and implement a few examples with scikit-learn, however, it's useful to introduce here two statistical learning approaches which are very diffused. Refer to *Russel S., Norvig P., Artificial Intelligence: A Modern Approach, Pearson* for further information.

MAP learning

When selecting the right hypothesis, a Bayesian approach is normally one of the best choices, because it takes into account all the factors and, as we'll see, even if it's based on conditional independence, such an approach works perfectly when some factors are partially dependent. However, its complexity (in terms of probabilities) can easily grow because all terms must always be taken into account. For example, a real coin is a very short cylinder, so, in tossing a coin, we should also consider the probability of even. Let's say, it's 0.001. It means that we have three possible outcomes: *P(head)* = *P(tail)* = (1.0 - 0.001) / 2.0 and *P(even)* = 0.001. The latter event is obviously unlikely, but in Bayesian learning it must be considered (even if it'll be squeezed by the strength of the other terms).

An alternative is picking the most probable hypothesis in terms of **a posteriori** probability:

$$h_{MAP} : \; P(h_{MAP}|X) = max_i\{\, P(h_{pi}|X)\,\}$$

This approach is called **MAP (maximum a posteriori)** and it can really simplify the scenario when some hypotheses are quite unlikely (for example, in tossing a coin, a MAP hypothesis will discard *P(even)*). However, it still does have an important drawback: it depends on Apriori probabilities (remember that maximizing the a posteriori implies considering also the Apriori). As Russel and Norvig (Russel S., Norvig P., *Artificial Intelligence: A Modern Approach*, Pearson) pointed out, this is often a delicate part of an inferential process, because there's always a theoretical background which can drive to a particular choice and exclude others. In order to rely only on data, it's necessary to have a different approach.

Maximum-likelihood learning

We have defined likelihood as a filtering term in the Bayes formula. In general, it has the form of:

$$L\big(h_{pi}|X\big) = P(X|h_{pi})$$

Here the first term expresses the actual likelihood of a hypothesis, given a dataset X. As you can imagine, in this formula there are no more Apriori probabilities, so, maximizing it doesn't imply accepting a theoretical preferential hypothesis, nor considering unlikely ones. A very common approach, known as **expectation-maximization** and used in many algorithms (we're going to see an example in logistic regression), is split into two main parts:

- Determining a log-likelihood expression based on model parameters (they will be optimized accordingly)

- Maximizing it until residual error is small enough

A log-likelihood (normally called **L**) is a useful trick that can simplify gradient calculations. A generic likelihood expression is:

$$L(h_i|X) = \prod_k P(X|h)$$

As all parameters are inside h_i, the gradient is a complex expression which isn't very manageable. However our goal is maximizing the likelihood, but it's easier minimizing its reciprocal:

$$max_i\, L(h_i|X) = min_i\, \frac{1}{L(h_i|X)} = min_i\, \frac{1}{\prod_i P(X|h_i)}$$

This can be turned into a very simple expression by applying natural logarithm (which is monotonic):

$$max_i\, \log L(h_i|X) = min_i\, -\log L(h_i|X) = min_i\, \sum_i -\log P(X|h_i)$$

The last term is a summation which can be easily derived and used in most of the optimization algorithms. At the end of this process, we can find a set of parameters which provides the maximum likelihood without any strong statement about prior distributions. This approach can seem very technical, but its logic is really simple and intuitive. To understand how it works, I propose a simple exercise, which is part of Gaussian mixture technique discussed also in Russel S., Norvig P., *Artificial Intelligence: A Modern Approach*, Pearson.

Let's consider 100 points drawn from a Gaussian distribution with zero mean and a standard deviation equal to 2.0 (quasi-white noise made of independent samples):

```
import numpy as np

nb_samples = 100
X_data = np.random.normal(loc=0.0, scale=np.sqrt(2.0), size=nb_samples)
```

The plot is shown next:

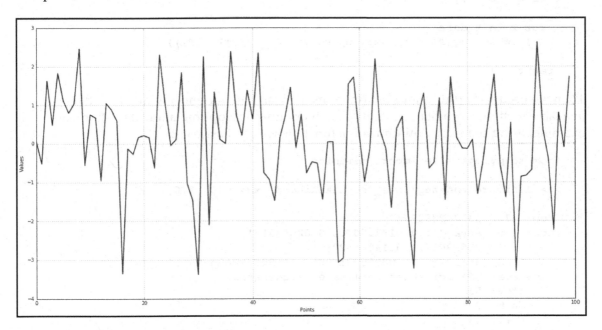

In this case, there's no need for a deep exploration (we know how they are generated), however, after restricting the hypothesis space to the Gaussian family (the most suitable considering only the graph), we'd like to find the best value for mean and variance. First of all, we need to compute the log-likelihood (which is rather simple thanks to the exponential function):

$$L(\mu, \sigma^2 | X) = \log P(X | \mu, \sigma^2) = \sum_i \log \frac{1}{\sqrt{2\pi\sigma^2}} e^{-\frac{(x_i - \mu)^2}{2\sigma^2}}$$

A simple Python implementation is provided next (for ease of use, there's only a single array which contains both mean (0) and variance (1)):

```python
def negative_log_likelihood(v):
    l = 0.0
    f1 = 1.0 / np.sqrt(2.0 * np.pi * v[1])
    f2 = 2.0 * v[1]

    for x in X_data:
        l += np.log(f1 * np.exp(-np.square(x - v[0]) / f2))

    return -l
```

Then we need to find its minimum (in terms of mean and variance) with any of the available methods (gradient descent or another numerical optimization algorithm). For example, using the `scipy` minimization function, we can easily get:

```python
from scipy.optimize import minimize

>>> minimize(fun=negative_log_likelihood, x0=[0.0, 1.0])

        fun: 172.33380423827057
   hess_inv: array([[ 0.01571807,  0.02658017],
        [ 0.02658017,  0.14686427]])
        jac: array([ 0.00000000e+00, -1.90734863e-06])
    message: 'Optimization terminated successfully.'
       nfev: 52
        nit: 9
       njev: 13
     status: 0
    success: True
          x: array([ 0.04088792,  1.83822255])
```

A graph of the negative log-likelihood function is plotted next. The global minimum of this function corresponds to an optimal likelihood given a certain distribution. It doesn't mean that the problem has been completely solved, because the first step of this algorithm is determining an expectation, which must be always realistic. The likelihood function, however, is quite sensitive to wrong distributions because it can easily get close to zero when the probabilities are low. For this reason, **maximum-likelihood (ML)** learning is often preferable to MAP learning, which needs Apriori distributions and can fail when they are not selected in the most appropriate way:

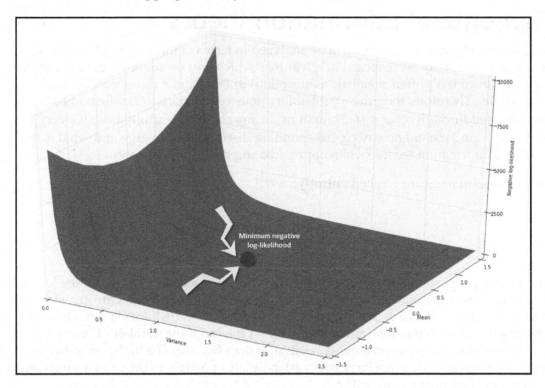

This approach has been applied to a specific distribution family (which is indeed very easy to manage), but it also works perfectly when the model is more complex. Of course, it's always necessary to have an initial awareness about how the likelihood should be determined because more than one feasible family can generate the same dataset. In all these cases, **Occam's razor** is the best way to proceed: the simplest hypothesis should be considered first. If it doesn't fit, an extra level of complexity can be added to our model. As we'll see, in many situations, the easiest solution is the winning one, and increasing the number of parameters or using a more detailed model can only add noise and a higher possibility of overfitting.

SciPy (https://www.scipy.org) is a set of high-end scientific and data-oriented libraries available for Python. It includes NumPy, Pandas, and many other useful frameworks. If you want to read more about Python scientific computing, refer to Johansson R., *Numerical Python*, Apress or Landau R. H., Pàez M. J., Bordeianu C. C., *Computational Physics. Problem Solving with Python*, Wiley-VCH.

Elements of information theory

A machine learning problem can also be analyzed in terms of information transfer or exchange. Our dataset is composed of n features, which are considered independent (for simplicity, even if it's often a realistic assumption) drawn from n different statistical distributions. Therefore, there are n probability density functions $p_i(x)$ which must be approximated through other n $q_i(x)$ functions. In any machine learning task, it's very important to understand how two corresponding distributions diverge and what is the amount of information we lose when approximating the original dataset.

The most useful measure is called **entropy**:

$$H(X) = -\sum_{x \in X} p(x) log_2 p(x)$$

This value is proportional to the uncertainty of X and it's measured in **bits** (if the logarithm has another base, this unit can change too). For many purposes, a high entropy is preferable, because it means that a certain feature contains more information. For example, in tossing a coin (two possible outcomes), $H(X) = 1$ bit, but if the number of outcomes grows, even with the same probability, $H(X)$ also does because of a higher number of different values and therefore increased variability. It's possible to prove that for a Gaussian distribution (using natural logarithm):

$$H(X) = \frac{1}{2}(1 + \ln(2\pi\sigma^2))$$

So, the entropy is proportional to the variance, which is a measure of the amount of information carried by a single feature. In the next chapter, we're going to discuss a method for feature selection based on variance threshold. Gaussian distributions are very common, so this example can be considered just as a general approach to feature filtering: low variance implies low information level and a model could often discard all those features.

In the following figure, there's a plot of *H(X)* for a Gaussian distribution expressed in **nats** (which is the corresponding unit measure when using natural logarithms):

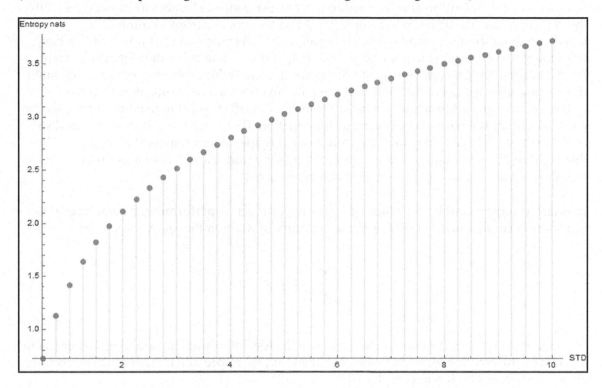

For example, if a dataset is made up of some features whose variance (here it's more convenient talking about standard deviation) is bounded between 8 and 10 and a few with *STD < 1.5*, the latter could be discarded with a limited loss in terms of information. These concepts are very important in real-life problems when large datasets must be cleaned and processed in an efficient way.

If we have a target probability distribution *p(x)*, which is approximated by another distribution *q(x)*, a useful measure is **cross-entropy** between *p* and *q* (we are using the discrete definition as our problems must be solved using numerical computations):

$$H(P,Q) = -\sum_{x \in X} p(x) log_2 q(x)$$

If the logarithm base is 2, it measures the number of bits requested to decode an event drawn from P when using a code optimized for Q. In many machine learning problems, we have a source distribution and we need to train an estimator to be able to identify correctly the class of a sample. If the error is null, $P = Q$ and the cross-entropy is minimum (corresponding to the entropy $H(P)$). However, as a null error is almost impossible when working with Q, we need to *pay* a price of $H(P, Q)$ bits, to determine the right class starting from a prediction. Our goal is often to minimize it, so to reduce this *price* under a threshold that cannot alter the predicted output if not paid. In other words, think about a binary output and a sigmoid function: we have a threshold of 0.5 (this is the maximum *price* we can pay) to identify the correct class using a step function (0.6 -> 1, 0.1 -> 0, 0.4999 -> 0, and so on). As we're not able to pay this *price*, since our classifier doesn't know the original distribution, it's necessary to reduce the cross-entropy under a tolerable noise-robustness threshold (which is always the smallest achievable one).

In order to understand how a machine learning approach is performing, it's also useful to introduce a **conditional** entropy or the uncertainty of X given the knowledge of Y:

$$H(X|Y) = - \sum_{x \in X, y \in Y} p(x, y) log_2 \frac{p(x, y)}{p(y)}$$

Through this concept, it's possible to introduce the idea of mutual information, which is the amount of information shared by both variables and therefore, the reduction of uncertainty about X provided by the knowledge of Y:

$$I(X; Y) = H(X) - H(X|Y)$$

Intuitively, when X and Y are independent, they don't share any information. However, in machine learning tasks, there's a very tight dependence between an original feature and its prediction, so we want to maximize the information shared by both distributions. If the conditional entropy is small enough (so Y is able to describe X quite well), the mutual information gets close to the marginal entropy $H(X)$, which measures the amount of information we want to learn.

An interesting learning approach based on the information theory, called **Minimum Description Length** (MDL), is discussed in Russel S., Norvig P., *Artificial Intelligence: A Modern Approach*, Pearson, where I suggest you look for any further information about these topics.

References

- Russel S., Norvig P., *Artificial Intelligence: A Modern Approach*, Pearson
- Valiant L., *A Theory of the Learnable, Communications of the ACM*, Vol. 27, No. 11 (Nov. 1984)
- Hastie T., Tibshirani R., Friedman J., *The Elements of Statistical Learning: Data Mining, Inference and, Prediction*, Springer
- Aleksandrov A.D., Kolmogorov A.N, Lavrent'ev M.A., *Mathematics: Its contents, Methods, and Meaning*, Courier Corporation

Summary

In this chapter, we have introduced some main concepts about machine learning. We started with some basic mathematical definitions, to have a clear view about data formats, standards, and kind of functions. This notation will be adopted in all the other chapters and it's also the most diffused in technical publications. We discussed how scikit-learn seamlessly works with multi-class problems, and when a strategy is preferable to another.

The next step was the introduction of some fundamental theoretical concepts about learnability. The main questions we tried to answer were: how can we decide if a problem can be learned by an algorithm and what is the maximum precision we can achieve. PAC learning is a generic but powerful definition that can be adopted when defining the boundaries of an algorithm. A PAC learnable problem, in fact, is not only manageable by a suitable algorithm but is also fast enough to be computed in polynomial time. Then we introduced some common statistical learning concepts, in particular, MAP and maximum likelihood learning approaches. The former tries to pick the hypothesis which maximizes the a posteriori probability, while the latter works the likelihood, looking for the hypothesis that best fits the data. This strategy is one of the most diffused in many machine learning problems because it's not affected by Apriori probabilities and it's very easy to implement in many different contexts. We also gave a physical interpretation of a loss function as an energy function. The goal of a training algorithm is to always try to find the global minimum point, which corresponds to the deepest valley in the error surface. At the end of this chapter, there was a brief introduction to information theory and how we can reinterpret our problems in terms of information gain and entropy. Every machine learning approach should work to minimize the amount of information needed to start from prediction and recover original (desired) outcomes.

In the next chapter, we're going to discuss the fundamental concepts of feature engineering, which is the first step in almost every machine learning pipeline. We're going to show how to manage different kinds of data (numerical and categorical) and how it's possible to reduce the dimensionality without a dramatic loss of information.

3
Feature Selection and Feature Engineering

Feature engineering is the first step in a machine learning pipeline and involves all the techniques adopted to clean existing datasets, increase their signal-noise ratio, and reduce their dimensionality. Most algorithms have strong assumptions about the input data, and their performances can be negatively affected when raw datasets are used. Moreover, the data is seldom isotropic; there are often features that determine the general behavior of a sample, while others that are correlated don't provide any additional pieces of information. So, it's important to have a clear view of a dataset and know the most common algorithms used to reduce the number of features or select only the best ones.

scikit-learn toy datasets

scikit-learn provides some built-in datasets that can be used for testing purposes. They're all available in the package `sklearn.datasets` and have a common structure: the data instance variable contains the whole input set X while target contains the labels for classification or target values for regression. For example, considering the Boston house pricing dataset (used for regression), we have:

```
from sklearn.datasets import load_boston

>>> boston = load_boston()
>>> X = boston.data
>>> Y = boston.target

>>> X.shape
(506, 13)
>>> Y.shape
```

```
(506,)
```

In this case, we have 506 samples with 13 features and a single target value. In this book, we're going to use it for regressions and the MNIST handwritten digit dataset (`load_digits()`) for classification tasks. scikit-learn also provides functions for creating dummy datasets from scratch: `make_classification()`, `make_regression()`, and `make_blobs()` (particularly useful for testing cluster algorithms). They're very easy to use and in many cases, it's the best choice to test a model without loading more complex datasets.

 Visit `http://scikit-learn.org/stable/datasets/` for further information.

 The MNIST dataset provided by scikit-learn is limited for obvious reasons. If you want to experiment with the original one, refer to the website managed by Y. LeCun, C. Cortes, C. Burges: `http://yann.lecun.com/exd b/mnist/`. Here you can download a full version made up of 70,000 handwritten digits already split into training and test sets.

Creating training and test sets

When a dataset is large enough, it's a good practice to split it into training and test sets; the former to be used for training the model and the latter to test its performances. In the following figure, there's a schematic representation of this process:

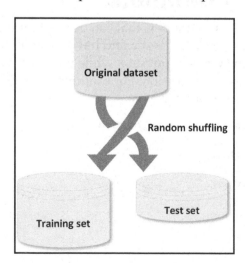

There are two main rules in performing such an operation:

- Both datasets must reflect the original distribution
- The original dataset must be randomly shuffled before the split phase in order to avoid a correlation between consequent elements

With scikit-learn, this can be achieved using the `train_test_split()` function:

```
from sklearn.model_selection import train_test_split

>>> X_train, X_test, Y_train, Y_test = train_test_split(X, Y,
test_size=0.25, random_state=1000)
```

The parameter `test_size` (as well as `training_size`) allows specifying the percentage of elements to put into the test/training set. In this case, the ratio is 75 percent for training and 25 percent for the test phase. Another important parameter is `random_state` which can accept a NumPy `RandomState` generator or an integer seed. In many cases, it's important to provide reproducibility for the experiments, so it's also necessary to avoid using different seeds and, consequently, different random splits:

My suggestion is to always use the same number (it can also be 0 or completely omitted), or define a global `RandomState` which can be passed to all requiring functions.

```
from sklearn.utils import check_random_state

>>> rs = check_random_state(1000)
<mtrand.RandomState at 0x12214708>

>>> X_train, X_test, Y_train, Y_test = train_test_split(X, Y,
test_size=0.25, random_state=rs)
```

In this way, if the seed is kept equal, all experiments have to lead to the same results and can be easily reproduced in different environments by other scientists.

For further information about NumPy random number generation, visit `ht tps://docs.scipy.org/doc/numpy/reference/generated/numpy.rando m.RandomState.html`.

Managing categorical data

In many classification problems, the target dataset is made up of categorical labels which cannot immediately be processed by any algorithm. An encoding is needed and scikit-learn offers at least two valid options. Let's consider a very small dataset made of 10 categorical samples with two features each:

```
import numpy as np

>>> X = np.random.uniform(0.0, 1.0, size=(10, 2))
>>> Y = np.random.choice(('Male','Female'), size=(10))
>>> X[0]
array([ 0.8236887 ,   0.11975305])
>>> Y[0]
'Male'
```

The first option is to use the `LabelEncoder` class, which adopts a dictionary-oriented approach, associating to each category label a progressive integer number, that is an index of an instance array called `classes_`:

```
from sklearn.preprocessing import LabelEncoder

>>> le = LabelEncoder()
>>> yt = le.fit_transform(Y)
>>> print(yt)
[0 0 0 1 0 1 1 0 0 1]

>>> le.classes_array(['Female', 'Male'], dtype='|S6')
```

The inverse transformation can be obtained in this simple way:

```
>>> output = [1, 0, 1, 1, 0, 0]
>>> decoded_output = [le.classes_[i] for i in output]
['Male', 'Female', 'Male', 'Male', 'Female', 'Female']
```

This approach is simple and works well in many cases, but it has a drawback: all labels are turned into sequential numbers. A classifier which works with real values will then consider similar numbers according to their distance, without any concern for semantics. For this reason, it's often preferable to use so-called **one-hot encoding**, which binarizes the data. For labels, it can be achieved using the `LabelBinarizer` class:

```
from sklearn.preprocessing import LabelBinarizer

>>> lb = LabelBinarizer()
>>> Yb = lb.fit_transform(Y)
array([[1],
```

```
        [0],
        [1],
        [1],
        [1],
        [1],
        [0],
        [1],
        [1],
        [1]])
>>> lb.inverse_transform(Yb)
array(['Male', 'Female', 'Male', 'Male', 'Male', 'Male', 'Female', 'Male',
       'Male', 'Male'], dtype='|S6')
```

In this case, each categorical label is first turned into a positive integer and then transformed into a vector where only one feature is 1 while all the others are 0. It means, for example, that using a softmax distribution with a peak corresponding to the main class can be easily turned into a discrete vector where the only non-null element corresponds to the right class. For example:

```
import numpy as np

>>> Y = lb.fit_transform(Y)
array([[0, 1, 0, 0, 0],
       [0, 0, 0, 1, 0],
       [1, 0, 0, 0, 0]])

>>> Yp = model.predict(X[0])
array([[0.002, 0.991, 0.001, 0.005, 0.001]])

>>> Ypr = np.round(Yp)
array([[ 0.,   1.,   0.,   0.,   0.]])

>>> lb.inverse_transform(Ypr)
array(['Female'], dtype='|S6')
```

Another approach to categorical features can be adopted when they're structured like a list of dictionaries (not necessarily dense, they can have values only for a few features). For example:

```
data = [
    { 'feature_1': 10.0, 'feature_2': 15.0 },
    { 'feature_1': -5.0, 'feature_3': 22.0 },
    { 'feature_3': -2.0, 'feature_4': 10.0 }
]
```

In this case, scikit-learn offers the classes DictVectorizer and FeatureHasher; they both produce sparse matrices of real numbers that can be fed into any machine learning model. The latter has a limited memory consumption and adopts **MurmurHash 3** (read https://en.wikipedia.org/wiki/MurmurHash, for further information). The code for these two methods is shown as follows:

```
from sklearn.feature_extraction import DictVectorizer, FeatureHasher

>>> dv = DictVectorizer()
>>> Y_dict = dv.fit_transform(data)

>>> Y_dict.todense()
matrix([[ 10.,   15.,    0.,    0.],
        [ -5.,    0.,   22.,    0.],
        [  0.,    0.,   -2.,   10.]])

>>> dv.vocabulary_
{'feature_1': 0, 'feature_2': 1, 'feature_3': 2, 'feature_4': 3}

>>> fh = FeatureHasher()
>>> Y_hashed = fh.fit_transform(data)

>>> Y_hashed.todense()
matrix([[ 0.,   0.,   0.,   ...,   0.,   0.,   0.],
        [ 0.,   0.,   0.,   ...,   0.,   0.,   0.],
        [ 0.,   0.,   0.,   ...,   0.,   0.,   0.]])
```

In both cases, I suggest you read the original scikit-learn documentation to know all possible options and parameters.

When working with categorical features (normally converted into positive integers through LabelEncoder), it's also possible to filter the dataset in order to apply one-hot encoding using the OneHotEncoder class. In the following example, the first feature is a binary index which indicates 'Male' or 'Female':

```
from sklearn.preprocessing import OneHotEncoder

>>> data = [
    [0, 10],
    [1, 11],
    [1, 8],
    [0, 12],
    [0, 15]
]

>>> oh = OneHotEncoder(categorical_features=[0])
>>> Y_oh = oh.fit_transform(data1)
```

```
>>> Y_oh.todense()
matrix([[  1.,    0.,   10.],
        [  0.,    1.,   11.],
        [  0.,    1.,    8.],
        [  1.,    0.,   12.],
        [  1.,    0.,   15.]])
```

Considering that these approaches increase the number of values (also exponentially with binary versions), all the classes adopt sparse matrices based on SciPy implementation. See h ttps://docs.scipy.org/doc/scipy-0.18.1/reference/sparse.html for further information.

Managing missing features

Sometimes a dataset can contain missing features, so there are a few options that can be taken into account:

- Removing the whole line
- Creating sub-model to predict those features
- Using an automatic strategy to input them according to the other known values

The first option is the most drastic one and should be considered only when the dataset is quite large, the number of missing features is high, and any prediction could be risky. The second option is much more difficult because it's necessary to determine a supervised strategy to train a model for each feature and, finally, to predict their value. Considering all pros and cons, the third option is likely to be the best choice. scikit-learn offers the class Imputer, which is responsible for filling the holes using a strategy based on the mean (default choice), median, or frequency (the most frequent entry will be used for all the missing ones).

The following snippet shows an example using the three approaches (the default value for a missing feature entry is NaN. However, it's possible to use a different placeholder through the parameter missing_values):

```
from sklearn.preprocessing import Imputer

>>> data = np.array([[1, np.nan, 2], [2, 3, np.nan], [-1, 4, 2]])

>>> imp = Imputer(strategy='mean')
>>> imp.fit_transform(data)
array([[ 1. ,   3.5,   2. ],
       [ 2. ,   3. ,   2. ],
       [-1. ,   4. ,   2. ]])
```

```
>>> imp = Imputer(strategy='median')
>>> imp.fit_transform(data)
array([[ 1. ,   3.5,   2. ],
       [ 2. ,   3. ,   2. ],
       [-1. ,   4. ,   2. ]])

>>> imp = Imputer(strategy='most_frequent')
>>> imp.fit_transform(data)
array([[ 1.,   3.,   2.],
       [ 2.,   3.,   2.],
       [-1.,   4.,   2.]])
```

Data scaling and normalization

A generic dataset (we assume here that it is always numerical) is made up of different values which can be drawn from different distributions, having different scales and, sometimes, there are also outliers. A machine learning algorithm isn't naturally able to distinguish among these various situations, and therefore, it's always preferable to standardize datasets before processing them. A very common problem derives from having a non-zero mean and a variance greater than one. In the following figure, there's a comparison between a raw dataset and the same dataset scaled and centered:

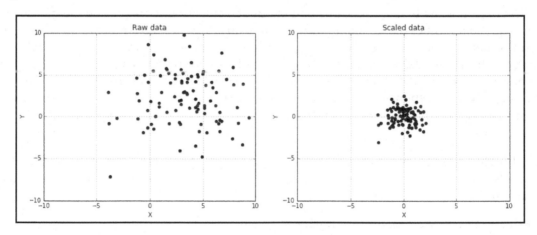

This result can be achieved using the StandardScaler class:

```
from sklearn.preprocessing import StandardScaler

>>> ss = StandardScaler()
>>> scaled_data = ss.fit_transform(data)
```

It's possible to specify if the scaling process must include both mean and standard deviation using the parameters `with_mean=True/False` and `with_std=True/False` (by default they're both active). If you need a more powerful scaling feature, with a superior control on outliers and the possibility to select a quantile range, there's also the class `RobustScaler`. Here are some examples with different quantiles:

```
from sklearn.preprocessing import RobustScaler

>>> rb1 = RobustScaler(quantile_range=(15, 85))
>>> scaled_data1 = rb1.fit_transform(data)

>>> rb1 = RobustScaler(quantile_range=(25, 75))
>>> scaled_data1 = rb1.fit_transform(data)

>>> rb2 = RobustScaler(quantile_range=(30, 60))
>>> scaled_data2 = rb2.fit_transform(data)
```

The results are shown in the following figures:

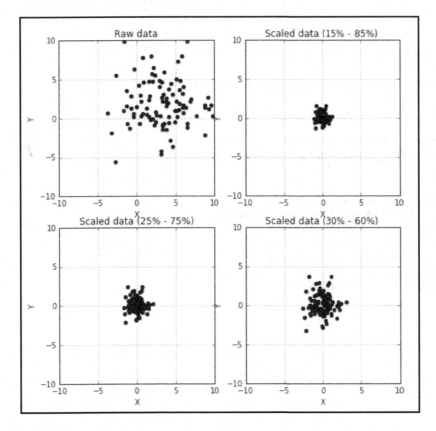

Other options include `MinMaxScaler` and `MaxAbsScaler`, which scale data by removing elements that don't belong to a given range (the former) or by considering a maximum absolute value (the latter).

scikit-learn also provides a class for per-sample normalization, `Normalizer`. It can apply `max`, `l1` and `l2` norms to each element of a dataset. In a Euclidean space, they are defined in the following way:

$$Max\ norm: \quad \|X\|_{max} = \frac{X}{|max_i\{X\}|}$$

$$L1\ norm: \quad \|X\|_{L1} = \frac{X}{\Sigma_i|x_i|}$$

$$L2\ norm: \quad \|X\|_{L2} = \frac{X}{\sqrt{\Sigma_i|x_i|^2}}$$

An example of every normalization is shown next:

```
from sklearn.preprocessing import Normalizer

>>> data = np.array([1.0, 2.0])

>>> n_max = Normalizer(norm='max')
>>> n_max.fit_transform(data.reshape(1, -1))
[[ 0.5, 1. ]]

>>> n_l1 = Normalizer(norm='l1')
>>> n_l1.fit_transform(data.reshape(1, -1))
[[ 0.33333333,  0.66666667]]

>>> n_l2 = Normalizer(norm='l2')
>>> n_l2.fit_transform(data.reshape(1, -1))
[[ 0.4472136 ,  0.89442719]]
```

Feature selection and filtering

An unnormalized dataset with many features contains information proportional to the independence of all features and their variance. Let's consider a small dataset with three features, generated with random Gaussian distributions:

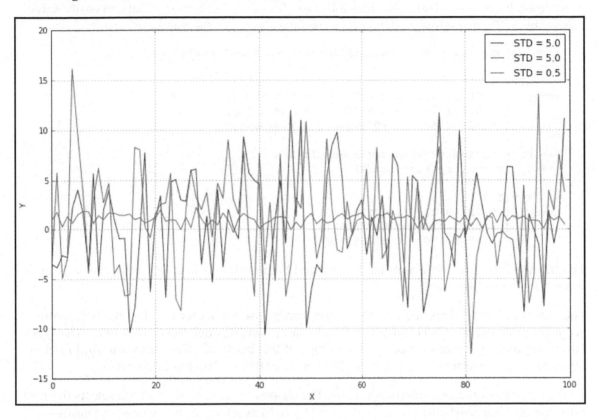

Even without further analysis, it's obvious that the central line (with the lowest variance) is almost constant and doesn't provide any useful information. If you remember the previous chapter, the entropy H(X) is quite small, while the other two variables carry more information. A variance threshold is, therefore, a useful approach to remove all those elements whose contribution (in terms of variability and so, information) is under a predefined level. scikit-learn provides the class `VarianceThreshold` that can easily solve this problem. By applying it on the previous dataset, we get the following result:

```
from sklearn.feature_selection import VarianceThreshold

>>> X[0:3, :]
array([[-3.5077778 , -3.45267063,  0.9681903 ],
       [-3.82581314,  5.77984656,  1.78926338],
       [-2.62090281, -4.90597966,  0.27943565]])

>>> vt = VarianceThreshold(threshold=1.5)
>>> X_t = vt.fit_transform(X)

>>> X_t[0:3, :]
array([[-0.53478521, -2.69189452],
       [-5.33054034, -1.91730367],
       [-1.17004376,  6.32836981]])
```

The third feature has been completely removed because its variance is under the selected threshold (1.5 in this case).

There are also many univariate methods that can be used in order to select the best features according to specific criteria based on F-tests and p-values, such as chi-square or ANOVA. However, their discussion is beyond the scope of this book and the reader can find further information in Freedman D., Pisani R., Purves R., *Statistics*, Norton & Company.

Two examples of feature selection that use the classes `SelectKBest` (which selects the best *K* high-score features) and `SelectPercentile` (which selects only a subset of features belonging to a certain percentile) are shown next. It's possible to apply them both to regression and classification datasets, being careful to select appropriate score functions:

```
from sklearn.datasets import load_boston, load_iris
from sklearn.feature_selection import SelectKBest, SelectPercentile, chi2, f_regression

>>> regr_data = load_boston()
>>> regr_data.data.shape
(506L, 13L)

>>> kb_regr = SelectKBest(f_regression)
>>> X_b = kb_regr.fit_transform(regr_data.data, regr_data.target)
```

```
>>> X_b.shape
(506L, 10L)

>>> kb_regr.scores_
array([  88.15124178,   75.2576423 ,  153.95488314,   15.97151242,
        112.59148028,  471.84673988,   83.47745922,   33.57957033,
         85.91427767,  141.76135658,  175.10554288,   63.05422911,
        601.61787111])

>>> class_data = load_iris()
>>> class_data.data.shape
(150L, 4L)

>>> perc_class = SelectPercentile(chi2, percentile=15)
>>> X_p = perc_class.fit_transform(class_data.data, class_data.target)

>>> X_p.shape
(150L, 1L)

>>> perc_class.scores_
array([  10.81782088,    3.59449902,  116.16984746,   67.24482759])
```

For further details about all scikit-learn score functions and their usage, visit `http://scikit-learn.org/stable/modules/feature_selection.html#univariate-feature-selection`.

Principal component analysis

In many cases, the dimensionality of the input dataset X is high and so is the complexity of every related machine learning algorithm. Moreover, the information is seldom spread uniformly across all the features and, as discussed in the previous chapter, there will be high entropy features together with low entropy ones, which, of course, don't contribute dramatically to the final outcome. In general, if we consider a Euclidean space, we have:

$$X = \{\bar{x}_1, \bar{x}_2, \ldots, \bar{x}_n\} \; where \; \bar{x}_i \in \mathbb{R}^m \; and \; \bar{x}_i = x_{i1}\overrightarrow{e_1} + x_{i2}\overrightarrow{e_2} + \cdots + x_{im}\overrightarrow{e_m}$$

So each point is expressed using an orthonormal basis made of m linearly independent vectors. Now, considering a dataset X, a natural question arises: is it possible to reduce m without a drastic loss of information? Let's consider the following figure (without any particular interpretation):

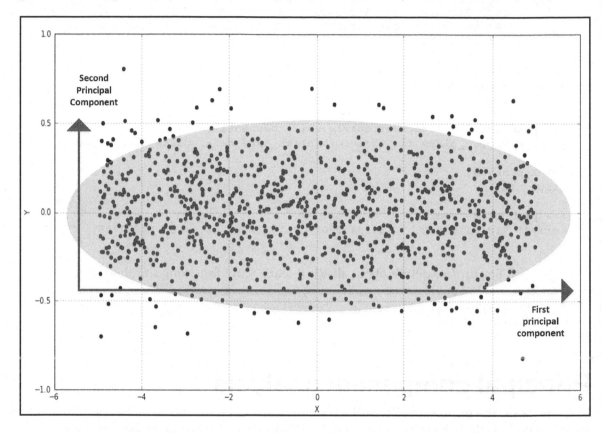

It doesn't matter which distributions generated $X=(x,y)$, however, the variance of the horizontal component is clearly higher than the vertical one. As discussed, it means that the amount of information provided by the first component is higher and, for example, if the x axis is stretched horizontally keeping the vertical one fixed, the distribution becomes similar to a segment where the depth has lower and lower importance.

In order to assess how much information is brought by each component, and the correlation among them, a useful tool is the covariance matrix (if the dataset has zero mean, we can use the correlation matrix):

$$C = \begin{pmatrix} \sigma_1{}^2 & \cdots & \sigma_{1m} \\ \vdots & \ddots & \vdots \\ \sigma_{m1} & \cdots & \sigma_m{}^2 \end{pmatrix}$$

$$where \ \sigma_{ij} = \frac{1}{m} \sum_k (x_{ki} - E[X_i])(x_{kj} - E[X_j])$$

C is symmetric and positive semidefinite, so all the eigenvalues are non-negative, but what's the meaning of each value? The covariance matrix for the previous example is:

$$C = \begin{pmatrix} 8.31 & -0.02 \\ -0.02 & 0.06 \end{pmatrix}$$

As expected, the horizontal variance is quite a bit higher than the vertical one. Moreover, the other values are close to zero. If you remember the definition and, for simplicity, remove the mean term, they represent the cross-correlation between couples of components. It's obvious that in our example, X and Y are uncorrelated (they're orthogonal), but in real-life examples, there could be features which present a residual cross-correlation. In terms of information theory, it means that knowing Y gives us some information about X (which we already know), so they share information which is indeed doubled. So our goal is also to decorrelate X while trying to reduce its dimensionality.

This can be achieved considering the sorted eigenvalues of C and selecting $g < m$ values:

$$Let \ be \ \Lambda = \{\lambda_1 \geq \lambda_2 \geq \cdots \lambda_m\} \ and \ \Lambda_g \subseteq \Lambda \ with \ \dim(\Lambda_g) \leq \dim(\Lambda)$$

$$W = (\vec{w}_{\lambda 1}, \vec{w}_{\lambda 2}, ..., \vec{w}_{\lambda g}) \ so \ that \ \bar{y}_R = W\bar{y} \ where \ \bar{y}_R \in \mathbb{R}^g$$

So, it's possible to project the original feature vectors into this new (sub-)space, where each component carries a portion of total variance and where the new covariance matrix is decorrelated to reduce useless information sharing (in terms of correlation) among different features. In scikit-learn, there's the PCA class which can do all this in a very smooth way:

```
from sklearn.datasets import load_digits
from sklearn.decomposition import PCA

>>> digits = load_digits()
```

A figure with a few random MNIST handwritten digits is shown as follows:

Each image is a vector of 64 unsigned int (8 bit) numbers (0, 255), so the initial number of components is indeed 64. However, the total amount of black pixels is often predominant and the basic signs needed to write 10 digits are similar, so it's reasonable to assume both high cross-correlation and a low variance on several components. Trying with 36 principal components, we get:

```
>>> pca = PCA(n_components=36, whiten=True)
>>> X_pca = pca.fit_transform(digits.data / 255)
```

In order to improve performance, all integer values are normalized into the range [0, 1] and, through the parameter `whiten=True`, the variance of each component is scaled to one. As also the official scikit-learn documentation says, this process is particularly useful when an isotropic distribution is needed for many algorithms to perform efficiently. It's possible to access the explained variance ratio through the instance variable `explained_variance_ratio_`, which shows which part of the total variance is carried by each single component:

```
>>> pca.explained_variance_ratio_
array([ 0.14890594,  0.13618771,  0.11794594,  0.08409979,  0.05782415,
        0.0491691 ,  0.04315987,  0.03661373,  0.03353248,  0.03078806,
        0.02372341,  0.02272697,  0.01821863,  0.01773855,  0.01467101,
        0.01409716,  0.01318589,  0.01248138,  0.01017718,  0.00905617,
        0.00889538,  0.00797123,  0.00767493,  0.00722904,  0.00695889,
        0.00596081,  0.00575615,  0.00515158,  0.00489539,  0.00428887,
        0.00373606,  0.00353274,  0.00336684,  0.00328029,  0.0030832 ,
        0.00293778])
```

A plot for the example of MNIST digits is shown next. The left graph represents the variance ratio while the right one is the cumulative variance. It can be immediately seen how the first components are normally the most important ones in terms of information, while the following ones provide details that a classifier could also discard:

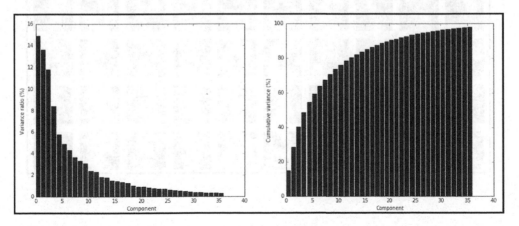

As expected, the contribution to the total variance decreases dramatically starting from the fifth component, so it's possible to reduce the original dimensionality without an unacceptable loss of information, which could drive an algorithm to learn wrong classes. In the preceding graph, there are the same handwritten digits rebuilt using the first 36 components with whitening and normalization between 0 and 1. To obtain the original images, we need to inverse-transform all new vectors and project them into the original space:

```
>>> X_rebuilt = pca.inverse_transform(X_pca)
```

The result is shown in the following figure:

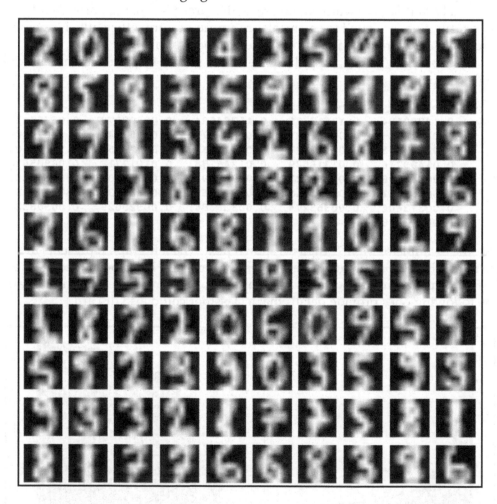

This process can also partially denoise the original images by removing residual variance, which is often associated with noise or unwanted contributions (almost every calligraphy distorts some of the structural elements which are used for recognition).

I suggest the reader try different numbers of components (using the explained variance data) and also `n_components='mle'`, which implements an automatic selection of the best dimensionality (Minka T.P, *Automatic Choice of Dimensionality for PCA*, NIPS 2000: 598-604).

 scikit-learn solves the PCA problem with **SVD (Singular Value Decomposition)**, which can be studied in detail in Poole D., *Linear Algebra*, Brooks Cole. It's possible to control the algorithm through the parameter `svd_solver`, whose values are `'auto'`, `'full'`, `'arpack'`, `'randomized'`. Arpack implements a truncated SVD. Randomized is based on an approximate algorithm which drops many singular vectors and can achieve very good performances also with high-dimensional datasets where the actual number of components is sensibly smaller.

Non-negative matrix factorization

When the dataset is made up of non-negative elements, it's possible to use **non-negative matrix factorization** (**NNMF**) instead of standard PCA. The algorithm optimizes a loss function (alternatively on *W* and *H*) based on the Frobenius norm:

$$L = \frac{1}{2} \|X - WH\|_{Frob}^2 \ where \ \|A\|_{Frob}^2 = \sqrt{\sum_i \sum_j |a_{ij}|^2}$$

If *dim(X)* = *n x m*, then *dim(W)* = *n x p* and *dim(H)* = *p x m* with *p* equal to the number of requested components (the `n_components` parameter), which is normally smaller than the original dimensions *n* and *m*.

The final reconstruction is purely additive and it has been shown that it's particularly efficient for images or text where there are normally no non-negative elements. In the following snippet, there's an example using the Iris dataset (which is non-negative). The `init` parameter can assume different values (see the documentation) which determine how the data matrix is initially processed. A random choice is for non-negative matrices which are only scaled (no SVD is performed):

```
from sklearn.datasets import load_iris
from sklearn.decomposition import NMF

>>> iris = load_iris()
>>> iris.data.shape
(150L, 4L)

>>> nmf = NMF(n_components=3, init='random', l1_ratio=0.1)
>>> Xt = nmf.fit_transform(iris.data)

>>> nmf.reconstruction_err_
1.8819327624141866

>>> iris.data[0]
array([ 5.1,   3.5,   1.4,   0.2])
>>> Xt[0]
array([ 0.20668461,  1.09973772,  0.0098996 ])
>>> nmf.inverse_transform(Xt[0])
array([ 5.10401653,  3.49666967,  1.3965409 ,  0.20610779])
```

NNMF, together with other factorization methods, will be very useful for more advanced techniques, such as recommendation systems and topic modeling.

 NNMF is very sensitive to its parameters (in particular, initialization and regularization), so I suggest reading the original documentation for further information: http://scikit-learn.org/stable/modules/genera ted/sklearn.decomposition.NMF.html.

Sparse PCA

scikit-learn provides different PCA variants that can solve particular problems. I do suggest reading the original documentation. However, I'd like to mention `SparsePCA`, which allows exploiting the natural sparsity of data while extracting principal components. If you think about the handwritten digits or other images that must be classified, their initial dimensionality can be quite high (a 10x10 image has 100 features). However, applying a standard PCA selects only the average most important features, assuming that every sample can be rebuilt using the same components. Simplifying, this is equivalent to:

$$y_R = c_1 y_{R1} + c_2 y_{R2} + \cdots + c_g y_{Rg}$$

On the other hand, we can always use a limited number of components, but without the limitation given by a dense projection matrix. This can be achieved by using sparse matrices (or vectors), where the number of non-zero elements is quite low. In this way, each element can be rebuilt using its specific components (in most cases, they will be always the most important), which can include elements normally discarded by a dense PCA. The previous expression now becomes:

$$y_R = (c_1 y_{R1} + c_2 y_{R2} + \cdots + c_g y_{Rg}) + (0 \cdot y_{Rg+1} + 0 \cdot y_{Rg+2} + \cdots + 0 \cdot y_{Rm})$$

Here the non-null components have been put into the first block (they don't have the same order as the previous expression), while all the other zero terms have been separated. In terms of linear algebra, the vectorial space now has the original dimensions. However, using the power of sparse matrices (provided by `scipy.sparse`), scikit-learn can solve this problem much more efficiently than a classical PCA.

The following snippet shows a sparse PCA with 60 components. In this context, they're usually called atoms and the amount of sparsity can be controlled via *L1*-norm regularization (higher `alpha` parameter values lead to more sparse results). This approach is very common in classification algorithms and will be discussed in the next chapters:

```
from sklearn.decomposition import SparsePCA

>>> spca = SparsePCA(n_components=60, alpha=0.1)
>>> X_spca = spca.fit_transform(digits.data / 255)

>>> spca.components_.shape
(60L, 64L)
```

For further information about SciPy sparse matrices, visit `https://docs.scip y.org/doc/scipy-0.18.1/reference/sparse.html`.

Kernel PCA

We're going to discuss kernel methods in Chapter 7, *Support Vector Machines*, however, it's useful to mention the class `KernelPCA`, which performs a PCA with non-linearly separable data sets. Just to understand the logic of this approach (the mathematical formulation isn't very simple), it's useful to consider a projection of each sample into a particular space where the dataset becomes linearly separable. The components of this space correspond to the first, second, ... principal components and a kernel PCA algorithm, therefore, computes the projection of our samples onto each of them.

Let's consider a dataset made up of a circle with a blob inside:

```
from sklearn.datasets import make_circles

>>> Xb, Yb = make_circles(n_samples=500, factor=0.1, noise=0.05)
```

The graphical representation is shown in the following picture. In this case, a classic PCA approach isn't able to capture the non-linear dependency of existing components (the reader can verify that the projection is equivalent to the original dataset). However, looking at the samples and using polar coordinates (therefore, a space where it's possible to project all the points), it's easy to separate the two sets, only considering the radius:

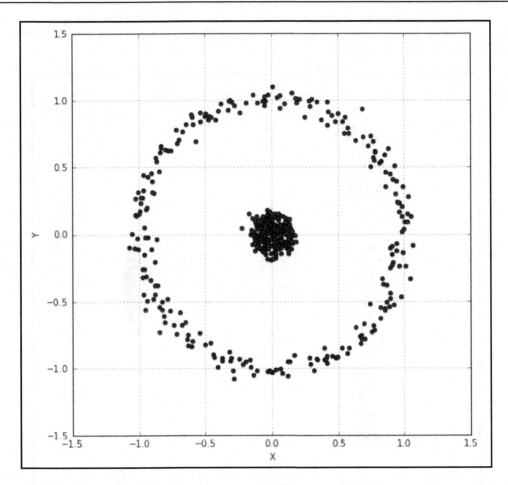

Considering the structure of the dataset, it's possible to investigate the behavior of a PCA with a radial basis function kernel. As the default value for gamma is 1.0/number of features (for now, consider this parameter as inversely proportional to the variance of a Gaussian), we need to increase it to capture the external circle. A value of 1.0 is enough:

```
from sklearn.decomposition import KernelPCA

>>> kpca = KernelPCA(n_components=2, kernel='rbf',
fit_inverse_transform=True, gamma=1.0)
>>> X_kpca = kpca.fit_transform(Xb)
```

The instance variable `X_transformed_fit_` will contain the projection of our dataset into the new space. Plotting it, we get:

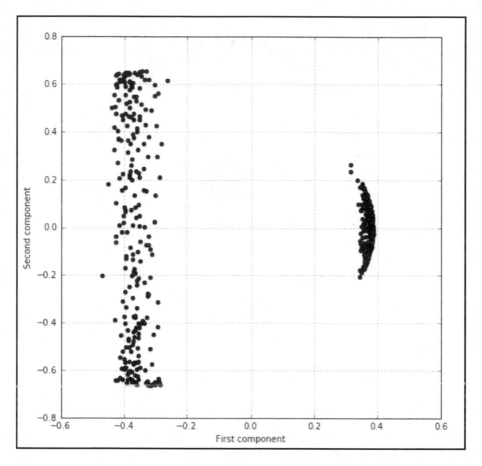

The plot shows a separation just like expected, and it's also possible to see that the points belonging to the central blob have a curve distribution because they are more sensitive to the distance from the center.

Kernel PCA is a powerful instrument when we think of our dataset as made up of elements that can be a function of components (in particular, radial-basis or polynomials) but we aren't able to determine a linear relationship among them.

For more information about the different kernels supported by scikit-learn, visit `http://scikit-learn.org/stable/modules/metrics.html#l inear-kernel`.

Atom extraction and dictionary learning

Dictionary learning is a technique which allows rebuilding a sample starting from a sparse dictionary of atoms (similar to principal components). In Mairal J., Bach F., Ponce J., Sapiro G., *Online Dictionary Learning for Sparse Coding*, Proceedings of the 29th International Conference on Machine Learning, 2009 there's a description of the same online strategy adopted by scikit-learn, which can be summarized as a double optimization problem where:

$$X = \{\bar{x}_1, \bar{x}_2, \dots, \bar{x}_n\} \; where \; \bar{x}_i \in \mathbb{R}^m$$

Is an input dataset and the target is to find both a dictionary D and a set of weights for each sample:

$$\boldsymbol{D} \in \mathbb{R}^{m \times k} \; and \; A = \{\bar{\alpha}_1, \bar{\alpha}_2, \dots, \bar{\alpha}_m\} \; where \; \bar{\alpha}_i \in \mathbb{R}^k$$

After the training process, an input vector can be computed as:

$$\bar{x}_i = \boldsymbol{D}\bar{\alpha}_i$$

The optimization problem (which involves both D and alpha vectors) can be expressed as the minimization of the following loss function:

$$L(\boldsymbol{D}, A) = \frac{1}{2} \sum_i \|x_i - D\bar{\alpha}_i\|_2^2 + c\|\bar{\alpha}_i\|_1$$

Here the parameter c controls the level of sparsity (which is proportional to the strength of *L1* normalization). This problem can be solved by alternating the least square variable until a stable point is reached.

In scikit-learn, we can implement such an algorithm with the class `DictionaryLearning` (using the usual MNIST datasets), where `n_components`, as usual, determines the number of atoms:

```
from sklearn.decomposition import DictionaryLearning

>>> dl = DictionaryLearning(n_components=36, fit_algorithm='lars',
transform_algorithm='lasso_lars')
>>> X_dict = dl.fit_transform(digits.data)
```

A plot of each atom (component) is shown in the following figure:

This process can be very long on low-end machines. In such a case, I suggest limiting the number of samples to 20 or 30.

References

- Freedman D., Pisani R., Purves R., *Statistics*, Norton & Company
- Gareth J., Witten D., Hastie T., Tibshirani R., *An Introduction to Statistical Learning: With Application in R*, Springer
- Poole D., *Linear Algebra*, Brooks Cole
- Minka T.P, *Automatic Choice of Dimensionality for PCA*, NIPS 2000: 598-604
- Mairal J., Bach F., Ponce J., Sapiro G., *Online Dictionary Learning for Sparse Coding*, Proceedings of the 29th International Conference on Machine Learning, 2009

Summary

Feature selection is the first (and sometimes the most important) step in a machine learning pipeline. Not all the features are useful for our purposes and some of them are expressed using different notations, so it's often necessary to preprocess our dataset before any further operations.

We saw how to split the data into training and test sets using a random shuffle and how to manage missing elements. Another very important section covered the techniques used to manage categorical data or labels, which are very common when a certain feature assumes only a discrete set of values.

Then we analyzed the problem of dimensionality. Some datasets contain many features which are correlated with each other, so they don't provide any new information but increase the computational complexity and reduce the overall performances. Principal component analysis is a method to select only a subset of features which contain the largest amount of total variance. This approach, together with its variants, allows to decorrelate the features and reduce the dimensionality without a drastic loss in terms of accuracy. Dictionary learning is another technique used to extract a limited number of building blocks from a dataset, together with the information needed to rebuild each sample. This approach is particularly useful when the dataset is made up of different versions of similar elements (such as images, letters, or digits).

In the next chapter, we're going to discuss linear regression, which is the most diffused and simplest supervised approach to predict continuous values. We'll also analyze how to overcome some limitations and how to solve non-linear problems using the same algorithms.

4
Linear Regression

Linear models are the simplest parametric methods and always deserve the right attention, because many problems, even intrinsically non-linear ones, can be easily solved with these models. As discussed previously, a regression is a prediction where the target is continuous and its applications are several, so it's important to understand how a linear model can fit the data, what its strengths and weaknesses are, and when it's preferable to pick an alternative. In the last part of the chapter, we're going to discuss an interesting method to work efficiently with non-linear data using the same models.

Linear models

Consider a dataset of real-values vectors:

$$X = \{\bar{x}_1, \bar{x}_2, \dots, \bar{x}_n\} \text{ where } \bar{x}_i \in \mathbb{R}^m$$

Each input vector is associated with a real value y_i:

$$Y = \{y_1, y_2, \dots, y_n\} \text{ where } y_n \in \mathbb{R}$$

A linear model is based on the assumption that it's possible to approximate the output values through a regression process based on the rule:

$$\tilde{y} = \alpha_0 + \sum_{i=1}^{m} \alpha_i x_i \text{ where } A = \{\alpha_0, \alpha_1, \dots, \alpha_m\}$$

In other words, the strong assumption is that our dataset and all other unknown points lie on a hyperplane and the maximum error is proportional to both the training quality and the adaptability of the original dataset. One of the most common problems arises when the dataset is clearly non-linear and other models have to be considered (such as neural networks or kernel support vector machines).

A bidimensional example

Let's consider a small dataset built by adding some uniform noise to the points belonging to a segment bounded between -6 and 6. The original equation is: $y = x + 2 + n$, where n is a noise term.

In the following figure, there's a plot with a candidate regression function:

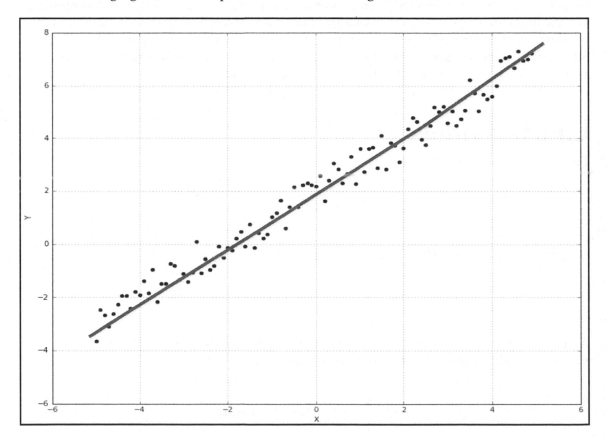

As we're working on a plane, the regressor we're looking for is a function of only two parameters:

$$\tilde{y} = \alpha + \beta x$$

In order to fit our model, we must find the best parameters and to do that we choose an ordinary least squares approach. The loss function to minimize is:

$$L = \frac{1}{2}\sum_{i=1}^{n}\|\tilde{y}_i - y_i\|_2^2 \quad \text{which becomes} \quad L = \frac{1}{2}\sum_{i=1}^{n}(\alpha + \beta x_i - y_i)^2$$

With an analytic approach, in order to find the global minimum, we must impose:

$$\begin{cases} \dfrac{\partial L}{\partial \alpha} = \displaystyle\sum_{i=1}^{n}(\alpha + \beta x_i - y_i) = 0 \\ \dfrac{\partial L}{\partial \beta} = \displaystyle\sum_{i=1}^{n}(\alpha + \beta x_i - y_i)x_i = 0 \end{cases}$$

So (for simplicity, it accepts a vector containing both variables):

```
import numpy as np

def loss(v):
    e = 0.0
    for i in range(nb_samples):
        e += np.square(v[0] + v[1]*X[i] - Y[i])
    return 0.5 * e
```

And the gradient can be defined as:

```
def gradient(v):
    g = np.zeros(shape=2)
    for i in range(nb_samples):
        g[0] += (v[0] + v[1]*X[i] - Y[i])
        g[1] += ((v[0] + v[1]*X[i] - Y[i]) * X[i])
    return g
```

The optimization problem can now be solved using SciPy:

```
from scipy.optimize import minimize

>>> minimize(fun=loss, x0=[0.0, 0.0], jac=gradient, method='L-BFGS-B')
fun: 9.7283268345966025
 hess_inv: <2x2 LbfgsInvHessProduct with dtype=float64>
      jac: array([  7.28577538e-06,  -2.35647522e-05])
  message: 'CONVERGENCE: REL_REDUCTION_OF_F_<=_FACTR*EPSMCH'
     nfev: 8
      nit: 7
   status: 0
  success: True
        x: array([ 2.00497209,   1.00822552])
```

As expected, the regression denoised our dataset, rebuilding the original equation: $y = x + 2$.

Linear regression with scikit-learn and higher dimensionality

scikit-learn offers the class `LinearRegression`, which works with n-dimensional spaces. For this purpose, we're going to use the Boston dataset:

```
from sklearn.datasets import load_boston

>>> boston = load_boston()

>>> boston.data.shape
(506L, 13L)
>>> boston.target.shape
(506L,)
```

It has 506 samples with 13 input features and one output. In the following figure, there' a collection of the plots of the first 12 features:

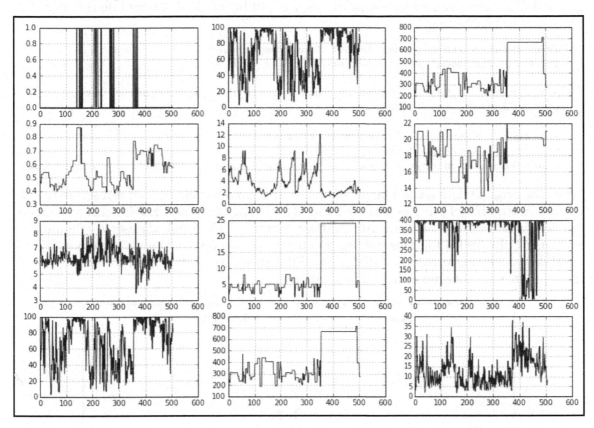

When working with datasets, it's useful to have a tabular view to manipulate data. pandas is a perfect framework for this task, and even though it's beyond the scope of this book, I suggest you create a data frame with the command `pandas.DataFrame(boston.data, columns=boston.feature_names)` and use Jupyter to visualize it. For further information, refer to Heydt M., *Learning pandas - Python Data Discovery and Analysis Made Easy*, Packt.

There are different scales and outliers (which can be removed using the methods studied in the previous chapters), so it's better to ask the model to normalize the data before processing it. Moreover, for testing purposes, we split the original dataset into training (90%) and test (10%) sets:

```
from sklearn.linear_model import LinearRegression
from sklearn.model_selection import train_test_split

>>> X_train, X_test, Y_train, Y_test = train_test_split(boston.data,
boston.target, test_size=0.1)

>>> lr = LinearRegression(normalize=True)
>>> lr.fit(X_train, Y_train)
LinearRegression(copy_X=True, fit_intercept=True, n_jobs=1, normalize=True)
```

When the original data set isn't large enough, splitting it into training and test sets may reduce the number of samples that can be used for fitting the model. k-fold cross-validation can help in solving this problem with a different strategy. The whole dataset is split into k folds using always k-1 folds for training and the remaining one to validate the model. K iterations will be performed, using always a different validation fold. In the following figure, there's an example with 3 folds/iterations:

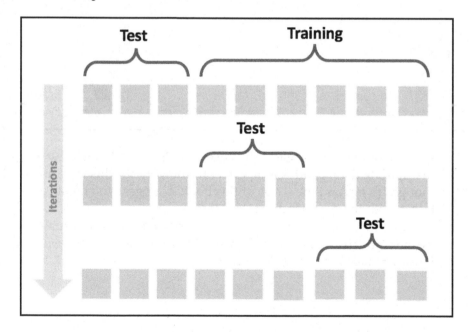

In this way, the final score can be determined as average of all values and all samples are selected for training k-1 times.

To check the accuracy of a regression, scikit-learn provides the internal method `score(X, y)` which evaluates the model on test data:

```
>>> lr.score(X_test, Y_test)
0.77371996006718879
```

So the overall accuracy is about 77%, which is an acceptable result considering the non-linearity of the original dataset, but it can be also influenced by the subdivision made by `train_test_split` (like in our case). Instead, for k-fold cross-validation, we can use the function `cross_val_score()`, which works with all the classifiers. The scoring parameter is very important because it determines which metric will be adopted for tests. As `LinearRegression` works with ordinary least squares, we preferred the negative mean squared error, which is a cumulative measure that must be evaluated according to the actual values (it's not relative).

```
from sklearn.model_selection import cross_val_score

>>> scores = cross_val_score(lr, boston.data, boston.target, cv=7,
scoring='neg_mean_squared_error')
array([ -11.32601065,  -10.96365388,  -32.12770594,  -33.62294354,
        -10.55957139, -146.42926647,  -12.98538412])

>>> scores.mean()
-36.859219426420601
>>> scores.std()
45.704973900600457
```

Another very important metric used in regressions is called the **coefficient of determination** or R^2. It measures the amount of variance on the prediction which is explained by the dataset. We define **residuals**, the following quantity:

$$\forall\, i \in (0, n) \quad r_i = x_i - \tilde{x}_i$$

In other words, it is the difference between the sample and the prediction. So the R^2 is defined as follows:

$$R^2 = 1 - \frac{\sum_i r_i^2}{\sum_i (x_i - E[X])^2}$$

For our purposes, R^2 values close to 1 mean an almost perfect regression, while values close to 0 (or negative) imply a bad model. Using this metric is quite easy with cross-validation:

```
>>> cross_val_score(lr, X, Y, cv=10, scoring='r2')
0.75
```

Regressor analytic expression

If we want to have an analytical expression of our model (a hyperplane), LinearRegression offers two instance variables, intercept_ and coef_:

```
>>> print('y = ' + str(lr.intercept_) + ' ')
>>> for i, c in enumerate(lr.coef_):
        print(str(c) + ' * x' + str(i))

y = 38.0974166342
-0.105375005552 * x0
0.0494815380304 * x1
0.0371643549528 * x2
3.37092201039 * x3
-18.9885299511 * x4
3.73331692311 * x5
0.00111437695492 * x6
-1.55681538908 * x7
0.325992743837 * x8
-0.01252057277 * x9
-0.978221746439 * x10
0.0101679515792 * x11
-0.550117114635 * x12
```

As for any other model, a prediction can be obtained through the method `predict(X)`. As an experiment, we can try to add some Gaussian noise to our training data and predict the value:

```
>>> X = boston.data[0:10] + np.random.normal(0.0, 0.1)

>>> lr.predict(X)
array([ 29.5588731 ,  24.49601998,  30.0981552 ,  28.01864586,
        27.28870704,  24.65881135,  22.46335968,  18.79690943,
        10.53493932,  18.18093544])

>>> boston.target[0:10]
array([ 24. ,  21.6,  34.7,  33.4,  36.2,  28.7,  22.9,  27.1,  16.5,
18.9])
```

It's obvious that the model is not performing in an ideal way and there are many possible reasons, the foremost being nonlinearities and the presence of outliers. However, in general, a linear regression model is not a perfectly robust solution. In Hastie T., Tibshirani R., Friedman J., *The Elements of Statistical Learning: Data Mining, Inference, and, Prediction,* Springer, you can find a very detailed discussion about its strengths and weaknesses. However, in this context, a common threat is represented by collinearities that lead to low-rank *X* matrix. This determines an ill-conditioned matrix that is particularly sensitive to noise, causing the explosion of some parameters as well. The following methods have been studied in order to mitigate this risk and provide more robust solutions.

Ridge, Lasso, and ElasticNet

Ridge regression imposes an additional shrinkage penalty to the ordinary least squares loss function to limit its squared *L2* norm:

$$L(\overline{w}) = \|X\overline{w} - \overline{y}\|_2^2 + \alpha\|\overline{w}\|_2^2$$

In this case, X is a matrix containing all samples as columns and the term w represents the weight vector. The additional term (through the coefficient alpha—if large it implies a stronger regularization and smaller values) forces the loss function to disallow an infinite growth of w, which can be caused by multicollinearity or ill-conditioning. In the following figure, there's a representation of what happens when a Ridge penalty is applied:

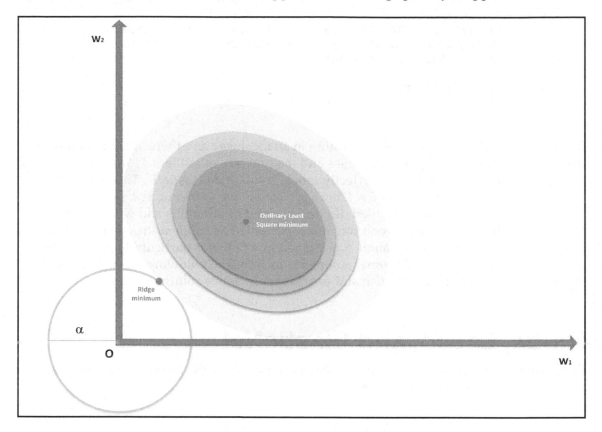

The gray surface represents the loss function (here, for simplicity, we're working with only two weights), while the circle center **O** is the boundary imposed by the Ridge condition. The minimum will have smaller w values and potential explosions are avoided.

In the following snippet, we're going to compare `LinearRegression` and `Ridge` with a cross-validation:

```
from sklearn.datasets import load_diabetes
from sklearn.linear_model import LinearRegression, Ridge

>>> diabetes = load_diabetes()

>>> lr = LinearRegression(normalize=True)
>>> rg = Ridge(0.001, normalize=True)

>>> lr_scores = cross_val_score(lr, diabetes.data, diabetes.target, cv=10)
>>> lr_scores.mean()
0.46196236195833718

>>> rg_scores = cross_val_score(rg, diabetes.data, diabetes.target, cv=10)
>>> rg_scores.mean()
0.46227174692391299
```

Sometimes, finding the right value for alpha (Ridge coefficient) is not so immediate. scikit-learn provides the class `RidgeCV`, which allows performing an automatic grid search (among a set and returning the best estimation):

```
from sklearn.linear_model import RidgeCV

>>> rg = RidgeCV(alphas=(1.0, 0.1, 0.01, 0.005, 0.0025, 0.001, 0.00025),
normalize=True)
>>> rg.fit(diabetes.data, diabetes.target)

>>> rg.alpha_
0.0050000000000000001
```

A Lasso regressor imposes a penalty on the *L1* norm of w to determine a potentially higher number of null coefficients:

$$L(\bar{w}) = \frac{1}{2n}\|X\bar{w} - \bar{y}\|_2^2 + \alpha\|\bar{w}\|_1$$

The sparsity is a consequence of the penalty term (the mathematical proof is non-trivial and will be omitted).

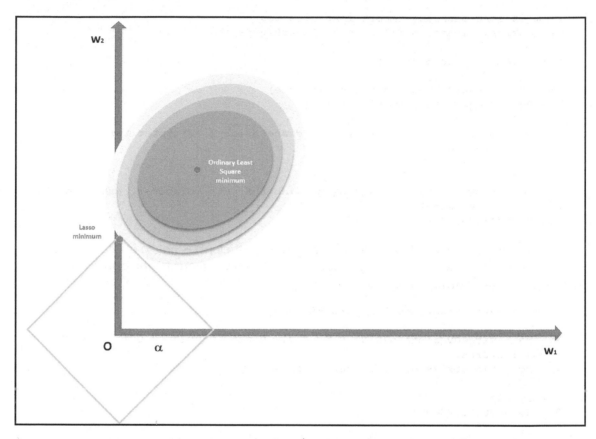

In this case, there are vertices where a component is non-null while all the other weights are zero. The probability of an intersection with a vertex is proportional to the dimensionality of w and, therefore, it's normal to discover a rather sparse model after training a Lasso regressor.

In the following snippet, the diabetes dataset is used to fit a Lasso model:

```
from sklearn.linear_model import Lasso

>>> ls = Lasso(alpha=0.001, normalize=True)
>>> ls_scores = cross_val_score(ls, diabetes.data, diabetes.target, cv=10)
>>> ls_scores.mean()
0.46215747851504058
```

Also for Lasso, there's the possibility of running a grid search for the best alpha parameter. The class, in this case, is `LassoCV` and its internal dynamics are similar to what was already seen for Ridge. Lasso can also perform efficiently on the sparse data generated through the `scipy.sparse` class, allowing for training bigger models without the need for partial fitting:

```
from scipy import sparse

>>> ls = Lasso(alpha=0.001, normalize=True)
>>> ls.fit(sparse.coo_matrix(diabetes.data), diabetes.target)
Lasso(alpha=0.001, copy_X=True, fit_intercept=True, max_iter=1000,
   normalize=True, positive=False, precompute=False, random_state=None,
   selection='cyclic', tol=0.0001, warm_start=False)
```

When working with a huge amount of data, some models cannot fit completely in memory, so it's impossible to train them. scikit-learn offers some models, such as **stochastic gradient descent (SGD)**, which work in a way quite similar to `LinearRegression` with `Ridge/Lasso`; however, they also implement the method `partial_fit()`, which also allows continuous training through Python generators. See `http://scikit-learn.org/stable/modules/linear_model.html#stochastic-gradient-descent-sgd`, for further details.

The last alternative is **ElasticNet**, which combines both Lasso and Ridge into a single model with two penalty factors: one proportional to *L1* norm and the other to *L2* norm. In this way, the resulting model will be sparse like a pure Lasso, but with the same regularization ability as provided by Ridge. The resulting loss function is:

$$L(\overline{w}) = \frac{1}{2n}\|X\overline{w} - \overline{y}\|_2^2 + \alpha\beta\|\overline{w}\|_1 + \frac{\alpha(1-\beta)}{2}\|\overline{w}\|_2^2$$

The `ElasticNet` class provides an implementation where the alpha parameter works in conjunction with `l1_ratio` (beta in the formula). The main peculiarity of `ElasticNet` is avoiding a selective exclusion of correlated features, thanks to the balanced action of the *L1* and *L2* norms.

In the following snippet, there's an example using both the `ElasticNet` and `ElasticNetCV` classes:

```
from sklearn.linear_model import ElasticNet, ElasticNetCV

>>> en = ElasticNet(alpha=0.001, l1_ratio=0.8, normalize=True)
>>> en_scores = cross_val_score(en, diabetes.data, diabetes.target, cv=10)
>>> en_scores.mean()
0.46358858847836454

>>> encv = ElasticNetCV(alphas=(0.1, 0.01, 0.005, 0.0025, 0.001),
l1_ratio=(0.1, 0.25, 0.5, 0.75, 0.8), normalize=True)
>>> encv.fit(dia.data, dia.target)
ElasticNetCV(alphas=(0.1, 0.01, 0.005, 0.0025, 0.001), copy_X=True,
cv=None,
        eps=0.001, fit_intercept=True, l1_ratio=(0.1, 0.25, 0.5, 0.75, 0.8),
        max_iter=1000, n_alphas=100, n_jobs=1, normalize=True,
        positive=False, precompute='auto', random_state=None,
        selection='cyclic', tol=0.0001, verbose=0)

>>> encv.alpha_
0.001
>>> encv.l1_ratio_
0.75
```

Robust regression with random sample consensus

A common problem with linear regressions is caused by the presence of outliers. An ordinary least square approach will take them into account and the result (in terms of coefficients) will be therefore biased. In the following figure, there's an example of such a behavior:

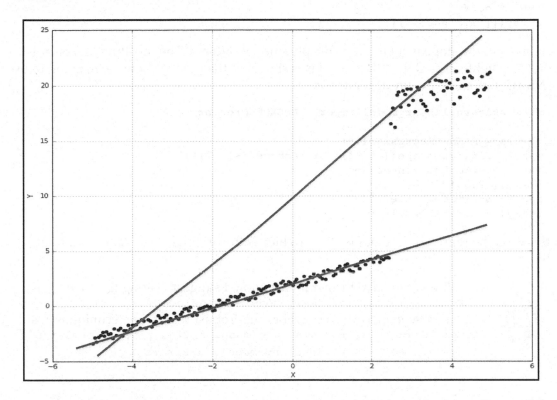

The less sloped line represents an acceptable regression which discards the outliers, while the other one is influenced by them. An interesting approach to avoid this problem is offered by **random sample consensus (RANSAC)**, which works with every regressor by subsequent iterations, after splitting the dataset into inliers and outliers. The model is trained only with valid samples (evaluated internally or through the callable is_data_valid()) and all samples are re-evaluated to verify if they're still inliers or they have become outliers. The process ends after a fixed number of iterations or when the desired score is achieved.

In the following snippet, there's an example of simple linear regression applied to the dataset shown in the previous figure.

```
from sklearn.linear_model import LinearRegression

>>> lr = LinearRegression(normalize=True)
>>> lr.fit(X.reshape((-1, 1)), Y.reshape((-1, 1)))
>>> lr.intercept_
array([ 5.500572])
>>> lr.coef_
array([[ 2.53688672]])
```

As imagined, the slope is high due to the presence of outliers. The resulting regressor is $y = 5.5 + 2.5x$ (slightly less sloped than what was shown in the figure). Now we're going to use RANSAC with the same linear regressor:

```
from sklearn.linear_model import RANSACRegressor

>>> rs = RANSACRegressor(lr)
>>> rs.fit(X.reshape((-1, 1)), Y.reshape((-1, 1)))
>>> rs.estimator_.intercept_
array([ 2.03602026])
>>> es.estimator_.coef_
array([[ 0.99545348]])
```

In this case, the regressor is about $y = 2 + x$ (which is the original clean dataset without outliers).

If you want to have further information, I suggest visiting the page `http ://scikit-learn.org/stable/modules/generated/sklearn.linear_mo del.RANSACRegressor.html`. **For other robust regression techniques, visit:** `http://scikit-learn.org/stable/modules/linear_model.html#robus tness-regression-outliers-and-modeling-errors`.

Polynomial regression

Polynomial regression is a technique based on a trick that allows using linear models even when the dataset has strong non-linearities. The idea is to add some extra variables computed from the existing ones and using (in this case) only polynomial combinations:

$$\hat{y} = \alpha_0 + \sum_{i=1}^{m} \alpha_i x_i + \sum_{j=m+1}^{k} \alpha_j f_{Pj}(x_1, x_2, \ldots, x_m) \; where \; f_{Pj} \; is \; a \; polynomial \; function$$

For example, with two variables, it's possible to extend to a second-degree problem by transforming the initial vector (whose dimension is equal to *m*) into another one with higher dimensionality (whose dimension is $k > m$):

$$\bar{x} = (x_1, x_2) \;\Rightarrow\; \bar{x}_t = (x_1, x_2, x_1^2, x_2^2, x_1 x_2)$$

In this case, the model remains externally linear, but it can capture internal non-linearities. To show how scikit-learn implements this technique, let's consider the dataset shown in the following figure:

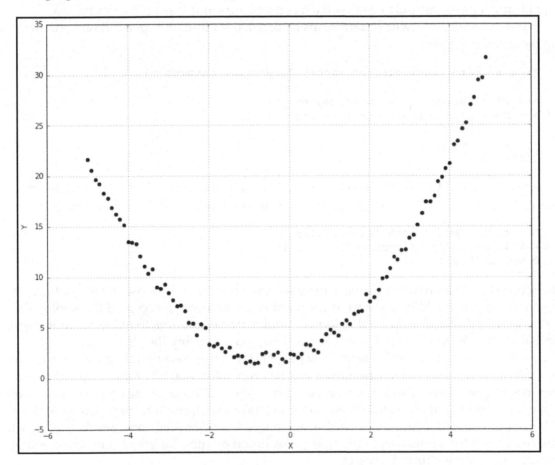

This is clearly a non-linear dataset, and any linear regression based only on the original two-dimensional points cannot capture the dynamics. Just to try, we can train a simple model (testing it on the same dataset):

```
from sklearn.linear_model import LinearRegression

>>> lr = LinearRegression(normalize=True)
>>> lr.fit(X.reshape((-1, 1)), Y.reshape((-1, 1)))
>>> lr.score(X.reshape((-1, 1)), Y.reshape((-1, 1)))
0.10888218817034558
```

Performances are poor, as expected. However, looking at the figure, we might suppose that a quadratic regression could easily solve this problem. scikit-learn provides the class `PolynomialFeatures`, which transforms an original set into an expanded one according to the parameter `degree`:

```
from sklearn.preprocessing import PolynomialFeatures

>>> pf = PolynomialFeatures(degree=2)
>>> Xp = pf.fit_transform(X.reshape(-1, 1))

>>> Xp.shape
(100L, 3L)
```

As expected, the old x_1 coordinate has been replaced by a triplet, which also contains the quadratic and mixed terms. At this point, a linear regression model can be trained:

```
>>> lr.fit(Xp, Y.reshape((-1, 1)))
>>> lr.score(Xp, Y.reshape((-1, 1)))
0.99692778265941961
```

The score is quite higher and the only price we have paid is an increase in terms of features. In general, this is feasible; however, if the number grows over an accepted threshold, it's useful to try a dimensionality reduction or, as an extreme solution, to move to a non-linear model (such as SVM-Kernel). Usually, a good approach is using the class `SelectFromModel` to let scikit-learn select the best features based on their importance. In fact, when the number of features increases, the probability that all of them have the same importance gets lower. This is the result of mutual correlation or of the co-presence of major and minor trends, which act like noise and don't have the strength to alter perceptibility the hyperplane slope. Moreover, when using a polynomial expansion, some weak features (that cannot be used for a linear separation) are substituted by their functions and so the actual number of strong features decreases.

In the following snippet, there's an example with the previous Boston dataset. The `threshold` parameter is used to set a minimum importance level. If missing, the class will try to maximize the efficiency by removing the highest possible number of features.

```
from sklearn.feature_selection import SelectFromModel

>>> boston = load_boston()

>>> pf = PolynomialFeatures(degree=2)
>>> Xp = pf.fit_transform(boston.data)
>>> Xp.shape
(506L, 105L)

>>> lr = LinearRegression(normalize=True)
>>> lr.fit(Xp, boston.target)
>>> lr.score(Xp, boston.target)
0.91795268869997404

>>> sm = SelectFromModel(lr, threshold=10)
>>> Xt = sm.fit_transform(Xp, boston.target)
>>> sm.estimator_.score(Xp, boston.target)
0.91795268869997404

>>> Xt.shape
(506L, 8L)
```

After selecting only the best features (with the threshold set to 10), the score remains the same, with a consistent dimensionality reduction (only 8 features are considered important for the prediction). If, after any other processing step, it's necessary to return to the original dataset, it's possible to use the inverse transformation:

```
>>> Xo = sm.inverse_transform(Xt)
>>> Xo.shape
(506L, 105L)
```

Isotonic regression

There are situations when we need to find a regressor for a dataset of non-decreasing points which can present low-level oscillations (such as noise). A linear regression can easily achieve a very high score (considering that the slope is about constant), but it works like a denoiser, producing a line that can't capture the internal dynamics we'd like to model. For these situations, scikit-learn offers the class IsotonicRegression, which produces a piecewise interpolating function minimizing the functional:

$$L = \sum_i w_i (y_i - \tilde{y}_i)^2 \ where \ y_0 \leq y_1 \leq \cdots \leq y_n$$

An example (with a toy dataset) is provided next:

```
>>> X = np.arange(-5, 5, 0.1)
>>> Y = X + np.random.uniform(-0.5, 1, size=X.shape)
```

Following is a plot of the dataset. As everyone can see, it can be easily modeled by a linear regressor, but without a high non-linear function, it is very difficult to capture the slight (and local) modifications in the slope:

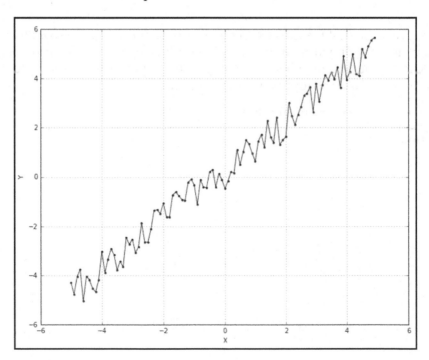

The class `IsotonicRegression` needs to know y_{min} and y_{max} (which correspond to the variables y_0 and y_n in the loss function). In this case, we impose -6 and 10:

```
from sklearn.isotonic import IsotonicRegression

>>> ir = IsotonicRegression(-6, 10)
>>> Yi = ir.fit_transform(X, Y)
```

The result is provided through three instance variables:

```
>>> ir.X_min_
-5.0
>>> ir.X_max_
4.8999999999999648
>>> ir.f_
<scipy.interpolate.interpolate.interp1d at 0x126edef8>
```

The last one, (`ir.f_`), is an interpolating function which can be evaluated in the domain $[x_{min}, x_{max}]$. For example:

```
>>> ir.f_(2)
array(1.7294334618146134)
```

A plot of this function (the green line), together with the original data set, is shown in the following figure:

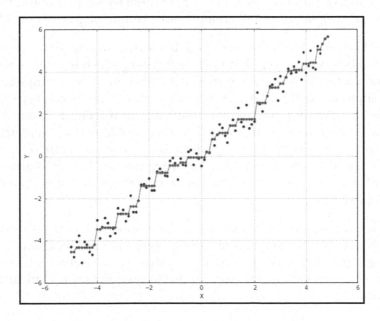

For further information about interpolation with SciPy, visit `https://docs` `.scipy.org/doc/scipy-0.18.1/reference/interpolate.html`.

References

Hastie T., Tibshirani R., Friedman J., *The Elements of Statistical Learning: Data Mining, Inference, and, Prediction*, Springer

Summary

In this chapter, we have introduced the important concepts of linear models and have described how linear regression works. In particular, we focused on the basic model and its main variants: Lasso, Ridge, and ElasticNet. They don't modify the internal dynamics but work as normalizers for the weights, in order to avoid common problems when the dataset contains unscaled samples. These penalties have specific peculiarities. While Lasso promotes sparsity, Ridge tries to find a minimum with the constraints that the weights must lay on a circle centered at the origin (whose radius is parametrized to increase/decrease the normalization strength). ElasticNet is a mix of both these techniques and it tries to find a minimum where the weights are small enough and a certain degree of sparsity is achieved.

We also discussed advanced techniques such as RANSAC, which allows coping with outliers in a very robust way, and polynomial regression, which is a very smart way to include virtual non-linear features into our model and continue working with them with the same linear approach. In this way, it's possible to create another dataset, containing the original columns together with polynomial combinations of them. This new dataset can be used to train a linear regression model, and then it's possible to select only those features that contributed towards achieving good performances. The last method we saw was isotonic regression, which is particularly useful when the function to interpolate is always not decreasing. Moreover it can capture the small oscillations that would be flattened by a generic linear regression.

In the next chapter, we're going to discuss some linear models for classifications. In particular, we'll focus our attention on the logistic regression and stochastic gradient descent algorithms. Moreover, we're going to introduce some useful metrics to evaluate the accuracy of a classification system, and a powerful technique to automatically find the best hyperparameters.

5
Logistic Regression

This chapter begins by analyzing linear classification problems, with particular focus on logistic regression (despite its name, it's a classification algorithm) and stochastic gradient descent approaches. Even if these strategies appear too simple, they're still the main choices in many classification tasks. Speaking of which, it's useful to remember a very important philosophical principle: **Occam's razor**. In our context, it states that the first choice must always be the simplest and only if it doesn't fit, it's necessary to move on to more complex models. In the second part of the chapter, we're going to discuss some common metrics useful to evaluate a classification task. They are not limited to linear models, so we use them when talking about different strategies as well.

Linear classification

Let's consider a generic linear classification problem with two classes. In the following figure, there's an example:

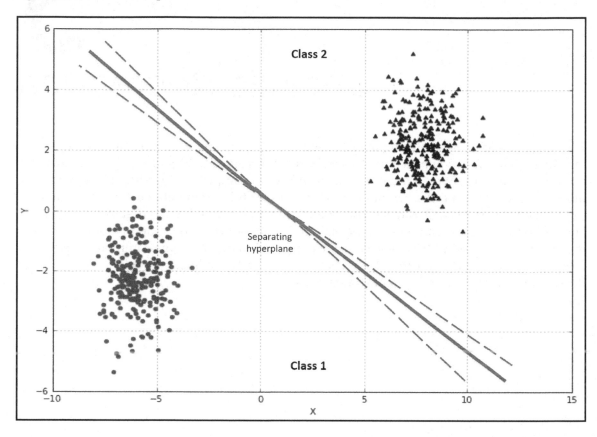

Our goal is to find an optimal hyperplane, which separates the two classes. In multi-class problems, the strategy one-vs-all is normally adopted, so the discussion can be focused only on binary classifications. Suppose we have the following dataset:

$$X = \{\bar{x}_1, \bar{x}_2, \dots, \bar{x}_n\} \; where \; \bar{x}_i \in \mathbb{R}^m$$

This dataset is associated with the following target set:

$$Y = \{y_1, y_2, \dots, y_n\} \; where \; y_n \in \{0, 1\}$$

We can now define a weight vector made of m continuous components:

$$W = \{w_1, w_2, \dots, w_m\} \; where \; w_i \in \mathbb{R}$$

We can also define the quantity z:

$$\forall \bar{x} \in \mathbb{R}^m \; z = \bar{x} \cdot \bar{w} = \sum_i x_i w_i$$

If x is a variable, z is the value determined by the hyperplane equation. Therefore, if the set of coefficients w that has been determined is correct, it happens that:

$$sign(z) = \begin{cases} +1 \; if \; x \in Class \; 1 \\ -1 \; if \; x \in Class \; 2 \end{cases}$$

Now we must find a way to optimize w, in order to reduce the classification error. If such a combination exists (with a certain error threshold), we say that our problem is **linearly separable**. On the other hand, when it's impossible to find a linear classifier, the problem is called **non-linearly separable**. A very simple but famous example is given by the logical operator XOR:

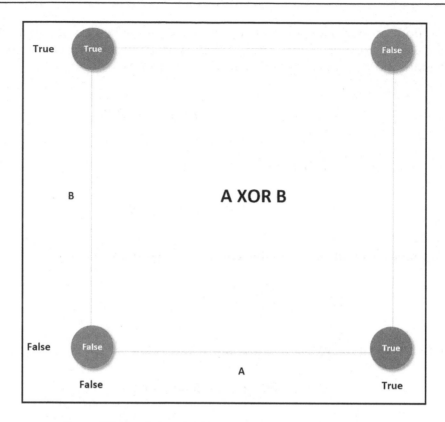

As you can see, any line will always include a wrong sample. Hence, in order to solve this problem, it is necessary to involve non-linear techniques. However, in many real-life cases, we use linear techniques (which are often simpler and faster) for non-linear problems too, accepting a tolerable misclassification error.

Logistic regression

Even if called regression, this is a classification method which is based on the probability for a sample to belong to a class. As our probabilities must be continuous in R and bounded between $(0, 1)$, it's necessary to introduce a threshold function to filter the term z. The name logistic comes from the decision to use the sigmoid (or logistic) function:

$$\sigma(z) = \frac{1}{1 + e^{-z}} \text{ which becomes } \sigma(\bar{x}; \bar{w}) = \frac{1}{1 + e^{-\bar{x} \cdot \bar{w}}}$$

A partial plot of this function is shown in the following figure:

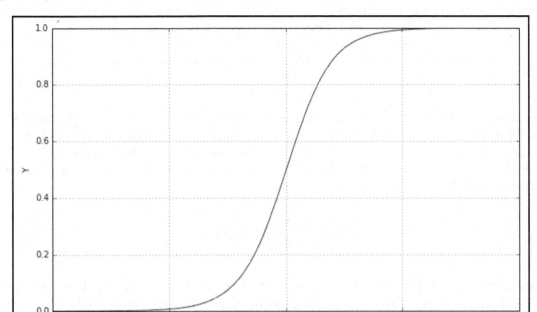

As you can see, the function intersects *x=0* in the ordinate 0.5, and *y<0.5* for *x<0* and *y>0.5* for *x>0*. Moreover, its domain is *R* and it has two asymptotes at 0 and 1. So, we can define the probability for a sample to belong to a class (from now on, we'll call them 0 and 1) as:

$$P(y|\bar{x}) = \sigma(\bar{x}; \bar{w})$$

At this point, finding the optimal parameters is equivalent to maximizing the log-likelihood given the output class:

$$L(\bar{w}; y) = \log P(y|\bar{w}) = \sum_i \log P(y_i|\bar{x}_i, \bar{w})$$

Therefore, the optimization problem can be expressed, using the indicator notation, as the minimization of the loss function:

$$J(\bar{w}) = -\sum_i \log P(y_i | \bar{x}_i, \bar{w}) = -\sum_i (y_i \log \sigma(z_i) + (1 - y_i) \log(1 - \sigma(z_i)))$$

If *y=0*, the first term becomes null and the second one becomes *log(1-x)*, which is the log-probability of the class 0. On the other hand, if *y=1*, the second term is 0 and the first one represents the log-probability of *x*. In this way, both cases are embedded in a single expression. In terms of information theory, it means minimizing the cross-entropy between a target distribution and an approximated one:

$$H(X) = -\sum_{x \in X} p(x) log_2 q(x)$$

In particular, if log_2 is adopted, the functional expresses the number of extra bits requested to encode the original distribution with the predicted one. It's obvious that when *J(w) = 0*, the two distributions are equal. Therefore, minimizing the cross-entropy is an elegant way to optimize the prediction error when the target distributions are categorical.

Implementation and optimizations

scikit-learn implements the `LogisticRegression` class, which can solve this problem using optimized algorithms. Let's consider a toy dataset made of 500 samples:

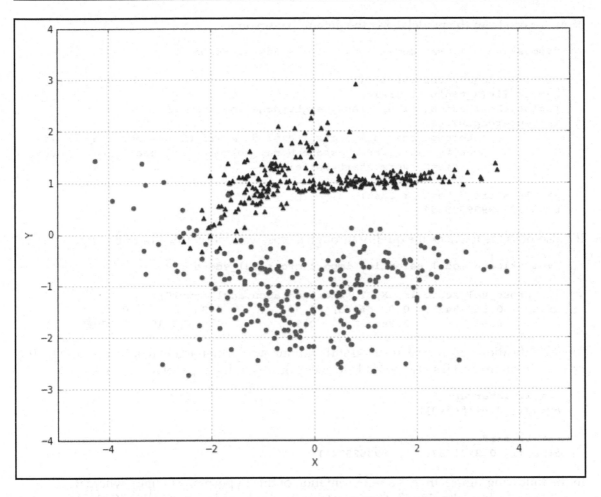

The dots belong to the class 0, while the triangles belong to the class 1. In order to immediately test the accuracy of our classification, it's useful to split the dataset into training and test sets:

```
from sklearn.model_selection import train_test_split

>>> X_train, X_test, Y_train, Y_test = train_test_split(X, Y,
test_size=0.25)
```

Now we can train the model using the default parameters:

```
from sklearn.linear_model import LogisticRegression

>>> lr = LogisticRegression()
>>> lr.fit(X_train, Y_train)
LogisticRegression(C=1.0, class_weight=None, dual=False,
fit_intercept=True,
        intercept_scaling=1, max_iter=100, multi_class='ovr', n_jobs=1,
        penalty='l2', random_state=None, solver='liblinear', tol=0.0001,
        verbose=0, warm_start=False)

>>> lr.score(X_test, Y_test)
0.95199999999999996
```

It's also possible to check the quality through a cross-validation (like for linear regression):

```
from sklearn.model_selection import cross_val_score

>>> cross_val_score(lr, X, Y, scoring='accuracy', cv=10)
array([ 0.96078431,  0.92156863,  0.96      ,  0.98      ,  0.96      ,
        0.98      ,  0.96      ,  0.96      ,  0.91836735,  0.97959184])
```

The classification task has been successful without any further action (confirmed also by the cross-validation) and it's also possible to check the resulting hyperplane parameters:

```
>>> lr.intercept_
array([-0.64154943])

>>> lr.coef_
array([[ 0.34417875,  3.89362924]])
```

In the following figure, there's a representation of this hyperplane (a line), where it's possible to see how the classification works and what samples are misclassified. Considering the local density of the two blocks, it's easy to see that the misclassifications happened for outliers and for some borderline samples. The latter can be controlled by adjusting the hyperparameters, even if a trade-off is often necessary. For example, if we want to include the four right dots on the separation line, this could exclude some elements in the right part. Later on, we're going to see how to find the optimal solution. However, when a linear classifier can easily find a separating hyperplane (even with a few outliers), we can say that the problem is linearly modelable; otherwise, more sophisticated non-linear techniques must be taken into account.

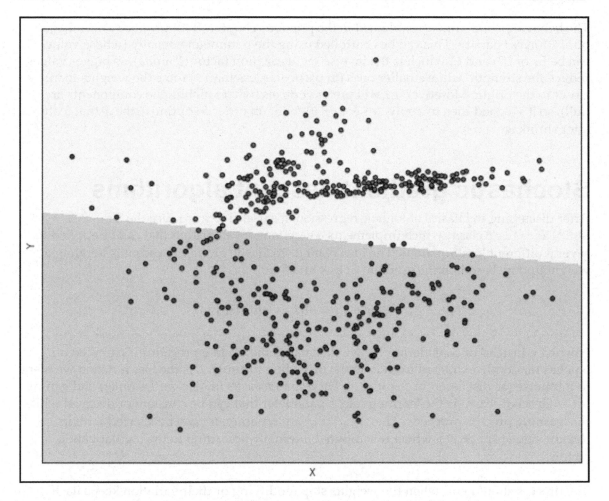

Just like for linear regression, it's possible to impose norm conditions on the weights. In particular, the actual functional becomes:

$$\tilde{J}(\overline{w}) = \begin{cases} J(\overline{w}) + \alpha\|\overline{w}\|_1 \\ J(\overline{w}) + \alpha\|\overline{w}\|_2 \end{cases}$$

The behavior is the same as explained in the previous chapter. Both produce a shrinkage, but *L1* forces sparsity. This can be controlled using the parameters penalty (whose values can be *L1* or *L2*) and *C*, which is the inverse regularization factor (1/alpha), so bigger values reduce the strength, while smaller ones (in particular less than 1) force the weights to move closer to the origin. Moreover, *L1* will prefer vertexes (where all but one components are null), so it's a good idea to apply `SelectFromModel` in order to optimize the actual features after shrinkage.

Stochastic gradient descent algorithms

After discussing the basics of logistic regression, it's useful to introduce the `SGDClassifier` class , which implements a very famous algorithm that can be applied to several different loss functions. The idea behind stochastic gradient descent is iterating a weight update based on the gradient of loss function:

$$\overline{w}(k + 1) = \overline{w}(k) - \gamma \nabla L(\overline{w})$$

However, instead of considering the whole dataset, the update procedure is applied on batches randomly extracted from it. In the preceding formula, *L* is the loss function we want to minimize (as discussed in `Chapter 2`, *Important Elements in Machine Learning*) and gamma (`eta0` in scikit-learn) is the learning rate, a parameter that can be constant or decayed while the learning process proceeds. The `learning_rate` parameter can be also left with its default value (`optimal`), which is computed internally according to the regularization factor.

The process should end when the weights stop modifying or their variation keeps itself under a selected threshold. The scikit-learn implementation uses the `n_iter` parameter to define the number of desired iterations.

There are many possible loss functions, but in this chapter, we consider only `log` and `perceptron`. Some of the other ones will be discussed in the next chapters. The former implements a logistic regression, while the latter (which is also available as the autonomous class `Perceptron`) is the simplest neural network, composed of a single layer of weights w, a fixed constant called bias, and a binary output function:

$$z = \overline{w} \cdot \overline{x} + b$$

The output function (which classifies in two classes) is:

$$y = \begin{cases} 1 & if\ z > 0 \\ 0 & if\ z \leq 0 \end{cases}$$

The differences between a `Perceptron` and a `LogisticRegression` are the output function (sign versus sigmoid) and the training model (with the loss function). A perceptron, in fact, is normally trained by minimizing the mean square distance between the actual value and prediction:

$$L = \frac{1}{n} \sum_i \| y_i - \hat{y}_i \|^2$$

Just like any other linear classifier, a perceptron is not able to solve nonlinear problems; hence, our example will be generated using the built-in function `make_classification`:

```
from sklearn.datasets import make_classification

>>> nb_samples = 500
>>> X, Y = make_classification(n_samples=nb_samples, n_features=2,
n_informative=2, n_redundant=0, n_clusters_per_class=1)
```

In this way, we can generate 500 samples split into two classes:

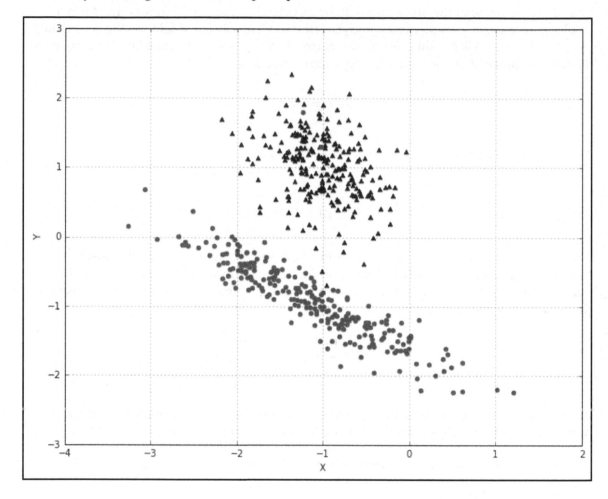

This problem, under a determined precision threshold, can be linearly solved, so our expectations are equivalent for both `Perceptron` and `LogisticRegression`. In the latter case, the training strategy is focused on maximizing the likelihood of a probability distribution. Considering the dataset, the probability of a red sample to belong to class 0 must be greater than 0.5 (it's equal to 0.5 when $z = 0$, so when the point lays on the separating hyperplane) and vice versa. On the other hand, a perceptron will adjust the hyperplane so that the dot product between a sample and the weights would be positive or negative, according to the class. In the following figure, there's a geometrical representation of a perceptron (where the bias is 0):

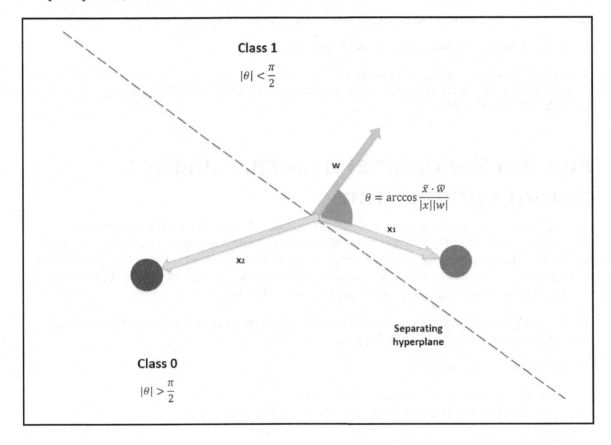

The weight vector is orthogonal to the separating hyperplane, so that the discrimination can happen only considering the sign of the dot product. An example of stochastic gradient descent with perceptron loss (without *L1/L2* constraints) is shown as follows:

```
from sklearn.linear_model import SGDClassifier

>>> sgd = SGDClassifier(loss='perceptron', learning_rate='optimal',
n_iter=10)
>>> cross_val_score(sgd, X, Y, scoring='accuracy', cv=10).mean()
0.98595918367346935
```

The same result can be obtained by directly using the `Perceptron` class:

```
from sklearn.linear_model import Perceptron

>>> perc = Perceptron(n_iter=10)
>>> cross_val_score(perc, X, Y, scoring='accuracy', cv=10).mean()
0.98195918367346935
```

Finding the optimal hyperparameters through grid search

Finding the best hyperparameters (called this because they influence the parameters learned during the training phase) is not always easy and there are seldom good methods to start from. The personal experience (a fundamental element) must be aided by an efficient tool such as `GridSearchCV`, which automates the training process of different models and provides the user with optimal values using cross-validation.

As an example, we show how to use it to find the best penalty and strength factors for a linear regression with the Iris toy dataset:

```
import multiprocessing

from sklearn.datasets import load_iris
from sklearn.model_selection import GridSearchCV

>>> iris = load_iris()

>>> param_grid = [
    {
        'penalty': [ 'l1', 'l2' ],
        'C': [ 0.5, 1.0, 1.5, 1.8, 2.0, 2.5]
    }
]
```

```
>>> gs = GridSearchCV(estimator=LogisticRegression(),
param_grid=param_grid,
    scoring='accuracy', cv=10, n_jobs=multiprocessing.cpu_count())

>>> gs.fit(iris.data, iris.target)
GridSearchCV(cv=10, error_score='raise',
        estimator=LogisticRegression(C=1.0, class_weight=None, dual=False,
fit_intercept=True,
            intercept_scaling=1, max_iter=100, multi_class='ovr', n_jobs=1,
            penalty='12', random_state=None, solver='liblinear', tol=0.0001,
            verbose=0, warm_start=False),
        fit_params={}, iid=True, n_jobs=8,
        param_grid=[{'penalty': ['11', '12'], 'C': [0.1, 0.2, 0.4, 0.5, 1.0,
1.5, 1.8, 2.0, 2.5]}],
        pre_dispatch='2*n_jobs', refit=True, return_train_score=True,
        scoring='accuracy', verbose=0)

>>> gs.best_estimator_
LogisticRegression(C=1.5, class_weight=None, dual=False,
fit_intercept=True,
            intercept_scaling=1, max_iter=100, multi_class='ovr', n_jobs=1,
            penalty='11', random_state=None, solver='liblinear', tol=0.0001,
            verbose=0, warm_start=False)

>>> cross_val_score(gs.best_estimator_, iris.data, iris.target,
scoring='accuracy', cv=10).mean()
0.96666666666666679
```

It's possible to insert into the `param` dictionary any parameter supported by the model with a list of values. `GridSearchCV` will process in parallel and return the best estimator (through the instance variable `best_estimator_`, which is an instance of the same classifier specified through the parameter `estimator`).

> When working with parallel algorithms, scikit-learn provides the `n_jobs` parameter, which allows us to specify how many threads must be used. Setting `n_jobs=multiprocessing.cpu_count()` is useful to exploit all CPU cores available on the current machine.

In the next example, we're going to find the best parameters of an `SGDClassifier` trained with perceptron loss. The dataset is plotted in the following figure:

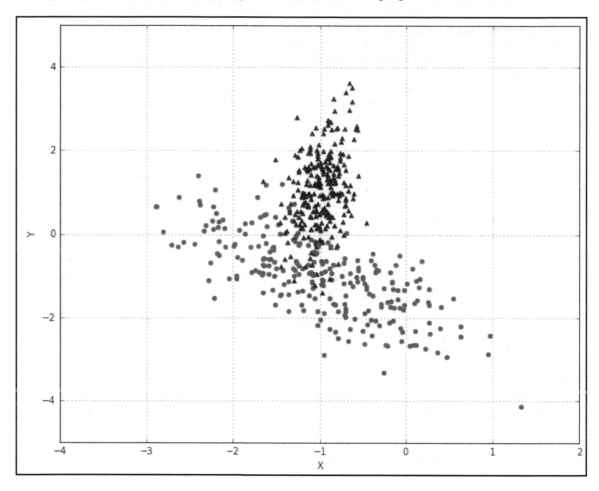

```
import multiprocessing

from sklearn.model_selection import GridSearchCV

>>> param_grid = [
    {
        'penalty': [ 'l1', 'l2', 'elasticnet' ],
        'alpha': [ 1e-5, 1e-4, 5e-4, 1e-3, 2.3e-3, 5e-3, 1e-2],
        'l1_ratio': [0.01, 0.05, 0.1, 0.15, 0.25, 0.35, 0.5, 0.75, 0.8]
    }
]
```

```
>>> sgd = SGDClassifier(loss='perceptron', learning_rate='optimal')
>>> gs = GridSearchCV(estimator=sgd, param_grid=param_grid,
scoring='accuracy', cv=10, n_jobs=multiprocessing.cpu_count())

>>> gs.fit(X, Y)
GridSearchCV(cv=10, error_score='raise',
        estimator=SGDClassifier(alpha=0.0001, average=False,
class_weight=None, epsilon=0.1,
        eta0=0.0, fit_intercept=True, l1_ratio=0.15,
        learning_rate='optimal', loss='perceptron', n_iter=5, n_jobs=1,
        penalty='l2', power_t=0.5, random_state=None, shuffle=True,
        verbose=0, warm_start=False),
        fit_params={}, iid=True, n_jobs=8,
        param_grid=[{'penalty': ['l1', 'l2', 'elasticnet'], 'alpha': [1e-05,
0.0001, 0.0005, 0.001, 0.0023, 0.005, 0.01], 'l1_ratio': [0.01, 0.05, 0.1,
0.15, 0.25, 0.35, 0.5, 0.75, 0.8]}],
        pre_dispatch='2*n_jobs', refit=True, return_train_score=True,
        scoring='accuracy', verbose=0)

>>> gs.best_score_
0.89400000000000002

>>> gs.best_estimator_
SGDClassifier(alpha=0.001, average=False, class_weight=None, epsilon=0.1,
        eta0=0.0, fit_intercept=True, l1_ratio=0.1, learning_rate='optimal',
        loss='perceptron', n_iter=5, n_jobs=1, penalty='elasticnet',
        power_t=0.5, random_state=None, shuffle=True, verbose=0,
        warm_start=False)
```

Classification metrics

A classification task can be evaluated in many different ways to achieve specific objectives. Of course, the most important metric is the accuracy, often expressed as:

$$Generic\ accuracy = 1 - \frac{Number\ of\ misclassified\ samples}{Total\ number\ of\ samples}$$

In scikit-learn, it can be assessed using the built-in `accuracy_score()` function:

```
from sklearn.metrics import accuracy_score

>>> accuracy_score(Y_test, lr.predict(X_test))
0.94399999999999995
```

Another very common approach is based on zero-one loss function, which we saw in Chapter 2, *Important Elements in Machine Learning*, which is defined as the normalized average of $L_{0/1}$ (where 1 is assigned to misclassifications) over all samples. In the following example, we show a normalized score (if it's close to 0, it's better) and then the same unnormalized value (which is the actual number of misclassifications):

```
from sklearn.metrics import zero_one_loss

>>> zero_one_loss(Y_test, lr.predict(X_test))
0.05600000000000005

>>> zero_one_loss(Y_test, lr.predict(X_test), normalize=False)
7L
```

A similar but opposite metric is the **Jaccard similarity coefficient**, defined as:

$$A = \{\, y_i \text{ where } y_i \text{ is a true label}\}$$

$$B = \{\, \hat{y}_i \text{ where } \hat{y}_i \text{ is predicted label}\}$$

$$J(A, B) = \frac{|A \cap B|}{|A \cup B|}$$

This index measures the similarity and is bounded between 0 (worst performances) and 1 (best performances). In the former case, the intersection is null, while in the latter, the intersection and union are equal because there are no misclassifications. In scikit-learn, the implementation is:

```
from sklearn.metrics import jaccard_similarity_score

>>> jaccard_similarity_score(Y_test, lr.predict(X_test))
0.94399999999999995
```

These measures provide a good insight into our classification algorithms. However, in many cases, it's necessary to be able to differentiate between different kinds of misclassifications (we're considering the binary case with the conventional notation: 0-negative, 1-positive), because the relative weight is quite different. For this reason, we introduce the following definitions:

- **True positive**: A positive sample correctly classified
- **False positive**: A negative sample classified as positive
- **True negative**: A negative sample correctly classified
- **False negative**: A positive sample classified as negative

At a glance, false positive and false negative can be considered as similar errors, but think about a medical prediction: while a false positive can be easily discovered with further tests, a false negative is often neglected, with repercussions following the consequences of this action. For this reason, it's useful to introduce the concept of a confusion matrix:

In scikit-learn, it's possible to build a confusion matrix using a built-in function. Let's consider a generic logistic regression on a dataset *X* with labels *Y*:

```
>>> X_train, X_test, Y_train, Y_test = train_test_split(X, Y,
test_size=0.25)
>>> lr = LogisticRegression()
>>> lr.fit(X_train, Y_train)
LogisticRegression(C=1.0, class_weight=None, dual=False,
fit_intercept=True,
          intercept_scaling=1, max_iter=100, multi_class='ovr', n_jobs=1,
          penalty='l2', random_state=None, solver='liblinear', tol=0.0001,
          verbose=0, warm_start=False)
```

Now we can compute our confusion matrix and immediately see how the classifier is working:

```
from sklearn.metrics import confusion_matrix

>>> cm = confusion_matrix(y_true=Y_test, y_pred=lr.predict(X_test))
cm[::-1, ::-1]
[[50  5]
 [ 2 68]]
```

The last operation is needed because scikit-learn adopts an inverse axle. However, in many books, the confusion matrix has true values on the main diagonal, so I preferred to invert the axle.

 In order to avoid mistakes, I suggest you visit the page at http://scikit-learn.org/stable/modules/generated/sklearn.metrics.confusion_matrix.html, and check for true/false positive/negative position.

So we have five false negatives and two false positives. If needed, a further analysis can allow for the detection of the misclassifications to decide how to treat them (for example, if their variance overcomes a predefined threshold, it's possible to consider them as outliers and remove them).

Another useful direct measure is:

$$Precision = \frac{True\ positives}{True\ positives + False\ positives}$$

This is directly connected with the ability to capture the features that determine the positiveness of a sample, to avoid the misclassification as negative. In scikit-learn, the implementation is:

```
from sklearn.metrics import precision_score

>>> precision_score(Y_test, lr.predict(X_test))
0.96153846153846156
```

 If you don't flip the confusion matrix, but want to get the same measures, it's necessary to add the `pos_label=0` parameter to all metric score functions.

The ability to detect true positive samples among all the potential positives can be assessed using another measure:

$$Recall = \frac{True\ positives}{True\ positives + False\ negatives}$$

The scikit-learn implementation is:

```
from sklearn.metrics import recall_score

>>> recall_score(Y_test, lr.predict(X_test))
0.90909090909090906
```

It's not surprising that we have a 90 percent recall with 96 percent precision, because the number of false negatives (which impact recall) is proportionally higher than the number of false positives (which impact precision). A weighted harmonic mean between precision and recall is provided by:

$$F_{Beta} = (\beta^2 + 1)\frac{Precision \cdot Recall}{(\beta^2 Precision) + Recall}$$

A beta value equal to 1 determines the so-called F_1 score, which is a perfect balance between the two measures. A beta less than 1 gives more importance to *precision* and a value greater than 1 gives more importance to *recall*. The following snippet shows how to implement it with scikit-learn:

```
from sklearn.metrics import fbeta_score

>>> fbeta_score(Y_test, lr.predict(X_test), beta=1)
0.93457943925233655

>>> fbeta_score(Y_test, lr.predict(X_test), beta=0.75)
0.94197437829691033

>>> fbeta_score(Y_test, lr.predict(X_test), beta=1.25)
0.92886270956048933
```

 For F_1 score, scikit-learn provides the function `f1_score()`, which is equivalent to `fbeta_score()` with `beta=1`.

The highest score is achieved by giving more importance to precision (which is higher), while the least one corresponds to a recall predominance. F_{Beta} is hence useful to have a compact picture of the accuracy as a trade-off between high precision and a limited number of false negatives.

ROC curve

The **ROC curve** (or receiver operating characteristics) is a valuable tool to compare different classifiers that can assign a score to their predictions. In general, this score can be interpreted as a probability, so it's bounded between 0 and 1. The plane is structured like in the following figure:

The x axis represents the increasing false positive rate (also known as **specificity**), while the y axis represents the true positive rate (also known as **sensitivity**). The dashed oblique line represents a perfectly random classifier, so all the curves below this threshold perform worse than a random choice, while the ones above it show better performances. Of course, the best classifier has an ROC curve split into the segments [0, 0] - [0, 1] and [0, 1] - [1, 1], and our goal is to find algorithms whose performances should be as close as possible to this limit. To show how to create a ROC curve with scikit-learn, we're going to train a model to determine the scores for the predictions (this can be achieved using the `decision_function()` or `predict_proba()` methods):

```
>>> X_train, X_test, Y_train, Y_test = train_test_split(X, Y,
test_size=0.25)

>>> lr = LogisticRegression()
>>> lr.fit(X_train, Y_train)
LogisticRegression(C=1.0, class_weight=None, dual=False,
fit_intercept=True,
        intercept_scaling=1, max_iter=100, multi_class='ovr', n_jobs=1,
        penalty='l2', random_state=None, solver='liblinear', tol=0.0001,
        verbose=0, warm_start=False)

>>> Y_scores = lr.decision_function(X_test)
```

Now we can compute the ROC curve:

```
from sklearn.metrics import roc_curve

>>> fpr, tpr, thresholds = roc_curve(Y_test, Y_scores)
```

The output is made up of the increasing true and false positive rates and the decreasing thresholds (which isn't normally used for plotting the curve). Before proceeding, it's also useful to compute the **area under the curve (AUC)**, whose value is bounded between 0 (worst performances) and 1 (best performances), with a perfectly random value corresponding to 0.5:

```
from sklearn.metrics import auc

>>> auc(fpr, tpr)
0.96961038961038959
```

We already know that our performances are rather good because the AUC is close to 1. Now we can plot the ROC curve using matplotlib. As this book is not dedicated to this powerful framework, I'm going to use a snippet that can be found in several examples:

```
import matplotlib.pyplot as plt

>>> plt.figure(figsize=(8, 8))
>>> plt.plot(fpr, tpr, color='red', label='Logistic regression (AUC: %.2f)'
% auc(fpr, tpr))
>>> plt.plot([0, 1], [0, 1], color='blue', linestyle='--')
>>> plt.xlim([0.0, 1.0])
>>> plt.ylim([0.0, 1.01])
>>> plt.title('ROC Curve')
>>> plt.xlabel('False Positive Rate')
>>> plt.ylabel('True Positive Rate')
>>> plt.legend(loc="lower right")
>>> plt.show()
```

The resulting ROC curve is the following plot:

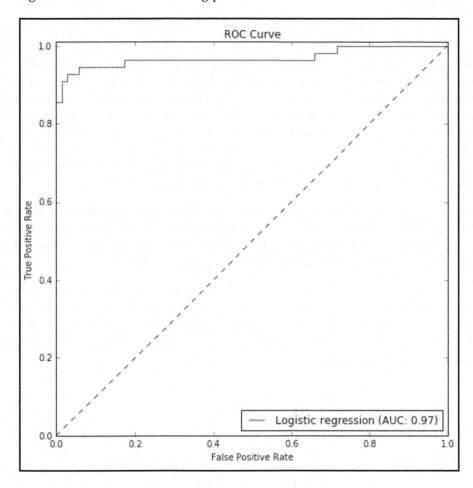

As confirmed by the AUC, our ROC curve shows very good performance. In later chapters, we're going to use the ROC curve to visually compare different algorithms. As an exercise, you can try different parameters of the same model and plot all the ROC curves, to immediately understand which setting is preferable.

 I suggest visiting http://matplotlib.org, for further information and tutorials. Moreover, an extraordinary tool is Jupyter (http://jupyter.org), which allows working with interactive notebooks, where you can immediately try your code and visualize in-line plots.

Summary

A linear model classifies samples using separating hyperplanes; hence, a problem is linearly separable if it's possible to find a linear model whose accuracy overcomes a predetermined threshold. Logistic regression is one of most famous linear classifiers, based on the principle of maximizing the probability of a sample belonging to the right class. Stochastic gradient descent classifiers are a more generic family of algorithms, determined by the different loss function that is adopted. SGD allows partial fitting, particularly when the amount of data is too huge to be loaded in memory. A perceptron is a particular instance of SGD, representing a linear neural network that cannot solve the XOR problem (for this reason, multi-layer perceptrons became the first choice for non-linear classification). However, in general, its performance is comparable to a logistic regression model.

All classifier performances must be measured using different approaches, in order to be able to optimize their parameters or to change them when the results don't meet our requirements. We discussed different metrics and, in particular, the ROC curve, which graphically shows how the different classifiers are performing.

In the next chapter, we're going to discuss naive Bayes classifiers, which are another very famous and powerful family of algorithms. Thanks to this simple approach, it's possible to build spam filtering systems and solve apparently complex problems using only probabilities and the quality of results. Even after decades, it's still superior or comparable to much more complex solutions.

6
Naive Bayes

Naive Bayes are a family of powerful and easy-to-train classifiers that determine the probability of an outcome given a set of conditions using Bayes' theorem. In other words, the conditional probabilities are inverted, so that the query can be expressed as a function of measurable quantities. The approach is simple, and the adjective "naive" has been attributed not because these algorithms are limited or less efficient, but because of a fundamental assumption about the causal factors that we're going to discuss. Naive Bayes are multipurpose classifiers and it's easy to find their application in many different contexts; however, their performance is particularly good in all those situations where the probability of a class is determined by the probabilities of some causal factors. A good example is natural language processing, where a piece of text can be considered as a particular instance of a dictionary and the relative frequencies of all terms provide enough information to infer a belonging class. We're going to discuss these concepts in later chapters. In this one, our examples will be always generic to let the reader understand how to apply naive Bayes in various contexts.

Bayes' theorem

Let's consider two probabilistic events A and B. We can correlate the marginal probabilities $P(A)$ and $P(B)$ with the conditional probabilities $P(A|B)$ and $P(B|A)$ using the product rule:

$$\begin{cases} P(A \cap B) = P(A|B)P(B) \\ P(B \cap A) = P(B|A)P(A) \end{cases}$$

Considering that the intersection is commutative, the first members are equal; so we can derive **Bayes' theorem**:

$$P(A|B) = \frac{P(B|A)P(A)}{P(B)}$$

This formula has very deep philosophical implications and it's a fundamental element of statistical learning. First of all, let's consider the marginal probability $P(A)$; this is normally a value that determines how probable a target event is, such as $P(Spam)$ or $P(Rain)$. As there are no other elements, this kind of probability is called **Apriori**, because it's often determined by mathematical considerations or simply by a frequency count. For example, imagine we want to implement a very simple spam filter and we've collected 100 emails. We know that 30 are spam and 70 are regular. So we can say that $P(Spam) = 0.3$.

However, we'd like to evaluate using some criteria (for simplicity, let's consider a single one), for example, email text is shorter than 50 characters. Therefore, our query becomes:

$$P(Spam|Text < 50\ chars) = \frac{P(Text < 50\ chars|Spam)P(Spam)}{P(Text < 50\ chars)}$$

The first term is similar to $P(Spam)$ because it's the probability of spam given a certain condition. For this reason, it's called **a posteriori** (in other words, it's a probability that we can estimate after knowing some additional elements). On the right-hand side, we need to calculate the missing values, but it's simple. Let's suppose that 35 emails have text shorter than 50 characters, so $P(Text < 50\ chars) = 0.35$. Looking only into our spam folder, we discover that only 25 spam emails have short text, so that $P(Text < 50\ chars\ |\ Spam) = 25/30 = 0.83$. The result is:

$$P(Spam|Text < 50\ chars) = \frac{0.83 \cdot 0.3}{0.35} = 0.71$$

So, after receiving a very short email, there is a 71% probability that it's spam. Now, we can understand the role of $P(Text < 50\ chars\ |\ Spam)$; as we have actual data, we can measure how probable is our hypothesis given the query. In other words, we have defined a likelihood (compare this with logistic regression), which is a weight between the Apriori probability and the a posteriori one (the term in the denominator is less important because it works as a normalizing factor):

$$P_{A-Posteriori} \propto Likelihood \cdot P_{A-Priori}$$

The normalization factor is often represented by the Greek letter alpha, so the formula becomes:

$$P(A|B) = \alpha P(B|A)P(A)$$

The last step is considering the case when there are more concurrent conditions (this is more realistic in real-life problems):

$$P(A|C_1 \cap C_2 \cap ... \cap C_n)$$

A common assumption is called **conditional independence** (in other words, the effects produced by every cause are independent of each other) and this allows us to write a simplified expression:

$$P(A|C_1 \cap C_2 \cap ... \cap C_n) = \alpha P(C_1|A)P(C_2|A) ... P(C_n|A)P(A)$$

Naive Bayes classifiers

A naive Bayes classifier is called so because it's based on a naive condition, which implies the conditional independence of causes. This can seem very difficult to accept in many contexts where the probability of a particular feature is strictly correlated to another one. For example, in spam filtering, a text shorter than 50 characters can increase the probability of the presence of an image, or if the domain has been already blacklisted for sending the same spam emails to million users, it's likely to find particular keywords. In other words, the presence of a cause isn't normally independent from the presence of other ones. However, in Zhang H., *The Optimality of Naive Bayes*, AAAI 1, no. 2 (2004): 3, the author showed that under particular conditions (not so rare to happen), different dependencies clears one another, and a naive Bayes classifier succeeds in achieving very high performances even if its naiveness is violated.

Let's consider a dataset:

$$X = \{\bar{x}_1, \bar{x}_2, ..., \bar{x}_n\} \; where \; \bar{x}_i \in \mathbb{R}^m$$

Every feature vector, for simplicity, will be represented as:

$$\bar{x}_i = [x_1, x_2, ..., x_m]$$

We need also a target dataset:

$$Y = \{y_1, y_2, ..., y_n\} \; where \; y_n \in (0,1,2, ... P)$$

Here, each y can belong to one of P different classes. Considering Bayes' theorem under conditional independence, we can write:

$$P(y|x_1, x_2, ..., x_m) = \alpha P(y) \prod_i P(x_i|y)$$

The values of the marginal Apriori probability $P(y)$ and of the conditional probabilities $P(x_i|y)$ is obtained through a frequency count; therefore, given an input vector x, the predicted class is the one for which the a posteriori probability is maximum.

Naive Bayes in scikit-learn

scikit-learn implements three naive Bayes variants based on the same number of different probabilistic distributions: Bernoulli, multinomial, and Gaussian. The first one is a binary distribution, useful when a feature can be present or absent. The second one is a discrete distribution and is used whenever a feature must be represented by a whole number (for example, in natural language processing, it can be the frequency of a term), while the third is a continuous distribution characterized by its mean and variance.

Bernoulli naive Bayes

If X is random variable and is Bernoulli-distributed, it can assume only two values (for simplicity, let's call them 0 and 1) and their probability is:

$$P(X) = \begin{cases} p & if \; X = 1 \\ q & if \; X = 0 \end{cases}$$

$$where \; q = 1 - p \; and \; 0 < p < 1$$

To try this algorithm with scikit-learn, we're going to generate a dummy dataset. Bernoulli naive Bayes expects binary feature vectors; however, the class `BernoulliNB` has a `binarize` parameter, which allows us to specify a threshold that will be used internally to transform the features:

```
from sklearn.datasets import make_classification

>>> nb_samples = 300
>>> X, Y = make_classification(n_samples=nb_samples, n_features=2,
n_informative=2, n_redundant=0)
```

We have generated the bidimensional dataset shown in the following figure:

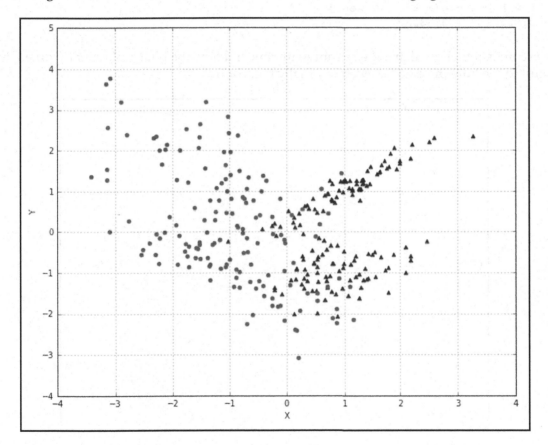

We have decided to use 0.0 as a binary threshold, so each point can be characterized by the quadrant where it's located. Of course, this is a rational choice for our dataset, but Bernoulli naive Bayes is envisaged for binary feature vectors or continuous values, which can be precisely split with a predefined threshold:

```
from sklearn.naive_bayes import BernoulliNB
from sklearn.model_selection import train_test_split

>>> X_train, X_test, Y_train, Y_test = train_test_split(X, Y,
test_size=0.25)

>>> bnb = BernoulliNB(binarize=0.0)
>>> bnb.fit(X_train, Y_train)
>>> bnb.score(X_test, Y_test)
0.85333333333333339
```

The score is rather good, but if we want to understand how the binary classifier worked, it's useful to see how the data has been internally binarized:

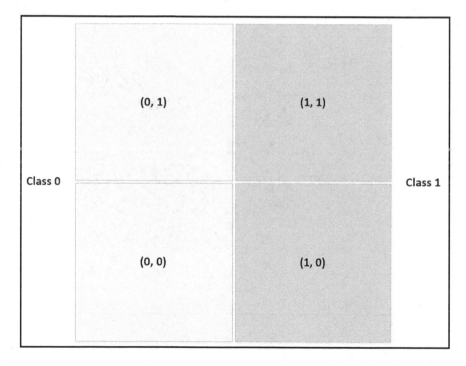

Now, checking the naive Bayes predictions, we obtain:

```
>>> data = np.array([[0, 0], [0, 1], [1, 0], [1, 1]])
>>> bnb.predict(data)
array([0, 0, 1, 1])
```

This is exactly what we expected.

Multinomial naive Bayes

A multinomial distribution is useful to model feature vectors where each value represents, for example, the number of occurrences of a term or its relative frequency. If the feature vectors have n elements and each of them can assume k different values with probability p_k, then:

$$P(X_1 = x_1 \cap X_2 = x_2 \cap ... \cap X_k = x_k) = \frac{n!}{\prod_i x_i!} \prod_i p_i^{x_i}$$

The conditional probabilities $P(x_i|y)$ are computed with a frequency count (which corresponds to applying a maximum likelihood approach), but in this case, it's important to consider the **alpha parameter** (called **Laplace smoothing factor**). Its default value is 1.0 and it prevents the model from setting null probabilities when the frequency is zero. It's possible to assign all non-negative values; however, larger values will assign higher probabilities to the missing features and this choice could alter the stability of the model. In our example, we're going to consider the default value of 1.0.

For our purposes, we're going to use `DictVectorizer`, already analyzed in Chapter 2 – Important Elements in Machine Learning. There are automatic instruments to compute the frequencies of terms, but we're going to discuss them later. Let's consider only two records: the first one representing a city, and the second one, the countryside. Our dictionary contains hypothetical frequencies, as if the terms were extracted from a text description:

```
from sklearn.feature_extraction import DictVectorizer

>>> data = [
    {'house': 100, 'street': 50, 'shop': 25, 'car': 100, 'tree': 20},
    {'house': 5, 'street': 5, 'shop': 0, 'car': 10, 'tree': 500, 'river': 1}
]
```

```
>>> dv = DictVectorizer(sparse=False)
>>> X = dv.fit_transform(data)
>>> Y = np.array([1, 0])

>>> X
array([[ 100.,  100.,    0.,   25.,   50.,   20.],
       [  10.,    5.,    1.,    0.,    5.,  500.]])
```

Note that the term 'river' is missing from the first set, so it's useful to keep alpha equal to 1.0 to give it a small probability. The output classes are 1 for city and 0 for the countryside. Now we can train a `MultinomialNB` instance:

```
from sklearn.naive_bayes import MultinomialNB

>>> mnb = MultinomialNB()
>>> mnb.fit(X, Y)
MultinomialNB(alpha=1.0, class_prior=None, fit_prior=True)
```

To test the model, we create a dummy city with a river and a dummy countryside place without any river:

```
>>> test_data = data = [
    {'house': 80, 'street': 20, 'shop': 15, 'car': 70, 'tree': 10, 'river':
1},
    {'house': 10, 'street': 5, 'shop': 1, 'car': 8, 'tree': 300, 'river': 0}
]

>>> mnb.predict(dv.fit_transform(test_data))
array([1, 0])
```

As expected, the prediction is correct. Later on, when discussing some elements of natural language processing, we're going to use multinomial naive Bayes for text classification with larger corpora. Even if a multinomial distribution is based on the number of occurrences, it can be used successfully with frequencies or more complex functions.

Gaussian naive Bayes

Gaussian naive Bayes is useful when working with continuous values whose probabilities can be modeled using a Gaussian distribution:

$$P(x) = \frac{1}{\sqrt{2\pi\sigma^2}} e^{-\frac{(x-\mu)^2}{2\sigma^2}}$$

The conditional probabilities $P(x_i|y)$ are also Gaussian distributed; therefore, it's necessary to estimate the mean and variance of each of them using the maximum likelihood approach. This quite easy; in fact, considering the property of a Gaussian, we get:

$$L(\mu; \sigma^2; x_i|y) = log \prod_k P(x_i^{(k)}|y) = \sum_k log\ P(x_i^{(k)}|y)$$

Here, the k index refers to the samples in our dataset and $P(x_i|y)$ is a Gaussian itself. By minimizing the inverse of this expression (in Russel S., Norvig P., *Artificial Intelligence: A Modern Approach*, Pearson, there's a complete analytical explanation), we get the mean and variance for each Gaussian associated with $P(x_i|y)$, and the model is hence trained.

As an example, we compare Gaussian naive Bayes with logistic regression using the ROC curves. The dataset has 300 samples with two features. Each sample belongs to a single class:

```
from sklearn.datasets import make_classification

>>> nb_samples = 300
>>> X, Y = make_classification(n_samples=nb_samples, n_features=2,
n_informative=2, n_redundant=0)
```

A plot of the dataset is shown in the following figure:

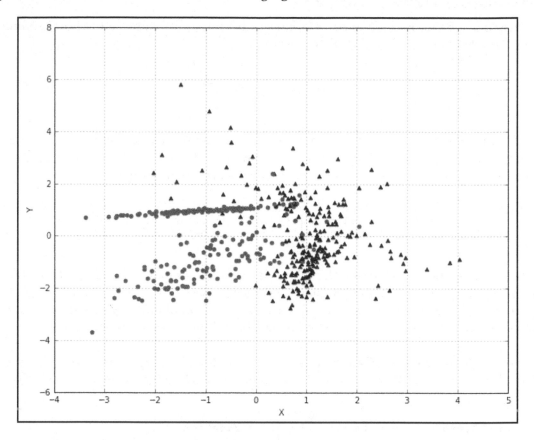

Now we can train both models and generate the ROC curves (the Y scores for naive Bayes are obtained through the `predict_proba` method):

```
from sklearn.naive_bayes import GaussianNB
from sklearn.linear_model import LogisticRegression
from sklearn.metrics import roc_curve, auc
from sklearn.model_selection import train_test_split

>>> X_train, X_test, Y_train, Y_test = train_test_split(X, Y,
test_size=0.25)

>>> gnb = GaussianNB()
>>> gnb.fit(X_train, Y_train)
>>> Y_gnb_score = gnb.predict_proba(X_test)

>>> lr = LogisticRegression()
```

```
>>> lr.fit(X_train, Y_train)
>>> Y_lr_score = lr.decision_function(X_test)

>>> fpr_gnb, tpr_gnb, thresholds_gnb = roc_curve(Y_test, Y_gnb_score[:, 1])
>>> fpr_lr, tpr_lr, thresholds_lr = roc_curve(Y_test, Y_lr_score)
```

The resulting ROC curves (generated in the same way shown in the previous chapter) are shown in the following figure:

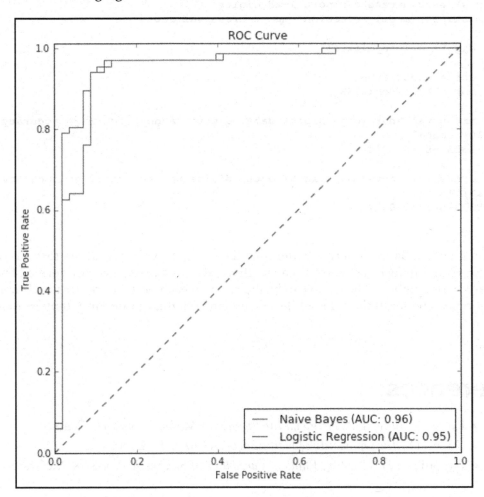

Naive Bayes' performance is slightly better than logistic regression; however, the two classifiers have similar accuracy and **Area Under the Curve** (**AUC**). It's interesting to compare the performances of Gaussian and multinomial naive Bayes with the MNIST digit dataset. Each sample (belonging to 10 classes) is an 8 x 8 image encoded as an unsigned integer (0-255); therefore, even if each feature doesn't represent an actual count, it can be considered as a sort of magnitude or frequency:

```
from sklearn.datasets import load_digits
from sklearn.model_selection import cross_val_score

>>> digits = load_digits()

>>> gnb = GaussianNB()
>>> mnb = MultinomialNB()

>>> cross_val_score(gnb, digits.data, digits.target, scoring='accuracy',
cv=10).mean()
0.81035375835678214

>>> cross_val_score(mnb, digits.data, digits.target, scoring='accuracy',
cv=10).mean()
0.88193962163008377
```

Multinomial naive Bayes performs better than the Gaussian variant and the result is not really surprising. In fact, each sample can be thought of as a feature vector derived from a dictionary of 64 symbols. The value can be the count of each occurrence, so a multinomial distribution can better fit the data, while a Gaussian is slightly more limited by its mean and variance.

References

- Russel S., Norvig P., *Artificial Intelligence: A Modern Approach*, Pearson
- Zhang H., *The Optimality of Naive Bayes, AAAI 1*, no. 2 (2004): 3
- Papoulis A., *Probability, Random Variables and Stochastic Processes*, McGraw-Hill

Summary

In this chapter, we exposed the generic naive Bayes approach, starting from the Bayes' theorem and its intrinsic philosophy. The naiveness of such algorithms is due to the choice to assume all the causes to be conditional independent. This means that each contribution is the same in every combination and the presence of a specific cause cannot alter the probability of the other ones. This is not so often realistic; however, under some assumptions, it's possible to show that internal dependencies clear each other so that the resulting probability appears unaffected by their relations.

scikit-learn provides three naive Bayes implementations: Bernoulli, multinomial and Gaussian. The only difference between them is in the probability distribution adopted. The first one is a binary algorithm, particularly useful when a feature can be present or not. Multinomial assumes having feature vectors, where each element represents the number of times it appears (or, very often, its frequency). This technique is very efficient in natural language processing or whenever the samples are composed starting from a common dictionary. Gaussian, instead, is based on a continuous distribution and it's suitable for more generic classification tasks.

In the next chapter, we're going to introduce a new classification technique called **support vector machines**. These algorithms are very powerful for solving both linear and non-linear problems. They're often the first choice for more complex scenarios because, despite their efficiency, the internal dynamics are very simple and they can be trained in a very short time.

7

Support Vector Machines

In this chapter, we're going to introduce another approach to classification using a family of algorithms called support vector machines. They can work with both linear and non-linear scenarios, allowing high performance in many different contexts. Together with neural networks, SVMs probably represent the best choice for many tasks where it's not easy to find out a good separating hyperplane. For example, for a long time, SVMs were the best choice for MNIST dataset classification, thanks to the fact that they can capture very high non-linear dynamics using a mathematical trick, without complex modifications in the algorithm. In the first part, we're going to discuss the basics of linear SVM, which then will be used for their non-linear extensions. We'll also discuss some techniques to control the number of parameters and, at the end, the application of support vector algorithms to regression problems.

Linear support vector machines

Let's consider a dataset of feature vectors we want to classify:

$$X = \{\bar{x}_1, \bar{x}_2, \ldots, \bar{x}_n\} \ where \ \bar{x}_i \in \mathbb{R}^m$$

For simplicity, we assume it as a binary classification (in all the other cases, it's possible to use automatically the one-versus-all strategy) and we set our class labels as -1 and 1:

$$Y = \{y_1, y_2, \ldots, y_n\} \ where \ y_n \in \{-1, 1\}$$

Our goal is to find the best separating hyperplane, for which the equation is:

$$\bar{w}^T \bar{x} + b = 0 \quad where \quad \bar{w} = \begin{pmatrix} w_1 \\ \vdots \\ w_m \end{pmatrix} \quad and \quad \bar{x} = \begin{pmatrix} x_1 \\ \vdots \\ x_m \end{pmatrix}$$

In the following figure, there's a bidimensional representation of such a hyperplane:

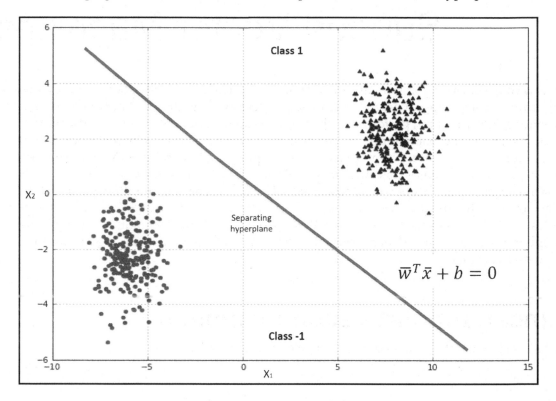

In this way, our classifier can be written as:

$$\hat{y} = f(\bar{x}) = sgn(\bar{w}^T \bar{x} + b)$$

In a realistic scenario, the two classes are normally separated by a margin with two boundaries where a few elements lie. Those elements are called **support vectors**. For a more generic mathematical expression, it's preferable to renormalize our dataset so that the support vectors will lie on two hyperplanes with equations:

$$\begin{cases} \bar{w}^T \bar{x} + b = -1 \\ \bar{w}^T \bar{x} + b = 1 \end{cases}$$

In the following figure, there's an example with two support vectors. The dashed line is the original separating hyperplane:

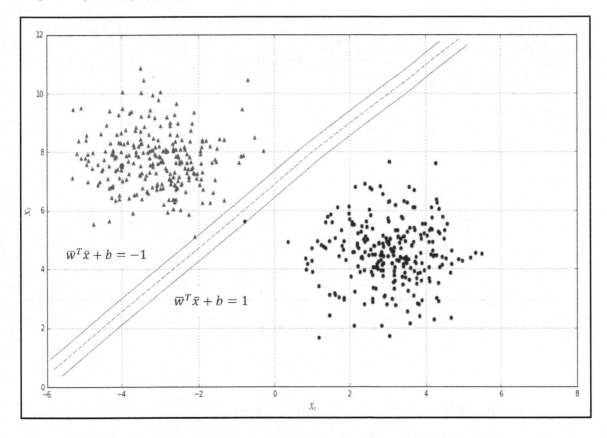

Our goal is to maximize the distance between these two boundary hyperplanes so as to reduce the probability of misclassification (which is higher when the distance is short, and there aren't two well-defined blobs as in the previous figure).

Considering that the boundaries are parallel, the distance between them is defined by the length of the segment perpendicular to both and connecting two points:

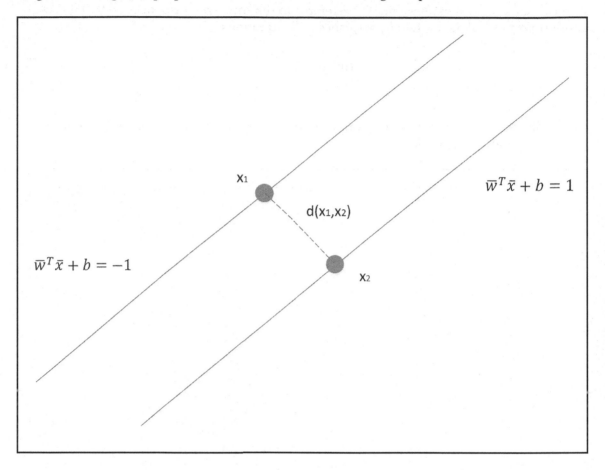

Considering the points as vectors, therefore, we have:

$$\bar{x}_2 - \bar{x}_1 = t\bar{w}$$

Now, considering the boundary hyperplane equations, we get:

$$\bar{w}^T \bar{x}_2 + b = \bar{w}^T(\bar{x}_1 + t\bar{w}) + b = (\bar{w}^T \bar{x}_1 + b) + t\|\bar{w}\|^2 = 1$$

The first term of the last part is equal to -1, so we solve for t:

$$t = \frac{2}{\|\overline{w}\|^2}$$

The distance between x_1 and x_2 is the length of the segment t; hence we get:

$$d(\bar{x}_1, \bar{x}_2) = t\|\overline{w}\| = \frac{2}{\|\overline{w}\|}$$

Now, considering all points of our dataset, we can impose the following constraint:

$$y_i(\overline{w}^T \bar{x}_i + b) \geq 1 \quad \forall\, (\bar{x}_i, y_i)$$

This is guaranteed by using -1, 1 as class labels and boundary margins. The equality is true only for the support vectors, while for all the other points it will greater than 1. It's important to consider that the model doesn't take into account vectors beyond this margin. In many cases, this can yield a very robust model, but in many datasets this can also be a strong limitation. In the next paragraph, we're going to use a trick to avoid this rigidness while keeping the same optimization technique.

At this point, we can define the function to minimize in order to train a support vector machine:

$$\begin{cases} min\, \dfrac{1}{2}\|\overline{w}\| \\ y_i(\overline{w}^T \bar{x}_i + b) \geq 1 \end{cases}$$

This can be further simplified (by removing the square root from the norm) in the following quadratic programming problem:

$$\begin{cases} min\, \dfrac{1}{2}\overline{w}^T \overline{w} \\ y_i(\overline{w}^T \bar{x}_i + b) \geq 1 \end{cases}$$

scikit-learn implementation

In order to allow the model to have a more flexible separating hyperplane, all scikit-learn implementations are based on a simple variant that includes so-called **slack variables** in the function to minimize:

$$min \frac{1}{2} \overline{w}^T \overline{w} + C \sum_i \zeta_i$$

In this case, the constraints become:

$$y_i(\overline{w}^T \overline{x}_i + b) \geq 1 - \zeta_i$$

The introduction of the slack variables allows us to create a flexible margin so that some vectors belonging to a class can also be found in the opposite part of the hyperspace and can be included in the model training. The strength of this flexibility can be set using the parameter C. Small values (close to zero) bring about very hard margins, while values greater than or equal to 1 allow more and more flexibility (also increasing the misclassification rate). The right choice of C is not immediate, but the best value can be found automatically by using a grid search as seen in the previous chapters. In our examples, we keep the default value of 1.

Linear classification

Our first example is based on a linear SVM, as described in the previous section. We start by creating a dummy dataset with 500 vectors subdivided into two classes:

```
from sklearn.datasets import make_classification

>>> nb_samples = 500
>>> X, Y = make_classification(n_samples=nb_samples, n_features=2,
n_informative=2, n_redundant=0, n_clusters_per_class=1)
```

In the following figure, there's a plot of our dataset. Notice that some points overlap the two main blobs. For this reason, a positive C value is needed to allow the model to capture a more complex dynamic.

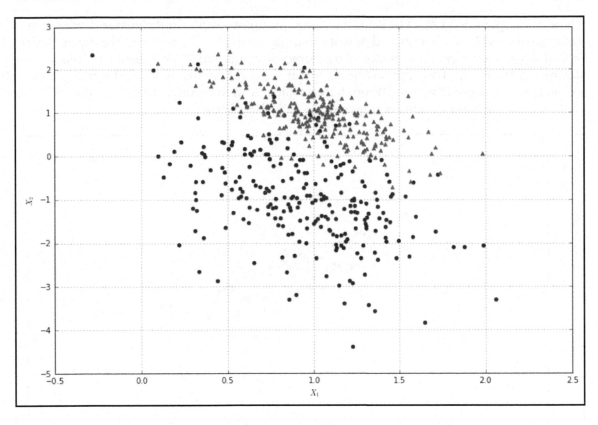

scikit-learn provides the SVC class, which is a very efficient implementation that can be used in most cases. We're going to use it together with cross-validation to validate performance:

```
from sklearn.svm import SVC
from sklearn.model_selection import cross_val_score

>>> svc = SVC(kernel='linear')
>>> cross_val_score(svc, X, Y, scoring='accuracy', cv=10).mean()
0.93191356542617032
```

The `kernel` parameter must be set to `'linear'` in this example. In the next section, we're going to discuss how it works and how it can improve the SVM's performance dramatically in non-linear scenarios. As expected, the accuracy is comparable to a logistic regression, as this model tries to find an optimal linear separator. After training a model, it's possible to get an array of support vectors, through the instance variable called `support_vectors_`. A plot of them, for our example, is shown in the following figure:

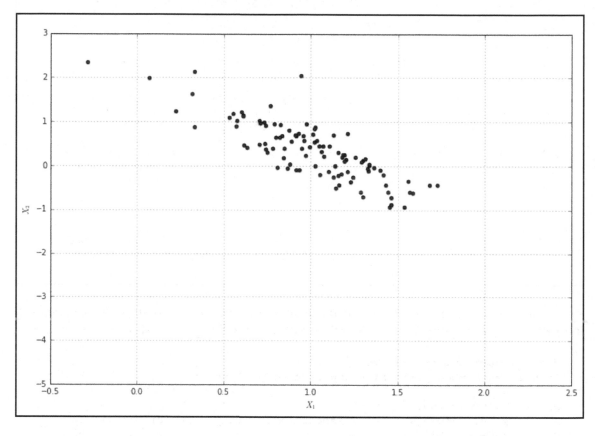

As it's possible to see, they are placed in a strip along the separating line. The effect of `C` and the slack variables determined a movable margin that partially captured the existing overlap. Of course, it's impossible to separate the sets in a perfect way with a linear classifier and, on the other hand, most real-life problems are non-linear; for this reason, it's a necessary further step.

Kernel-based classification

When working with non-linear problems, it's useful to transform the original vectors by projecting them into a higher dimensional space where they can be linearly separated. We saw a similar approach when we discussed polynomial regression. SVMs also adopt the same approach, even if there's now a complexity problem that we need to overcome. Our mathematical formulation becomes:

$$\begin{cases} min \dfrac{1}{2}\overline{w}^T\overline{w} + C\sum_{i}\zeta_i \\ y_i(\overline{w}^T\phi(\bar{x}_i) + b) \geq 1 - \zeta_i \end{cases}$$

Every feature vector is now filtered by a non-linear function that can completely reshape the scenario. However, the introduction of such a function increased the computational complexity in a way that could apparently discourage this approach. To understand what has happened, it's necessary to express the quadratic problem using Lagrange multipliers. The entire procedure is beyond the scope of this book (in Nocedal J., Wright S. J., *Numerical Optimization*, Springer, you can find a complete and formal description of quadratic programming problems); however, the final formulation is:

$$\begin{cases} max \left(\sum_{i}\alpha_i - \dfrac{1}{2}\sum_{i,j}\alpha_i\alpha_j y_i y_j \phi(\bar{x}_i)^T\phi(\bar{x}_j)\right) \\ \sum_{i}\alpha_i y_i = 0 \end{cases}$$

Therefore it's necessary to compute the following for every couple of vectors:

$$\phi(\bar{x}_i)^T\phi(\bar{x}_j)$$

And this procedure can be a bottleneck, unacceptable for large problems. However, it's now that the so-called **kernel trick** takes place. There are particular functions (called kernels) that have the following property:

$$K(\bar{x}_i, \bar{x}_j) = \phi(\bar{x}_i)^T\phi(\bar{x}_j)$$

In other words, the value of the kernel for two feature vectors is the product of the two projected vectors. With this trick, the computational complexity remains almost the same, but we can benefit from the power of non-linear projections even in a very large number of dimensions.

Excluding the linear kernel, which is a simple product, scikit-learn supports three different kernels that can solve many real-life problems.

Radial Basis Function

The RBF kernel is the default value for SVC and is based on the function:

$$K(\bar{x}_i, \bar{x}_j) = e^{-\gamma|\bar{x}_i - \bar{x}_j|^2}$$

The gamma parameter determines the amplitude of the function, which is not influenced by the direction but only by the distance.

Polynomial kernel

The polynomial kernel is based on the function:

$$K(\bar{x}_i, \bar{x}_j) = (\gamma \bar{x}_i^T \cdot \bar{x}_j + r)^c$$

The exponent c is specified through the parameter degree, while the constant term r is called `coef0`. This function can easily expand the dimensionality with a large number of support variables and overcome very non-linear problems; however, the requirements in terms of resources are normally higher. Considering that a non-linear function can often be approximated quite well for a bounded area (by adopting polynomials), it's not surprising that many complex problems become easily solvable using this kernel.

Sigmoid kernel

The sigmoid kernel is based on this function:

$$K\left(\bar{x}_i, \bar{x}_j\right) = \frac{1 - e^{-2(\gamma \bar{x}_i^T \cdot \bar{x}_j + r)}}{1 + e^{-2(\gamma \bar{x}_i^T \cdot \bar{x}_j + r)}}$$

The constant term r is specified through the parameter `coef0`.

Custom kernels

Normally, built-in kernels can efficiently solve most real-life problems; however scikit-learn allows us to create custom kernels as normal Python functions:

```
import numpy as np

>>> def custom_kernel(x1, x2):
        return np.square(np.dot(x1, x2) + 1)
```

The function can be passed to SVC through the `kernel` parameter, which can assume fixed string values (`'linear'`, `'rbf'`, `'poly'` and `'sigmoid'`) or a callable (such as `kernel=custom_kernel`).

Non-linear examples

To show the power of kernel SVMs, we're going to solve two problems. The first one is simpler but purely non-linear and the dataset is generated through the `make_circles()` built-in function:

```
from sklearn.datasets import make_circles

>>> nb_samples = 500
>>> X, Y = make_circles(n_samples=nb_samples, noise=0.1)
```

A plot of this dataset is shown in the following figure:

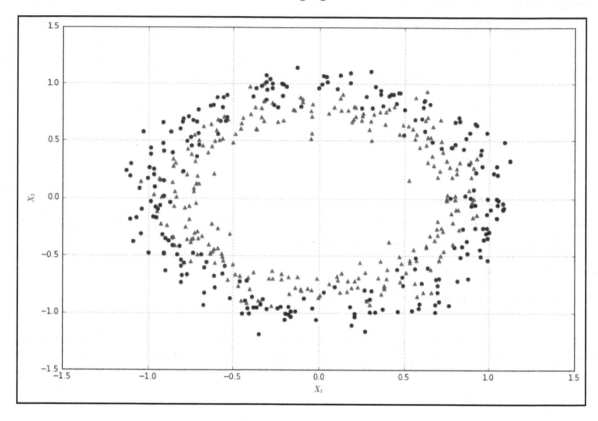

As it's possible to see, a linear classifier can never separate the two sets and every approximation will contain on average 50% misclassifications. A logistic regression example is shown here:

```
from sklearn.linear_model import LogisticRegression

>>> lr = LogisticRegression()
>>> cross_val_score(lr, X, Y, scoring='accuracy', cv=10).mean()
0.438
```

As expected, the accuracy is below 50% and no other optimizations can increase it dramatically. Let's consider, instead, a grid search with an SVM and different kernels (keeping the default values of each one):

```
import multiprocessing
from sklearn.model_selection import GridSearchCV

>>> param_grid = [
    {
        'kernel': ['linear', 'rbf', 'poly', 'sigmoid'],
        'C': [ 0.1, 0.2, 0.4, 0.5, 1.0, 1.5, 1.8, 2.0, 2.5, 3.0 ]
    }
]

>>> gs = GridSearchCV(estimator=SVC(), param_grid=param_grid,
                    scoring='accuracy', cv=10,
n_jobs=multiprocessing.cpu_count())

>>> gs.fit(X, Y)
GridSearchCV(cv=10, error_score='raise',
        estimator=SVC(C=1.0, cache_size=200, class_weight=None, coef0=0.0,
  decision_function_shape=None, degree=3, gamma='auto', kernel='rbf',
  max_iter=-1, probability=False, random_state=None, shrinking=True,
  tol=0.001, verbose=False),
        fit_params={}, iid=True, n_jobs=8,
        param_grid=[{'kernel': ['linear', 'rbf', 'poly', 'sigmoid'], 'C':
[0.1, 0.2, 0.4, 0.5, 1.0, 1.5, 1.8, 2.0, 2.5, 3.0]}],
        pre_dispatch='2*n_jobs', refit=True, return_train_score=True,
        scoring='accuracy', verbose=0)

>>> gs.best_estimator_
SVC(C=2.0, cache_size=200, class_weight=None, coef0=0.0,
  decision_function_shape=None, degree=3, gamma='auto', kernel='rbf',
  max_iter=-1, probability=False, random_state=None, shrinking=True,
  tol=0.001, verbose=False)

>>> gs.best_score_
0.87
```

As expected from the geometry of our dataset, the best kernel is a radial basis function, which yields 87% accuracy. Further refinements on gamma could slightly increase this value, but as there is a partial overlap between the two subsets, it's very difficult to achieve an accuracy close to 100%. However, our goal is not to overfit our model; it is to guarantee an appropriate level of generalization. So, considering the shape, a limited number of misclassifications is acceptable to ensure that the model captures sub-oscillations in the boundary surface.

Another interesting example is provided by the MNIST handwritten digit dataset. We have already seen it and classified it using linear models. Now we can try to find the best kernel with an SVM:

```
from sklearn.datasets import load_digits

>>> digits = load_digits()

>>> param_grid = [
    {
        'kernel': ['linear', 'rbf', 'poly', 'sigmoid'],
        'C': [ 0.1, 0.2, 0.4, 0.5, 1.0, 1.5, 1.8, 2.0, 2.5, 3.0 ]
    }
]

>>> gs = GridSearchCV(estimator=SVC(), param_grid=param_grid,
                  scoring='accuracy', cv=10,
n_jobs=multiprocessing.cpu_count())

>>> gs.fit(digits.data, digits.target)
GridSearchCV(cv=10, error_score='raise',
        estimator=SVC(C=1.0, cache_size=200, class_weight=None, coef0=0.0,
  decision_function_shape=None, degree=3, gamma='auto', kernel='rbf',
  max_iter=-1, probability=False, random_state=None, shrinking=True,
  tol=0.001, verbose=False),
        fit_params={}, iid=True, n_jobs=8,
        param_grid=[{'kernel': ['linear', 'rbf', 'poly', 'sigmoid'], 'C':
[0.1, 0.2, 0.4, 0.5, 1.0, 1.5, 1.8, 2.0, 2.5, 3.0]}],
        pre_dispatch='2*n_jobs', refit=True, return_train_score=True,
        scoring='accuracy', verbose=0)

>>> gs.best_estimator_
SVC(C=0.1, cache_size=200, class_weight=None, coef0=0.0,
  decision_function_shape=None, degree=3, gamma='auto', kernel='poly',
  max_iter=-1, probability=False, random_state=None, shrinking=True,
  tol=0.001, verbose=False)

>>> gs.best_score_
0.97885364496382865
```

Hence the best classifier (with almost 98% accuracy) is based on a polynomial kernel and a very low C value. This means that a non-linear transformation with very hard margins can easily capture the dynamics of all digits. Indeed, SVMs (with various internal alternatives) have always shown excellent performance with this dataset and their usage can easily be extended to similar problems.

Another interesting example is based on the Olivetti face dataset, which is not part of scikit-learn but can be automatically downloaded and set up using a built-in function called `fetch_olivetti_faces()`:

```
from sklearn.datasets import fetch_olivetti_faces

>>> faces = fetch_olivetti_faces(data_home='/ML/faces/')
```

Through the `data_home` parameter, it is possible to specify in which local folder the dataset must be placed. A subset of samples is shown in the following figure:

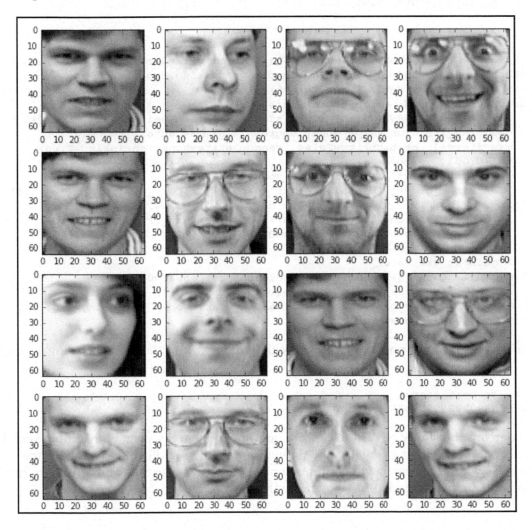

There are 40 different people and each of them is represented with 10 pictures of 64 x 64 pixels. The number of classes (40) is not high, but considering the similarity of many photos, a good classifier should be able to capture some specific anatomical details. Performing a grid search with non-linear kernels, we get:

```
>>> param_grid = [
  {
    'kernel': ['rbf', 'poly'],
    'C': [ 0.1, 0.5, 1.0, 1.5 ],
    'degree': [2, 3, 4, 5],
    'gamma': [0.001, 0.01, 0.1, 0.5]
  }
]

>>> gs = GridSearchCV(estimator=SVC(), param_grid=param_grid,
scoring='accuracy', cv=8,  n_jobs=multiprocessing.cpu_count())
>>> gs.fit(faces.data, faces.target)
GridSearchCV(cv=8, error_score='raise',
        estimator=SVC(C=1.0, cache_size=200, class_weight=None, coef0=0.0,
   decision_function_shape=None, degree=3, gamma='auto', kernel='rbf',
   max_iter=-1, probability=False, random_state=None, shrinking=True,
   tol=0.001, verbose=False),
        fit_params={}, iid=True, n_jobs=8,
        param_grid=[{'kernel': ['rbf', 'poly'], 'C': [0.1, 0.5, 1.0, 1.5],
 'gamma': [0.001, 0.01, 0.1, 0.5], 'degree': [2, 3, 4, 5]}],
        pre_dispatch='2*n_jobs', refit=True, return_train_score=True,
        scoring='accuracy', verbose=0)

>>> gs.best_estimator_
SVC(C=0.1, cache_size=200, class_weight=None, coef0=0.0,
   decision_function_shape=None, degree=2, gamma=0.1, kernel='poly',
   max_iter=-1, probability=False, random_state=None, shrinking=True,
   tol=0.001, verbose=False)
```

So the best estimator is polynomial-based with `degree=2`, and the corresponding accuracy is:

```
>>> gs.best_score_
0.9699999999999997
```

This confirms the ability of SVM to capture non-linear dynamics even with simple kernels that can be computed in a very limited amount of time. It would be interesting for the reader to try different parameter combinations or preprocess the data and apply principal component analysis to reduce its dimensionality.

Controlled support vector machines

With real datasets, SVM can extract a very large number of support vectors to increase accuracy, and that can slow down the whole process. To allow finding out a trade-off between precision and number of support vectors, scikit-learn provides an implementation called NuSVC, where the parameter nu (bounded between 0—not included—and 1) can be used to control at the same time the number of support vectors (greater values will increase their number) and training errors (lower values reduce the fraction of errors). Let's consider an example with a linear kernel and a simple dataset. In the following figure, there's a scatter plot of our set:

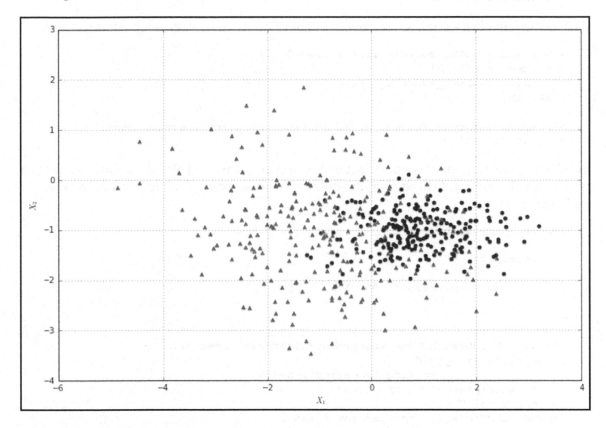

Let's start checking the number of support vectors for a standard SVM:

```
>>> svc = SVC(kernel='linear')
>>> svc.fit(X, Y)
>>> svc.support_vectors_.shape
(242L, 2L)
```

So the model has found 242 support vectors. Let's now try to optimize this number using cross-validation. The default value is 0.5, which is an acceptable trade-off:

```
from sklearn.svm import NuSVC

>>> nusvc = NuSVC(kernel='linear', nu=0.5)
>>> nusvc.fit(X, Y)
>>> nusvc.support_vectors_.shape
(251L, 2L)

>>> cross_val_score(nusvc, X, Y, scoring='accuracy', cv=10).mean()
0.80633213285314143
```

As expected, the behavior is similar to a standard SVC. Let's now reduce the value of nu:

```
>>> nusvc = NuSVC(kernel='linear', nu=0.15)
>>> nusvc.fit(X, Y)
>>> nusvc.support_vectors_.shape
(78L, 2L)

>>> cross_val_score(nusvc, X, Y, scoring='accuracy', cv=10).mean()
0.67584393757503003
```

In this case, the number of support vectors is less than before and also the accuracy has been affected by this choice. Instead of trying different values, we can look for the best choice with a grid search:

```
import numpy as np

>>> param_grid = [
    {
        'nu': np.arange(0.05, 1.0, 0.05)
    }
]

>>> gs = GridSearchCV(estimator=NuSVC(kernel='linear'),
param_grid=param_grid,
                scoring='accuracy', cv=10,
n_jobs=multiprocessing.cpu_count())
>>> gs.fit(X, Y)
GridSearchCV(cv=10, error_score='raise',
      estimator=NuSVC(cache_size=200, class_weight=None, coef0=0.0,
   decision_function_shape=None, degree=3, gamma='auto', kernel='linear',
   max_iter=-1, nu=0.5, probability=False, random_state=None,
   shrinking=True, tol=0.001, verbose=False),
      fit_params={}, iid=True, n_jobs=8,
      param_grid=[{'nu': array([ 0.05,  0.1 ,  0.15,  0.2 ,  0.25,  0.3 ,
 0.35,  0.4 ,  0.45,
```

```
        0.5 ,  0.55,  0.6 ,  0.65,  0.7 ,  0.75,  0.8 ,  0.85,  0.9 ,
  0.95])}],
        pre_dispatch='2*n_jobs', refit=True, return_train_score=True,
        scoring='accuracy', verbose=0)

>>> gs.best_estimator_
NuSVC(cache_size=200, class_weight=None, coef0=0.0,
    decision_function_shape=None, degree=3, gamma='auto', kernel='linear',
    max_iter=-1, nu=0.5, probability=False, random_state=None,
    shrinking=True, tol=0.001, verbose=False)

>>> gs.best_score_
0.80600000000000005

>>> gs.best_estimator_.support_vectors_.shape
(251L, 2L)
```

Therefore, in this case as well, the default value of 0.5 yielded the most accurate results. Normally, this approach works quite well, but when it's necessary to reduce the number of support vectors, it can be a good starting point for progressively reducing the value of nu until the result is acceptable.

Support vector regression

scikit-learn provides a support vector regressor based on a very simple variant of the algorithm already described (see the original documentation for further information). The real power of this approach resides in the usage of non-linear kernels (in particular, polynomials); however, the user is advised to evaluate the degree progressively because the complexity can grow rapidly, together with the training time.

For our example, I've created a dummy dataset based on a second-order noisy function:

```
>>> nb_samples = 50

>>> X = np.arange(-nb_samples, nb_samples, 1)
>>> Y = np.zeros(shape=(2 * nb_samples,))

>>> for x in X:
        Y[int(x)+nb_samples] = np.power(x*6, 2.0) / 1e4 +
np.random.uniform(-2, 2)
```

The dataset in plotted in the following figure:

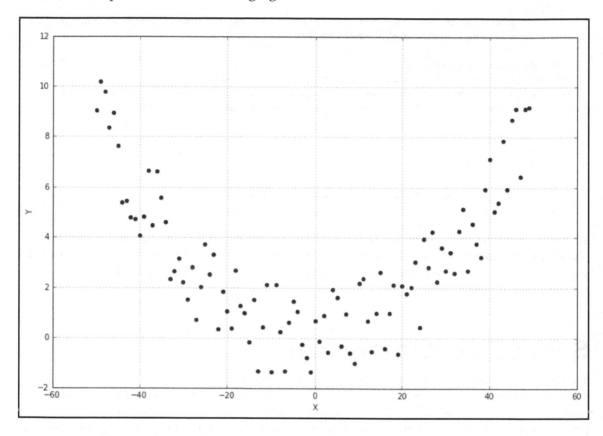

In order to avoid a very long training process, the model is evaluated with `degree` set to 2. The epsilon parameter allows us to specify a soft margin for predictions; if a predicted value is contained in the ball centered on the target value and the radius is equal to epsilon, no penalty is applied to the function to be minimized. The default value is 0.1:

```
from sklearn.svm import SVR

>>> svr = SVR(kernel='poly', degree=2, C=1.5, epsilon=0.5)
>>> cross_val_score(svr, X.reshape((nb_samples*2, 1)), Y,
scoring='neg_mean_squared_error', cv=10).mean()
-1.4641683636397234
```

References

Nocedal J., Wright S. J., *Numerical Optimization*, Springer

Summary

In this chapter, we discussed how a support vector machine works in both linear and non-linear scenarios, starting from the basic mathematical formulation. The main concept is to find the hyperplane that maximizes the distance between the classes by using a limited number of samples (called support vectors) that are closest to the separation margin.

We saw how to transform a non-linear problem using kernel functions, which allow remapping of the original space to a another high-dimensional one where the problem becomes linearly separable. We also saw how to control the number of support vectors and how to use SVMs for regression problems.

In the next chapter, we're going to introduce another classification method called decision trees, which is the last one explained in this book.

8
Decision Trees and Ensemble Learning

In this chapter, we're going to discuss binary decision trees and ensemble methods. Even if they're probably not the most common methods for classification, they offer a good level of simplicity and can be adopted in many tasks that don't require a high level of complexity. They're also quite useful when it's necessary to show how a decision process works because they are based on a structure that can be shown easily in presentations and described step by step.

Ensemble methods are a powerful alternative to complex algorithms because they try to exploit the statistical concept of majority vote. Many weak learners can be trained to capture different elements and make their own predictions, which are not globally optimal, but using a sufficient number of elements, it's statistically probable that a majority will evaluate correctly. In particular, we're going to discuss random forests of decision trees and some boosting methods that are slightly different algorithms that can optimize the learning process by focusing on misclassified samples or by continuously minimizing a target loss function.

Binary decision trees

A binary decision tree is a structure based on a sequential decision process. Starting from the root, a feature is evaluated and one of the two branches is selected. This procedure is repeated until a final leaf is reached, which normally represents the classification target we're looking for. Considering other algorithms, decision trees seem to be simpler in their dynamics; however, if the dataset is splittable while keeping an internal balance, the overall process is intuitive and rather fast in its predictions. Moreover, decision trees can work efficiently with unnormalized datasets because their internal structure is not influenced by the values assumed by each feature. In the following figure, there are plots of an unnormalized bidimensional dataset and the cross-validation scores obtained using a logistic regression and a decision tree:

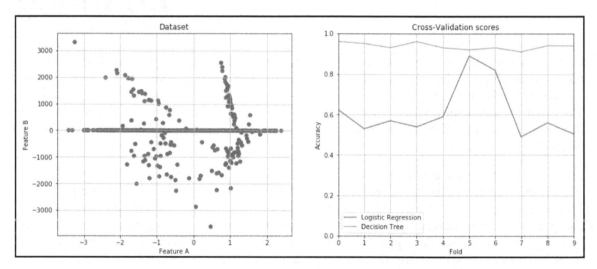

The decision tree always achieves a score close to 1.0, while the logistic regression has an average slightly greater than 0.6. However, without proper limitations, a decision tree could potentially grow until a single sample (or a very low number) is present in every node. This situation drives to overfit the model, and the tree becomes unable to generalize correctly. Using a consistent test set or cross-validation can help in avoiding this problem; however, in the section dedicated to scikit-learn implementation, we're going to discuss how to limit the growth of the tree.

Binary decisions

Let's consider an input dataset X:

$$X = \{\bar{x}_1, \bar{x}_2, \dots, \bar{x}_n\} \, where \; \bar{x}_i \in \mathbb{R}^m$$

Every vector is made up of m features, so each of them can be a good candidate to create a node based on the (feature, threshold) tuple:

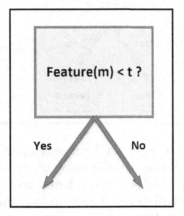

According to the feature and the threshold, the structure of the tree will change. Intuitively, we should pick the feature that best separates our data in other words, a perfect separating feature will be present only in a node and the two subsequent branches won't be based on it anymore. In real problems, this is often impossible, so it's necessary to find the feature that minimizes the number of following decision steps.

For example, let's consider a class of students where all males have dark hair and all females have blonde hair, while both subsets have samples of different sizes. If our task is to determine the composition of the class, we can start with the following subdivision:

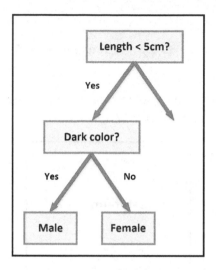

However, the block **Dark color?** will contain both males and females (which are the targets we want to classify). This concept is expressed using the term **purity** (or, more often, its opposite concept, **impurity**). An ideal scenario is based on nodes where the impurity is null so that all subsequent decisions will be taken only on the remaining features. In our example, we can simply start from the color block:

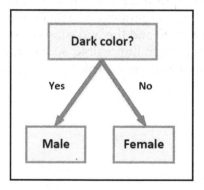

The two resulting sets are now pure according to the color feature, and this can be enough for our task. If we need further details, such as hair length, other nodes must be added; their impurity won't be null because we know that there are, for example, both male and female students with long hair.

More formally, suppose we define the selection tuple as:

$$\sigma = \langle i, t_k \rangle$$

Here, the first element is the index of the feature we want to use to split our dataset at a certain node (it will be the entire dataset only at the beginning; after each step, the number of samples decreases), while the second is the threshold that determines left and right branches. The choice of the best threshold is a fundamental element because it determines the structure of the tree and, therefore, its performance. The goal is to reduce the residual impurity in the least number of splits so as to have a very short decision path between the sample data and the classification result.

We can also define a total impurity measure by considering the two branches:

$$I(D, \sigma) = \frac{N_{left}}{N_D} I(D_{left}) + \frac{N_{right}}{N_D} I(D_{right})$$

Here, D is the whole dataset at the selected node, D_{left} and D_{right} are the resulting subsets (by applying the selection tuple), and the I are impurity measures.

Impurity measures

To define the most used impurity measures, we need to consider the total number of target classes:

$$Y = \{y_1, y_2, \ldots, y_n\} \; where \; y_n \in (0,1,2,\ldots P)$$

In a certain node j, we can define the probability $p(i|j)$ where i is an index [1, n] associated with each class. In other words, according to a frequentist approach, this value is the ratio between the number of samples belonging to class i and the total number of samples belonging to the selected node.

Gini impurity index

The Gini impurity index is defined as:

$$I_{Gini}(j) = \sum_i p(i|j)(1 - p(i|j))$$

Here, the sum is always extended to all classes. This is a very common measure and it's used as a default value by scikit-learn. Given a sample, the Gini impurity measures the probability of a misclassification if a label is randomly chosen using the probability distribution of the branch. The index reaches its minimum (0.0) when all the samples of a node are classified into a single category.

Cross-entropy impurity index

The cross-entropy measure is defined as:

$$I_{Cross-entropy}(j) = -\sum_i p(i|j)\log p(i|j)$$

This measure is based on information theory, and assumes null values only when samples belonging to a single class are present in a split, while it is maximum when there's a uniform distribution among classes (which is one of the worst cases in decision trees because it means that there are still many decision steps until the final classification). This index is very similar to the Gini impurity, even though, more formally, the cross-entropy allows you to select the split that minimizes the uncertainty about the classification, while the Gini impurity minimizes the probability of misclassification.

In Chapter 2, *Important Elements in Machine Learning*, we defined the concept of mutual information $I(X; Y) = H(X) - H(X|Y)$ as the amount of information shared by both variables, thereby reducing the uncertainty about X provided by the knowledge of Y. We can use this to define the information gain provided by a split:

$$IG(\sigma) = H(Parent) - H(Parent|Children)$$

When growing a tree, we start by selecting the split that provides the highest information gain and proceed until one of the following conditions is verified:

- All nodes are pure
- The information gain is null
- The maximum depth has been reached

Misclassification impurity index

The misclassification impurity is the simplest index, defined as:

$$I_{Misclassification}(j) = 1 - \max p(i|j)$$

In terms of quality performance, this index is not the best choice because it's not particularly sensitive to different probability distributions (which can easily drive the selection to a subdivision using Gini or cross-entropy indexes).

Feature importance

When growing a decision tree with a multidimensional dataset, it can be useful to evaluate the importance of each feature in predicting the output values. In `Chapter 3`, *Feature Selection and Feature Engineering*, we discussed some methods to reduce the dimensionality of a dataset by selecting only the most significant features. Decision trees offer a different approach based on the impurity reduction determined by every single feature. In particular, considering a feature x_i, its importance can be determined as:

$$Importance(x_i) = \sum_k \frac{N_k}{N} \Delta I_{x_i}$$

The sum is extended to all nodes where x_i is used, and N_k is the number of samples reaching the node k. Therefore, the importance is a weighted sum of all impurity reductions computed considering only the nodes where the feature is used to split them. If the Gini impurity index is adopted, this measure is also called **Gini importance**.

Decision tree classification with scikit-learn

scikit-learn contains the `DecisionTreeClassifier` class, which can train a binary decision tree with Gini and cross-entropy impurity measures. In our example, let's consider a dataset with three features and three classes:

```
from sklearn.datasets import make_classification

>>> nb_samples = 500
>>> X, Y = make_classification(n_samples=nb_samples, n_features=3,
n_informative=3, n_redundant=0, n_classes=3, n_clusters_per_class=1)
```

Let's first consider a classification with default Gini impurity:

```
from sklearn.tree import DecisionTreeClassifier
from sklearn.model_selection import cross_val_score

>>> dt = DecisionTreeClassifier()
>>> print(cross_val_score(dt, X, Y, scoring='accuracy', cv=10).mean())
0.970
```

A very interesting feature is given by the possibility of exporting the tree in `Graphviz` format and converting it into a PDF.

Graphviz is a free tool that can be downloaded from `http://www.graphviz.org`.

To export a trained tree, it is necessary to use the built-in function `export_graphviz()`:

```
from sklearn.tree import export_graphviz

>>> dt.fit(X, Y)
>>> with open('dt.dot', 'w') as df:
        df = export_graphviz(dt, out_file=df,
                                feature_names=['A','B','C'],
                                class_names=['C1', 'C2', 'C3'])
```

In this case, we have used A, B, and C as feature names and C1, C2, and C3 as class names. Once the file has been created, it's possible converting to PDF using the command-line tool:

```
>>> <Graphviz Home>bindot -Tpdf dt.dot -o dt.pdf
```

The graph for our example is rather large, so in the following feature you can see only a part of a branch:

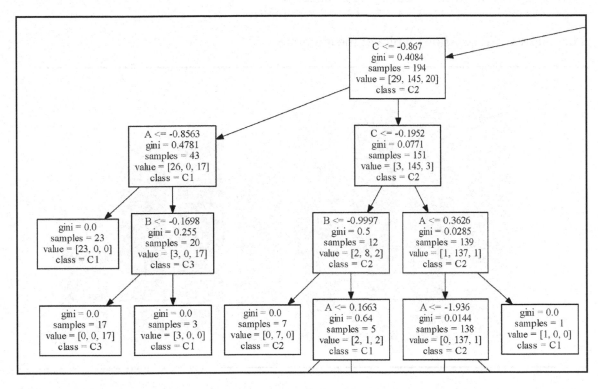

As you can see, there are two kinds of nodes:

- Nonterminal, which contains the splitting tuple (as feature <= threshold) and a positive impurity measure
- Terminal, where the impurity measure is null and a final target class is present

In both cases, you can always check the number of samples. This kind of graph is very useful in understanding how many decision steps are needed. Unfortunately, even if the process is quite simple, the dataset structure can lead to very complex trees, while other methods can immediately find out the most appropriate class. Of course, not all features have the same importance. If we consider the root of the tree and the first nodes, we find features that separate a lot of samples; therefore, their importance must be higher than that of all terminal nodes, where the residual number of samples is minimum. In scikit-learn, it's possible to assess the Gini importance of each feature after training a model:

```
>>> dt.feature_importances_
array([ 0.12066952,  0.12532507,  0.0577379 ,  0.14402762,  0.14382398,
```

```
        0.12418921,   0.14638565,   0.13784106])

>>> np.argsort(dt.feature_importances_)
array([2, 0, 5, 1, 7, 4, 3, 6], dtype=int64)
```

The following figure shows a plot of the importances:

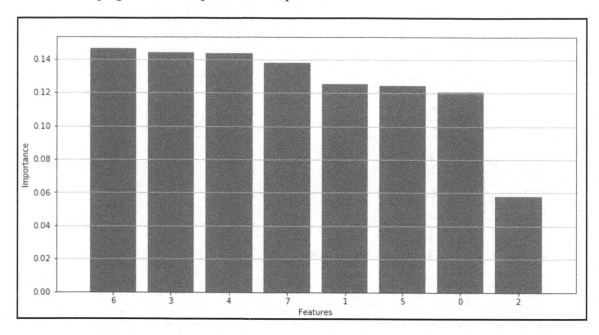

The most important features are 6, 3, 4, and 7, while feature 2, for example, separates a very small number of samples, and can be considered noninformative for the classification task.

In terms of efficiency, a tree can also be pruned using the `max_depth` parameter; however, it's not always so simple to understand which value is the best (grid search can help in this task). On the other hand, it's easier to decide what the maximum number of features to consider at each split should be. The parameter `max_features` can be used for this purpose:

- If it's a number, the value is directly taken into account at each split
- If it's `'auto'` or `'sqrt'`, the square root of the number of features will be adopted
- If it's `'log2'`, the logarithm (base 2) will be used
- If it's `'None'`, all the features will be used (this is the default value)

In general, when the number of total features is not too high, the default value is the best choice, although it's useful to introduce a small compression (via `sqrt` or `log2`) when too many features can interfere among themselves, reducing the efficiency. Another parameter useful for controlling both performance and efficiency is `min_samples_split`, which specifies the minimum number of samples to consider for a split. Some examples are shown in the following snippet:

```
>>> cross_val_score(DecisionTreeClassifier(), X, Y, scoring='accuracy',
cv=10).mean()
0.77308070807080698

>>> cross_val_score(DecisionTreeClassifier(max_features='auto'), X, Y,
scoring='accuracy', cv=10).mean()
0.76410071007100711

>>> cross_val_score(DecisionTreeClassifier(min_samples_split=100), X, Y,
scoring='accuracy', cv=10).mean()
0.72999969996999692
```

As already explained, finding the best parameters is generally a difficult task, and the best way to carry it out is to perform a grid search while including all the values that could affect the accuracy.

Using logistic regression on the previous set (only for comparison), we get:

```
from sklearn.linear_model import LogisticRegression

>>> lr = LogisticRegression()
>>> cross_val_score(lr, X, Y, scoring='accuracy', cv=10).mean()
0.9053368347338937
```

So the score is higher, as expected. However, the original dataset was quite simple, and based on the concept of having a single cluster per class. This allows a simpler and more precise linear separation. If we consider a slightly different scenario with more variables and a more complex structure (which is hard to capture by a linear classifier), we can compare an ROC curve for both linear regression and decision trees:

```
>>> nb_samples = 1000
>>> X, Y = make_classification(n_samples=nb_samples, n_features=8,
n_informative=6, n_redundant=2,    n_classes=2, n_clusters_per_class=4)
```

The resulting ROC curve is shown in the following figure:

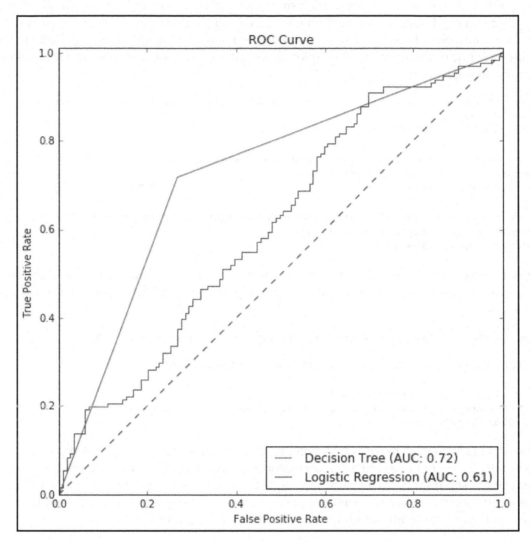

Using a grid search with the most common parameters on the MNIST digits dataset, we can get:

```python
from sklearn.model_selection import GridSearchCV

param_grid = [
 {
   'criterion': ['gini', 'entropy'],
   'max_features': ['auto', 'log2', None],
```

```
    'min_samples_split': [ 2, 10, 25, 100, 200 ],
    'max_depth': [5, 10, 15, None]
  }
]

>>> gs = GridSearchCV(estimator=DecisionTreeClassifier(),
param_grid=param_grid,
  scoring='accuracy', cv=10, n_jobs=multiprocessing.cpu_count())

>>> gs.fit(digits.data, digits.target)
GridSearchCV(cv=10, error_score='raise',
        estimator=DecisionTreeClassifier(class_weight=None,
criterion='gini', max_depth=None,
            max_features=None, max_leaf_nodes=None,
            min_impurity_split=1e-07, min_samples_leaf=1,
            min_samples_split=2, min_weight_fraction_leaf=0.0,
            presort=False, random_state=None, splitter='best'),
        fit_params={}, iid=True, n_jobs=8,
        param_grid=[{'max_features': ['auto', 'log2', None],
'min_samples_split': [2, 10, 25, 100, 200], 'criterion': ['gini',
'entropy'], 'max_depth': [5, 10, 15, None]}],
        pre_dispatch='2*n_jobs', refit=True, return_train_score=True,
        scoring='accuracy', verbose=0)

>>> gs.best_estimator_
DecisionTreeClassifier(class_weight=None, criterion='entropy',
max_depth=None,
            max_features=None, max_leaf_nodes=None,
            min_impurity_split=1e-07, min_samples_leaf=1,
            min_samples_split=2, min_weight_fraction_leaf=0.0,
            presort=False, random_state=None, splitter='best')

>>> gs.best_score_
0.8380634390651085
```

In this case, the element that impacted accuracy the most is the minimum number of samples to consider for a split. This is reasonable, considering the structure of this dataset and the need to have many branches to capture even small changes.

Ensemble learning

Until now, we have trained models on single instances, iterating an algorithm in order to minimize a target loss function. This approach is based on so-called strong learners, or methods that are optimized to solve a specific problem by looking for the best possible solution. Another approach is based on a set of weak learners that can be trained in parallel or sequentially (with slight modifications on the parameters) and used as an ensemble based on a majority vote or the averaging of results. These methods can be classified into two main categories:

- **Bagged (or Bootstrap) trees**: In this case, the ensemble is built completely. The training process is based on a random selection of the splits and the predictions are based on a majority vote. Random forests are an example of bagged tree ensembles.
- **Boosted trees**: The ensemble is built sequentially, focusing on the samples that have been previously misclassified. Examples of boosted trees are AdaBoost and gradient tree boosting.

Random forests

A random forest is a set of decision trees built on random samples with a different policy for splitting a node: Instead of looking for the best choice, in such a model, a random subset of features (for each tree) is used, trying to find the threshold that best separates the data. As a result, there will be many trees trained in a weaker way and each of them will produce a different prediction.

There are two ways to interpret these results; the more common approach is based on a majority vote (the most voted class will be considered correct). However, scikit-learn implements an algorithm based on averaging the results, which yields very accurate predictions. Even if they are theoretically different, the probabilistic average of a trained random forest cannot be very different from the majority of predictions (otherwise, there should be different stable points); therefore the two methods often drive to comparable results.

As an example, let's consider the MNIST dataset with random forests made of a different number of trees:

```
from sklearn.ensemble import RandomForestClassifier
>>> nb_classifications = 100
>>> accuracy = []

>>> for i in range(1, nb_classifications):
        a = cross_val_score(RandomForestClassifier(n_estimators=i),
digits.data, digits.target,  scoring='accuracy', cv=10).mean()
        rf_accuracy.append(a)
```

The resulting plot is shown in the following figure:

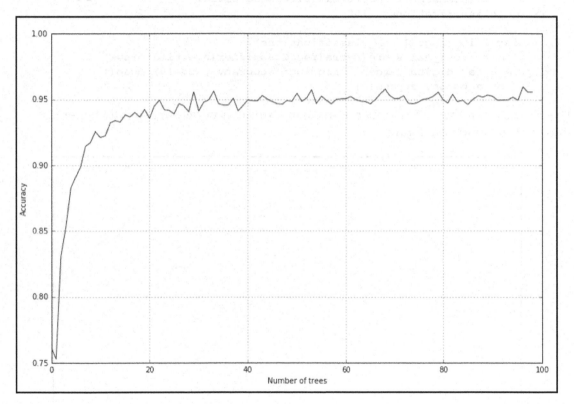

As expected, the accuracy is low when the number of trees is under a minimum threshold; however, it starts increasing rapidly with fewer than 10 trees. A value between 20 and 30 trees yields the optimal result (95%), which is higher than for a single decision tree. When the number of trees is low, the variance of the model is very high and the averaging process produces many incorrect results; however, increasing the number of trees reduces the variance and allows the model to converge to a very stable solution. scikit-learn also offers a variance that enhances the randomness in selecting the best threshold. Using the `ExtraTreesClassifier` class, it's possible to implement a model that randomly computes thresholds and picks the best one. As discussed in the official documentation, this allows us to further reduce the variance:

```
from sklearn.ensemble import ExtraTreesClassifier
>>> nb_classifications = 100

>>> for i in range(1, nb_classifications):
        a = cross_val_score(ExtraTreesClassifier(n_estimators=i),
    digits.data, digits.target,  scoring='accuracy', cv=10).mean()
        et_accuracy.append(a)
```

The results (with the same number of trees) in terms of accuracy are slightly better, as shown in the following figure:

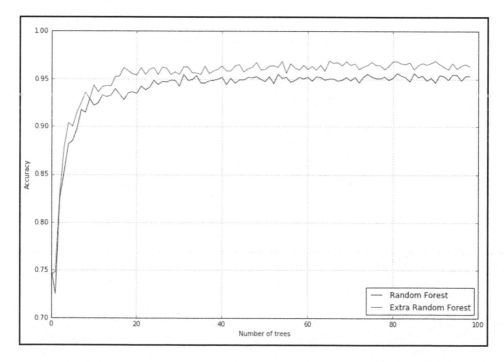

Feature importance in random forests

The concept of feature importance that we previously introduced can also be applied to random forests, computing the average over all trees in the forest:

$$Importance(x_i) = \frac{1}{N_{Trees}} \sum_t \sum_k \frac{N_k}{N} \Delta I_{x_i}$$

We can easily test the importance evaluation with a dummy dataset containing 50 features with 20 noninformative elements:

```
>>> nb_samples = 1000
>>> X, Y = make_classification(n_samples=nb_samples, n_features=50,
n_informative=30, n_redundant=20, n_classes=2, n_clusters_per_class=5)
```

The importance of the first 50 features according to a random forest with 20 trees is plotted in the following figure:

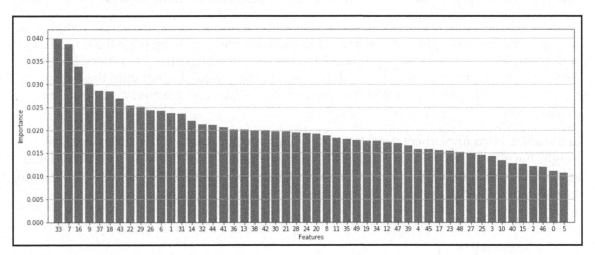

As expected, there are a few *very* important features, a block of features with a medium importance, and a tail containing features that have quite a low influence on the predictions. This type of plot is also useful during the analysis stage to better understand how the decision process is structured. With multidimensional datasets, it's rather difficult to understand the influence of every factor, and sometimes many important business decisions are made without a complete awareness of their potential impact. Using decision trees or random forests, it's possible to assess the "real" importance of all features and exclude all the elements under a fixed threshold. In this way, a complex decision process can be simplified and, at the same time, be partially denoised.

AdaBoost

Another technique is called **AdaBoost** (short for **Adaptive Boosting**) and works in a slightly different way than many other classifiers. The basic structure behind this can be a decision tree, but the dataset used for training is continuously adapted to force the model to focus on those samples that are misclassified. Moreover, the classifiers are added sequentially, so a new one boosts the previous one by improving the performance in those areas where it was not as accurate as expected.

At each iteration, a weight factor is applied to each sample so as to increase the importance of the samples that are wrongly predicted and decrease the importance of others. In other words, the model is repeatedly boosted, starting as a very weak learner until the maximum n_estimators number is reached. The predictions, in this case, are always obtained by majority vote.

In the scikit-learn implementation, there's also a parameter called learning_rate that weighs the effect of each classifier. The default value is 1.0, so all estimators are considered to have the same importance. However, as we can see with the MNIST dataset, it's useful to decrease this value so that each contribution is weakened:

```
from sklearn.ensemble import AdaBoostClassifier

>>> accuracy = []

>>> nb_classifications = 100

>>> for i in range(1, nb_classifications):
        a = cross_val_score(AdaBoostClassifier(n_estimators=i,
learning_rate=0.1), digits.data, digits.target, scoring='accuracy',
cv=10).mean()
>>> ab_accuracy.append(a)
```

The result is shown in the following figure:

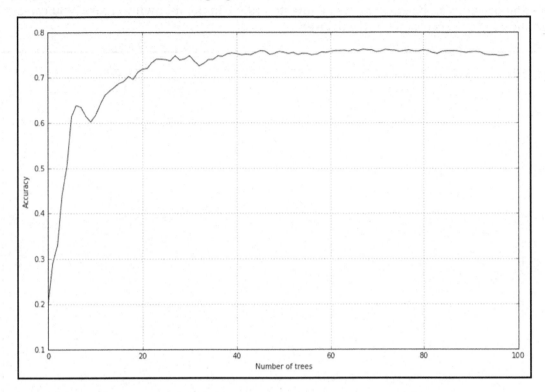

The accuracy is not so high as in the previous examples; however, it's possible to see that when the boosting adds about 20-30 trees, it reaches a stable value. A grid search on `learning_rate` could allow you to find the optimal value; however, the sequential approach in this case is not preferable. A classic random forest, which works with a fixed number of trees since the first iteration, performs better. This may well be due to the strategy adopted by AdaBoost; in this set, increasing the weight of the correctly classified samples and decreasing the strength of misclassifications can produce an oscillation in the loss function, with a final result that is not the optimal minimum point. Repeating the experiment with the Iris dataset (which is structurally much simpler) yields better results:

```
from sklearn.datasets import load_iris

>>> iris = load_iris()

>>> ada = AdaBoostClassifier(n_estimators=100, learning_rate=1.0)
>>> cross_val_score(ada, iris.data, iris.target, scoring='accuracy',
cv=10).mean()
0.94666666666666666
```

In this case, a learning rate of 1.0 is the best choice, and it's easy to understand that the boosting process can be stopped after a few iterations. In the following figure, you can see a plot showing the accuracy for this dataset:

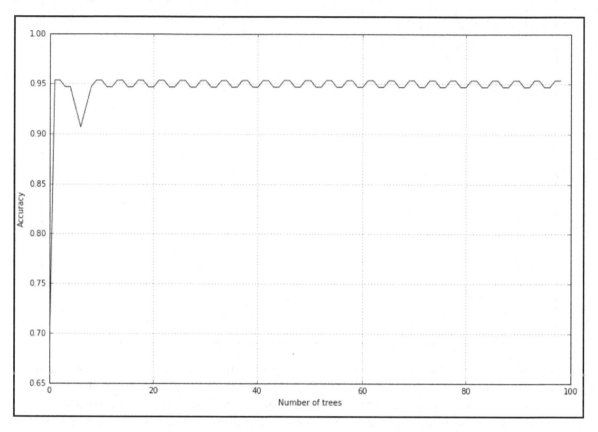

After about 10 iterations, the accuracy becomes stable (the residual oscillation can be discarded), reaching a value that is compatible with this dataset. The advantage of using AdaBoost can be appreciated in terms of resources; it doesn't work with a fully configured set of classifiers and the whole set of samples. Therefore, it can help save time when training on large datasets.

Gradient tree boosting

Gradient tree boosting is a technique that allows you to build a tree ensemble step by step with the goal of minimizing a target loss function. The generic output of the ensemble can be represented as:

$$y_E = \sum_i \alpha_i f_i(\bar{x})$$

Here, $f_i(x)$ is a function representing a weak learner. The algorithm is based on the concept of adding a new decision tree at each step so as to minimize the global loss function using the steepest gradient descent method (see `https://en.wikipedia.org/wiki/Method_of_s teepest_descent`, for further information):

$$y_E^{n+1} = y_E^n + \alpha_{n+1} f_{n+1}(\bar{x})$$

After introducing the gradient, the previous expression becomes:

$$y_E^{n+1} = y_E^n + \alpha_{n+1} \sum_i \nabla L(y_{T_i}, y_{E_i}) \ where \ y_{T_i} \ is \ a \ target \ class$$

scikit-learn implements the `GradientBoostingClassifier` class, supporting two classification loss functions:

- Binomial/multinomial negative log-likelihood (which is the default choice)
- Exponential (such as AdaBoost)

Let's evaluate the accuracy of this method using a more complex dummy dataset made up of 500 samples with four features (three informative and one redundant) and three classes:

```
from sklearn.datasets import make_classification

>>> nb_samples = 500

>>> X, Y = make_classification(n_samples=nb_samples, n_features=4,
n_informative=3, n_redundant=1, n_classes=3)
```

Now we can collect the cross-validation average accuracy for a number of estimators in the range (1, 50). The loss function is the default one (multinomial negative log-likelihood):

```
from sklearn.ensemble import GradientBoostingClassifier
from sklearn.model_selection import cross_val_score

>>> a = []
>>> max_estimators = 50

>>> for i in range(1, max_estimators):
>>> score = cross_val_score(GradientBoostingClassifier(n_estimators=i,
learning_rate=10.0/float(i)), X, Y, cv=10, scoring='accuracy').mean()
>>> a.append(score)
```

While increasing the number of estimators (parameter `n_estimators`), it's important to decrease the learning rate (parameter `learning_rate`). The optimal value cannot be easily predicted; therefore, it's often useful to perform a grid search. In our example, I've set a very high learning rate at the beginning (5.0), which converges to 0.05 when the number of estimators is equal to 100. This is not a perfect choice (unacceptable in most real cases!), and it has been made only to show the different accuracy performances. The results are shown in the following figure:

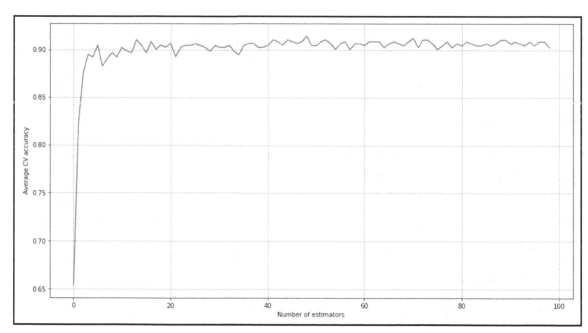

As it's possible to see, the optimal number of estimators is about 50, with a learning rate of 0.1. The reader can try different combinations and compare the performances of this algorithm with the other ensemble methods.

Voting classifier

A very interesting ensemble solution is offered by the class `VotingClassifier`, which isn't an actual classifier but a wrapper for a set of different ones that are trained and evaluated in parallel. The final decision for a prediction is taken by majority vote according to two different strategies:

- **Hard voting**: In this case, the class that received the major number of votes, $N_c(y_t)$, will be chosen:

$$\tilde{y} = argmax(Nc(y_t^1), Nc(y_t^2), ..., Nc(y_t^n))$$

- **Soft voting**: In this case, the probability vectors for each predicted class (for all classifiers) are summed up and averaged. The winning class is the one corresponding to the highest value:

$$\tilde{y} = argmax \frac{1}{Nclassifiers} \sum_{Classifier} (p_1, p_2, ..., p_n)$$

Let's consider a dummy dataset and compute the accuracy with a hard voting strategy:

```
from sklearn.datasets import make_classification

>>> nb_samples = 500

>>> X, Y = make_classification(n_samples=nb_samples, n_features=2,
n_redundant=0, n_classes=2)
```

For our examples, we are going to consider three classifiers: logistic regression, decision tree (with default Gini impurity), and an SVM (with a polynomial kernel and `probability=True` in order to generate the probability vectors). This choice has been made only for didactic purposes and may not be the best one. When creating an ensemble, it's useful to consider the different features of each involved classifier and avoid "duplicate" algorithms (for example, a logistic regression and a linear SVM or a perceptron are likely to yield very similar performances). In many cases, it can be useful to mix nonlinear classifiers with random forests or AdaBoost classifiers. The reader can repeat this experiment with other combinations, comparing the performance of each single estimator and the accuracy of the voting classifier:

```
from sklearn.linear_model import LogisticRegression
from sklearn.svm import SVC
from sklearn.tree import DecisionTreeClassifier
from sklearn.ensemble import VotingClassifier

>>> lr = LogisticRegression()
>>> svc = SVC(kernel='poly', probability=True)
>>> dt = DecisionTreeClassifier()

>>> classifiers = [('lr', lr),
                   ('dt', dt),
                   ('svc', svc)]

>>> vc = VotingClassifier(estimators=classifiers, voting='hard')
```

Computing the cross-validation accuracies, we get:

```
from sklearn.model_selection import cross_val_score

>>> a = []

>>> a.append(cross_val_score(lr, X, Y, scoring='accuracy', cv=10).mean())
>>> a.append(cross_val_score(dt, X, Y, scoring='accuracy', cv=10).mean())
>>> a.append(cross_val_score(svc, X, Y, scoring='accuracy', cv=10).mean())
>>> a.append(cross_val_score(vc, X, Y, scoring='accuracy', cv=10).mean())

>>> print(np.array(a))
[ 0.90182873  0.84990876  0.87386955  0.89982873]
```

The accuracies of each single classifier and of the ensemble are plotted in the following figure:

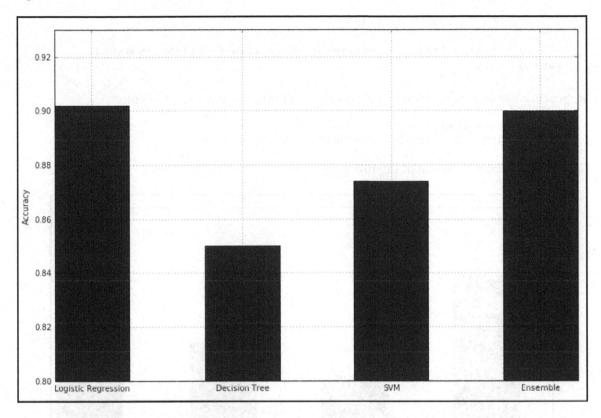

As expected, the ensemble takes advantage of the different algorithms and yields better performance than any single one. We can now repeat the experiment with soft voting, considering that it's also possible to introduce a weight vector (through the parameter `weights`) to give more or less importance to each classifier:

$$\tilde{y} = argmax \frac{1}{Nclassifiers} \sum_{Classifier} w_c(p_1, p_2, ..., p_n)$$

For example, considering the previous figure, we can decide to give more importance to the logistic regression and less to the decision tree and SVM:

```
>>> weights = [1.5, 0.5, 0.75]

>>> vc = VotingClassifier(estimators=classifiers, weights=weights,
voting='soft')
```

Repeating the same calculations for the cross-validation accuracies, we get:

```
>>> print(np.array(a))
[ 0.90182873  0.85386795  0.87386955  0.89578952]
```

The resulting plot is shown in the following figure:

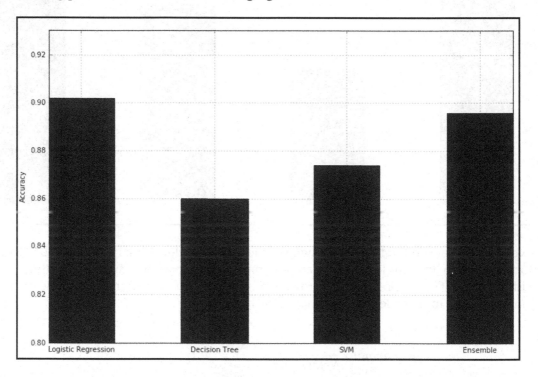

Weighting is not limited to the soft strategy. It can also be applied to hard voting, but in that case, it will be used to filter (reduce or increase) the number of actual occurrences.

$$\tilde{y} = argmax(Nc(y_t^1, \bar{w}), Nc(y_t^2, \bar{w}), \dots, Nc(y_t^n, \bar{w}))$$

Here, $N_c(y_i, w)$ is the number of votes for each target class, each of them multiplied by the corresponding classifier weighting factor.

A voting classifier can be a good choice whenever a single strategy is not able to reach the desired accuracy threshold; while exploiting the different approaches, it's possible to capture many microtrends using only a small set of strong (but sometimes limited) learners.

References

Louppe G., Wehenkel L., Sutera A., and Geurts P., *Understanding variable importances in forests of randomized trees*, NIPS Proceedings 2013.

Summary

In this chapter, we introduced decision trees as a particular kind of classifier. The basic idea behind their concept is that a decision process can become sequential by using splitting nodes, where, according to the sample, a branch is chosen until we reach a final leaf. In order to build such a tree, the concept of impurity was introduced; starting from a complete dataset, our goal is to find a split point that creates two distinct sets that should share the minimum number of features and, at the end of the process, should be associated with a single target class. The complexity of a tree depends on the intrinsic purity—in other words, when it's always easy to determine a feature that best separates a set, the depth will be lower. However, in many cases, this is almost impossible, so the resulting tree needs many intermediate nodes to reduce the impurity until it reaches the final leaves.

We also discussed some ensemble learning approaches: random forests, AdaBoost, gradient tree boosting and voting classifiers. They are all based on the idea of training several weak learners and evaluating their predictions using a majority vote or an average. However, while a random forest creates a set of decision trees that are partially randomly trained, AdaBoost and gradient boost trees adopt the technique of boosting a model by adding a new one, step after step, and focusing only on those samples that have been previously misclassified or by focusing on the minimization of a specific loss function. A voting classifier, instead, allows the mixing of different classifiers, adopting a majority vote to decide which class must be considered as the winning one during a prediction.
In the next chapter, we're going to introduce the first unsupervised learning approach, k-means, which is one of most diffused clustering algorithms. We will concentrate on its strengths and weaknesses, and explore some alternatives offered by scikit-learn.

9
Clustering Fundamentals

In this chapter, we're going to introduce the basic concepts of clustering and the structure of k-means, a quite common algorithm that can solve many problems efficiently. However, its assumptions are very strong, in particular those concerning the convexity of the clusters, and this can lead to some limitations in its adoption. We're going to discuss its mathematical foundation and how it can be optimized. Moreover, we're going to analyze two alternatives that can be employed when k-means fails to cluster a dataset. These alternatives are DBSCAN, (which works by considering the differences of sample density), and spectral clustering, a very powerful approach based on the affinity among points.

Clustering basics

Let's consider a dataset of points:

$$X = \{\bar{x}_1, \bar{x}_2, \dots, \bar{x}_n\} \text{ where } \bar{x}_i \in \mathbb{R}^m$$

We assume that it's possible to find a criterion (not unique) so that each sample can be associated with a specific group:

$$g_k = G(\bar{x}_i) \text{ where } k = \{0, 1, 2, \dots, t\}$$

Conventionally, each group is called a **cluster** and the process of finding the function *G* is called **clustering**. Right now, we are not imposing any restriction on the clusters; however, as our approach is unsupervised, there should be a similarity criterion to join some elements and separate other ones. Different clustering algorithms are based on alternative strategies to solve this problem, and can yield very different results. In the following figure, there's an example of clustering based on four sets of bidimensional samples; the decision to assign a point to a cluster depends only on its features and sometimes on the position of a set of other points (neighborhood):

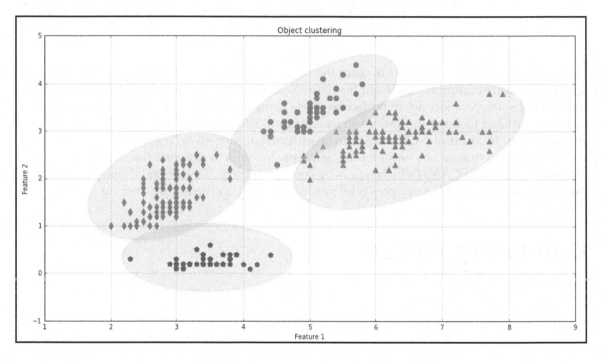

In this book, we're going to discuss **hard clustering** techniques, where each element must belong to a single cluster. The alternative approach, called **soft clustering** (or **fuzzy clustering**), is based on a membership score that defines how much the elements are "compatible" with each cluster. The generic clustering function becomes:

$$\bar{m}_i = F(\bar{x}_i) \ where \ \bar{m}_i = \left(m_i^0, m_i^2, \dots, m_i^t\right) and \ m_i^k \in [0,1]$$

A vector m_i represents the relative membership of x_i, and it's often normalized as a probability distribution.

K-means

The k-means algorithm is based on the (strong) initial condition to decide the number of clusters through the assignment of k initial **centroids** or **means**:

$$K^{(0)} = \left\{ \mu_1{}^{(0)}, \mu_2{}^{(0)}, \dots, \mu_k{}^{(0)} \right\}$$

Then the distance between each sample and each centroid is computed and the sample is assigned to the cluster where the distance is minimum. This approach is often called **minimizing the inertia** of the clusters, which is defined as follows:

$$SS_{W_i} = \sum_t \| x_t - \mu_i \|^2 \ \forall i \in (1, k)$$

The process is iterative—once all the samples have been processed, a new set of centroids $K^{(1)}$ is computed (now considering the actual elements belonging to the cluster), and all the distances are recomputed. The algorithm stops when the desired tolerance is reached, or in other words, when the centroids become stable and, therefore, the inertia is minimized. Of course, this approach is quite sensitive to the initial conditions, and some methods have been studied to improve the convergence speed. One of them is called **k-means++** (Karteeka Pavan K., Allam Appa Rao, Dattatreya Rao A. V., and Sridhar G.R., *Robust Seed Selection Algorithm for K-Means Type Algorithms*, International Journal of Computer Science and Information Technology 3, no. 5, October 30, 2011), which selects the initial centroids so that they are statistically close to the final ones. The mathematical explanation is quite difficult; however, this method is the default choice for scikit-learn, and it's normally the best choice for any clustering problem solvable with this algorithm.

Let's consider a simple example with a dummy dataset:

```
from sklearn.datasets import make_blobs

nb_samples = 1000
X, _ = make_blobs(n_samples=nb_samples, n_features=2, centers=3,
cluster_std=1.5)
```

We expect to have three clusters with bidimensional features and a partial overlap due to the standard deviation of each blob. In our example, we won't use the Y variable (which contains the expected cluster) because we want to generate only a set of locally coherent points to try our algorithms.

The resultant plot is shown in the following figure:

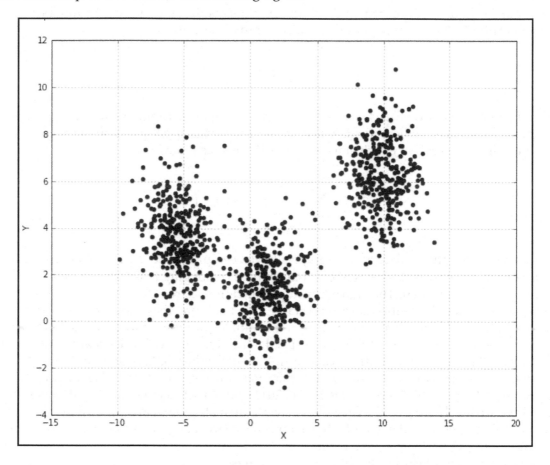

In this case, the problem is quite simple to solve, so we expect k-means to separate the three groups with minimum error in the region of X bounded between [-5, 0]. Keeping the default values, we get:

```
from sklearn.cluster import KMeans

>>> km = KMeans(n_clusters=3)
>>> km.fit(X)
KMeans(algorithm='auto', copy_x=True, init='k-means++', max_iter=300,
```

```
      n_clusters=3, n_init=10, n_jobs=1, precompute_distances='auto',
      random_state=None, tol=0.0001, verbose=0)

>>> print(km.cluster_centers_)
[[ 1.39014517,  1.38533993]
 [ 9.78473454,  6.1946332 ]
 [-5.47807472,  3.73913652]]
```

Replotting the data using three different markers, it's possible to verify how k-means successfully separated the data:

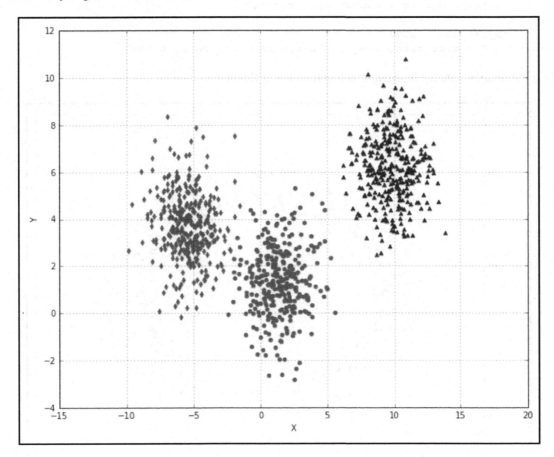

In this case, the separation was very easy because k-means is based on Euclidean distance, which is radial, and therefore the clusters are expected to be convex. When this doesn't happen, the problem cannot be solved using this algorithm. Most of the time, even if the convexity is not fully guaranteed, k-means can produce good results, but there are several situations when the expected clustering is impossible and letting k-means find out the centroid can lead to completely wrong solutions.

Let's consider the case of concentric circles. scikit-learn provides a built-in function to generate such datasets:

```
from sklearn.datasets import make_circles

>>> nb_samples = 1000
>>> X, Y = make_circles(n_samples=nb_samples, noise=0.05)
```

The plot of this dataset is shown in the following figure:

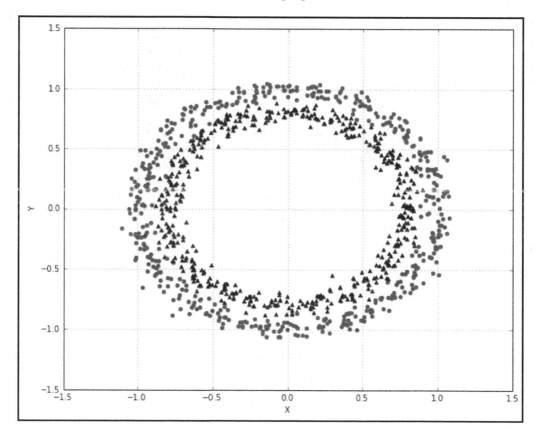

We would like to have an internal cluster (corresponding to the samples depicted with triangular markers) and an external one (depicted by dots). However, such sets are not convex, and it's impossible for k-means to separate them correctly (the means should be the same!). In fact, suppose we try to apply the algorithm to two clusters:

```
>>> km = KMeans(n_clusters=2)
>>> km.fit(X)
KMeans(algorithm='auto', copy_x=True, init='k-means++', max_iter=300,
    n_clusters=2, n_init=10, n_jobs=1, precompute_distances='auto',
    random_state=None, tol=0.0001, verbose=0)
```

We get the separation shown in the following figure:

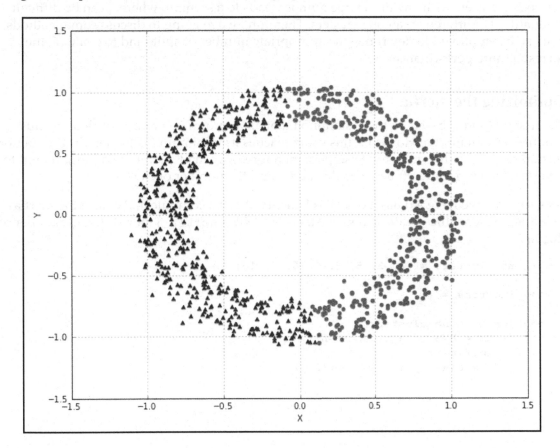

As expected, k-means converged on the two centroids in the middle of the two half-circles, and the resulting clustering is quite different from what we expected. Moreover, if the samples must be considered different according to the distance from the common center, this result will lead to completely wrong predictions. It's obvious that another method must be employed.

Finding the optimal number of clusters

One of the most common disadvantages of k-means is related to the choice of the optimal number of clusters. An excessively small value will determine large groupings that contain heterogeneous elements, while a large number leads to a scenario where it can be difficult to identify the differences among clusters. Therefore, we're going to discuss some methods that can be employed to determine the appropriate number of splits and to evaluate the corresponding performance.

Optimizing the inertia

The first method is based on the assumption that an appropriate number of clusters must produce a small inertia. However, this value reaches its minimum (0.0) when the number of clusters is equal to the number of samples; therefore, we can't look for the minimum, but for a value which is a trade-off between the inertia and the number of clusters.

Let's suppose we have a dataset of 1,000 elements. We can compute and collect the inertias (scikit-learn stores these values in the instance variable `inertia_`) for a different number of clusters:

```
>>> nb_clusters = [2, 3, 5, 6, 7, 8, 9, 10]

>>> inertias = []

>>> for n in nb_clusters:
>>>     km = KMeans(n_clusters=n)
>>>     km.fit(X)
>>>     inertias.append(km.inertia_)
```

Plotting the values, we get the result shown in the following figure:

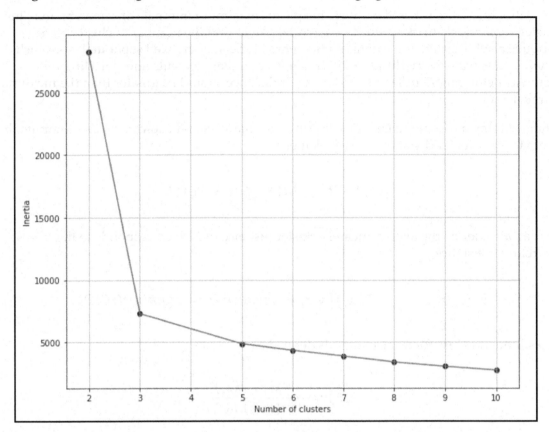

As you can see, there's a dramatic reduction between 2 and 3 and then the slope starts flattening. We want to find a value that, if reduced, leads to a great inertial increase and, if increased, produces a very small inertial reduction. Therefore, a good choice could be 4 or 5, while greater values are likely to produce unwanted intracluster splits (till the extreme situation where each point becomes a single cluster). This method is very simple, and can be employed as the first approach to determine a potential range. The next strategies are more complex, and can be used to find the final number of clusters.

Silhouette score

The silhouette score is based on the principle of "maximum internal cohesion and maximum cluster separation". In other words, we would like to find the number of clusters that produce a subdivision of the dataset into dense blocks that are well separated from each other. In this way, every cluster will contain very similar elements and, selecting two elements belonging to different clusters, their distance should be greater than the maximum intracluster one.

After defining a distance metric (Euclidean is normally a good choice), we can compute the average intracluster distance for each element:

$$a(\bar{x}_i) = E_{\bar{x}_{j \in C}}[d(\bar{x}_i, \bar{x}_j)] \; \forall \, \bar{x}_i \in C$$

We can also define the average nearest-cluster distance (which corresponds to the lowest intercluster distance):

$$b(\bar{x}_i) = E_{\bar{x}_{j \in D}}\left[d\left(\bar{x}_i, \bar{x}_j\right)\right] \forall \, \bar{x}_i \in C \; where \; D = argmin\{d(C, D)\}$$

The silhouette score for an element x_i is defined as:

$$s(\bar{x}_i) = \frac{b(\bar{x}_i) - a(\bar{x}_i)}{\max\{a(\bar{x}_i), b(\bar{x}_i)\}}$$

This value is bounded between -1 and 1, with the following interpretation:

- A value close to 1 is good (1 is the best condition) because it means that $a(x_i) \ll b(x_i)$
- A value close to 0 means that the difference between intra and inter cluster measures is almost null and therefore there's a cluster overlap
- A value close to -1 means that the sample has been assigned to a wrong cluster because $a(x_i) \gg b(x_i)$

scikit-learn allows computing the average silhouette score to have an immediate overview for different numbers of clusters:

```
from sklearn.metrics import silhouette_score

>>> nb_clusters = [2, 3, 5, 6, 7, 8, 9, 10]

>>> avg_silhouettes = []

>>> for n in nb_clusters:
>>>     km = KMeans(n_clusters=n)
>>>     Y = km.fit_predict(X)
>>>     avg_silhouettes.append(silhouette_score(X, Y))
```

The corresponding plot is shown in the following figure:

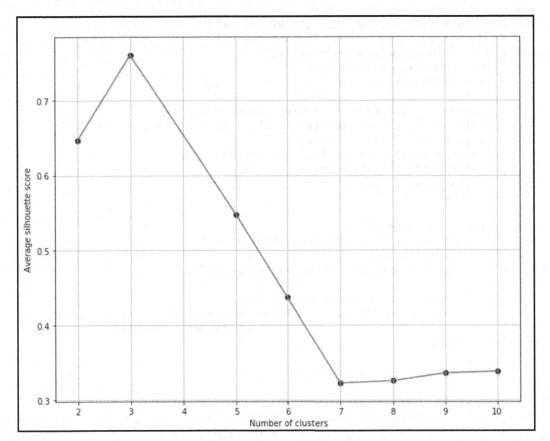

The best value is 3 (which is very close to 1.0), however, bearing in mind the previous method, 4 clusters provide a smaller inertia, together with a reasonable silhouette score. Therefore, a good choice could be 4 instead of 3. However, the decision between 3 and 4 is not immediate and should be evaluated by also considering the nature of the dataset. The silhouette score indicates that there are 3 dense agglomerates, but the inertia diagram suggests that one of them (at least) can probably be split into two clusters. To have a better understanding of how the clustering is working, it's also possible to graph the silhouette plots, showing the sorted score for each sample in all clusters. In the following snippet we create the plots for a number of clusters equal to 2, 3, 4, and 8:

```
from sklearn.metrics import silhouette_samples

>>> fig, ax = subplots(2, 2, figsize=(15, 10))

>>> nb_clusters = [2, 3, 4, 8]
>>> mapping = [(0, 0), (0, 1), (1, 0), (1, 1)]

>>> for i, n in enumerate(nb_clusters):
>>>     km = KMeans(n_clusters=n)
>>>     Y = km.fit_predict(X)

>>>     silhouette_values = silhouette_samples(X, Y)
>>>     ax[mapping[i]].set_xticks([-0.15, 0.0, 0.25, 0.5, 0.75, 1.0])
>>>     ax[mapping[i]].set_yticks([])
>>>     ax[mapping[i]].set_title('%d clusters' % n)
>>>     ax[mapping[i]].set_xlim([-0.15, 1])
>>>     ax[mapping[i]].grid()
>>>     y_lower = 20

>>>     for t in range(n):
>>>         ct_values = silhouette_values[Y == t]
>>>         ct_values.sort()
>>>         y_upper = y_lower + ct_values.shape[0]

>>>         color = cm.Accent(float(t) / n)
>>>         ax[mapping[i]].fill_betweenx(np.arange(y_lower, y_upper), 0,
                                        ct_values, facecolor=color,
edgecolor=color)

>>>         y_lower = y_upper + 20
```

The silhouette coefficients for each sample are computed using the function `silhouette_values` (which are always bounded between -1 and 1). In this case, we are limiting the graph between -0.15 and 1 because there are no smaller values. However, it's important to check the whole range before restricting it.

The resulting graph is shown in the following figure:

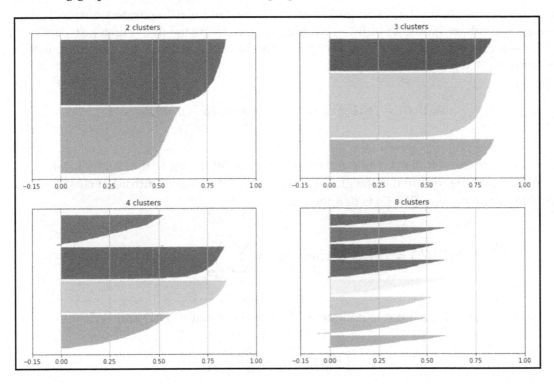

The width of each silhouette is proportional to the number of samples belonging to a specific cluster, and its shape is determined by the scores of each sample. An ideal plot should contain homogeneous and long silhouettes without peaks (they must be similar to trapezoids rather than triangles) because we expect to have a very low score variance among samples in the same cluster. For 2 clusters, the shapes are acceptable, but one cluster has an average score of 0.5, while the other has a value greater than 0.75; therefore, the first cluster has a low internal coherence. A completely different situation is shown in the plot corresponding to 8 clusters. All the silhouettes are triangular and their maximum score is slightly greater than 0.5. It means that all the clusters are internally coherent, but the separation is unacceptable. With 3 clusters, the plot is almost perfect, except for the width of the second silhouette. Without further metrics, we could consider this number as the best choice (confirmed also by the average score), but the inertia is lower for a higher numbers of clusters. With 4 clusters, the plot is slightly worse, with two silhouettes having a maximum score of about 0.5. This means that two clusters are perfectly coherent and separated, while the remaining two are rather coherent, but they aren't probably well separated. Right now, our choice should be made between 3 and 4. The next methods will help us in banishing all doubts.

Calinski-Harabasz index

Another method that is based on the concept of dense and well-separated clusters is the Calinski-Harabasz index. To build it, we need first to define the inter cluster dispersion. If we have k clusters with their relative centroids and the global centroid, the inter-cluster dispersion (BCD) is defined as:

$$BCD(k) = Tr(B_k) \ where \ B_k = \sum_t n_t \, (\mu - \mu_i)^T (\mu - \mu_j)$$

In the above expression, n_k is the number of elements belonging to the cluster k, *mu* (the Greek letter in the formula) is the global centroid, and mu_i is the centroid of cluster *i*. The intracluster dispersion (WCD) is defined as:

$$WCD(k) = Tr(X_k) \ where \ X_k = \sum_t \sum_{x \in C_k} (x - \mu_t)^T (x - \mu_t)$$

The Calinski-Harabasz index is defined as the ratio between *BCD(k)* and *WCD(k)*:

$$CH(k) = \frac{N - k}{k - 1} \cdot \frac{BCD(k)}{WCD(k)}$$

As we look for a low intracluster dispersion (dense agglomerates) and a high intercluster dispersion (well-separated agglomerates), we need to find the number of clusters that maximizes this index. We can obtain a graph in a way similar to what we have already done for the silhouette score:

```
from sklearn.metrics import calinski_harabaz_score

>>> nb_clusters = [2, 3, 5, 6, 7, 8, 9, 10]

>>> ch_scores = []

>>> km = KMeans(n_clusters=n)
>>> Y = km.fit_predict(X)

>>> for n in nb_clusters:
>>>     km = KMeans(n_clusters=n)
>>>     Y = km.fit_predict(X)
>>>     ch_scores.append(calinski_harabaz_score(X, Y))
```

The resulting plot is shown in the following figure:

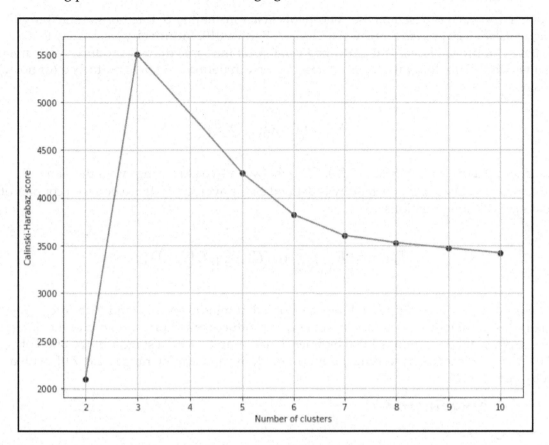

As expected, the highest value (5,500) is obtained with 3 clusters, while 4 clusters yield a value slightly below 5,000. Considering only this method, there's no doubt that the best choice is 3, even if 4 is still a reasonable value. Let's consider the last method, which evaluates the overall stability.

Cluster instability

Another approach is based on the concept of cluster instability defined in Von Luxburg U., *Cluster stability: an overview*, arXiv 1007:1075v1, 7 July 2010. Intuitively, we can say that a clustering approach is stable if perturbed versions of the same dataset produce very similar results. More formally, if we have a dataset X, we can define a set of m perturbed (or noisy) versions:

$$X_n = \{X_n^0, X_n^1, \dots, X_n^m\}$$

Considering a distance metric $d(C(X_1), C(X_2))$ between two clusterings with the same number (k) of clusters, the instability is defined as the average distance between couples of clusterings of noisy versions:

$$I(C) = E_{X_n^{i,j} \in X_n}[d(C(X_n^i), C(X_n^j))]$$

For our purposes, we need to find the value of k that minimizes $I(C)$ (and therefore maximizes the stability). First of all, we need to produce some noisy versions of the dataset. Let's suppose that X contains 1,000 bidimensional samples with a standard deviation of 10.0. We can perturb X by adding a uniform random value (in the range [-2.0, 2.0]) with a probability of 0.25:

```
>>> nb_noisy_datasets = 4

>>> X_noise = []

>>> for _ in range(nb_noisy_datasets):
>>>     Xn = np.ndarray(shape=(1000, 2))
>>>     for i, x in enumerate(X):
>>>         if np.random.uniform(0, 1) < 0.25:
>>>             Xn[i] = X[i] + np.random.uniform(-2.0, 2.0)
>>>         else:
>>>             Xn[i] = X[i]
>>>     X_noise.append(Xn)
```

Here we are assuming to have four perturbed versions. As a metric, we adopt the Hamming distance, which is proportional (if normalized) to the number of output elements that disagree. At this point, we can compute the instabilities for various numbers of clusters:

```
from sklearn.metrics.pairwise import pairwise_distances

>>> instabilities = []

>>> for n in nb_clusters:
>>>     Yn = []
>>>
>>>     for Xn in X_noise:
>>>         km = KMeans(n_clusters=n)
>>>         Yn.append(km.fit_predict(Xn))

>>> distances = []

>>> for i in range(len(Yn)-1):
>>>         for j in range(i, len(Yn)):
>>>             d = pairwise_distances(Yn[i].reshape(-1, 1),
Yn[j].reshape(-1, -1), 'hamming')
>>>             distances.append(d[0, 0])
>>>     instability = (2.0 * np.sum(distances)) / float(nb_noisy_datasets **
2)
>>>     instabilities.append(instability)
```

As the distances are symmetrical, we compute them only for the upper triangular part of the matrix. The result is shown in the following figure:

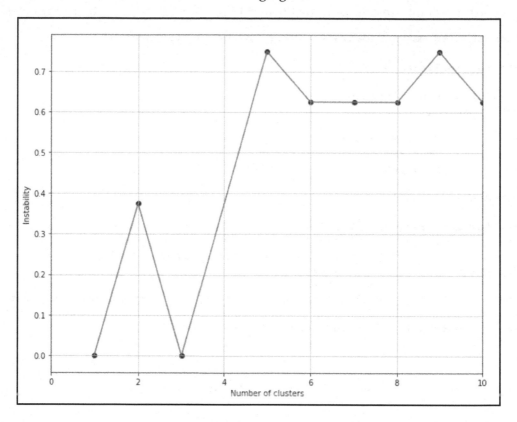

Excluding the configuration with 2 clusters, where the inertia is very high, we have a minimum for 3 clusters, a value that has already been confirmed by the three previous methods. Therefore, we can finally decide to set n_clusters=3, excluding the options of 4 or more clusters. This method is very powerful, but it's important to evaluate the stability with a reasonable number of noisy datasets, taking care not to excessively alter the original geometry. A good choice is to use Gaussian noise with a variance set to a fraction (for example 1/10) of the dataset variance. Alternative approaches are presented in Von Luxburg U., *Cluster stability: an overview*, arXiv 1007:1075v1, 7 July 2010.

Even if we have presented these methods with k-means, they can be applied to any clustering algorithm to evaluate the performance and compare them.

DBSCAN

DBSCAN or **Density-Based Spatial Clustering of Applications with Noise** is a powerful algorithm that can easily solve non-convex problems where k-means fails. The idea is simple: A cluster is a high-density area (there are no restrictions on its shape) surrounded by a low-density one. This statement is generally true, and doesn't need an initial declaration about the number of expected clusters. The procedure starts by analyzing a small area (formally, a point surrounded by a minimum number of other samples). If the density is enough, it is considered part of a cluster. At this point, the neighbors are taken into account. If they also have a high density, they are merged with the first area; otherwise, they determine a topological separation. When all the areas have been scanned, the clusters have also been determined because they are islands surrounded by empty space.

scikit-learn allows us to control this procedure with two parameters:

- `eps`: Responsible for defining the maximum distance between two neighbors. Higher values will aggregate more points, while smaller ones will create more clusters.
- `min_samples`: This determines how many surrounding points are necessary to define an area (also known as the core-point).

Let's try DBSCAN with a very hard clustering problem, called half-moons. The dataset can be created using a built-in function:

```
from sklearn.datasets import make_moons

>>> nb_samples = 1000
>>> X, Y = make_moons(n_samples=nb_samples, noise=0.05)
```

A plot of the dataset is shown in the following figure:

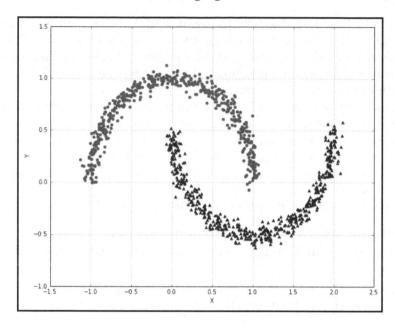

Just to understand, k-means will cluster by finding the optimal convexity, and the result is shown in the following figure:

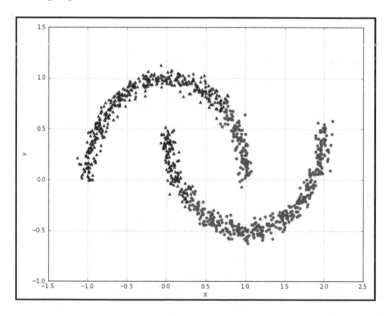

Of course, this separation is unacceptable, and there's no way to improve the accuracy. Let's try it with DBSCAN (with `eps` set to 0.1 and the default value of 5 for `min_samples`):

```
from sklearn.cluster import DBSCAN

>>> dbs = DBSCAN(eps=0.1)
>>> Y = dbs.fit_predict(X)
```

In a different manner than other implementations, DBSCAN predicts the label during the training process, so we already have an array `Y` containing the cluster assigned to each sample. In the following figure, there's a representation with two different markers:

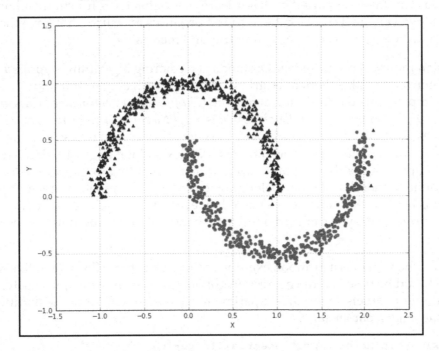

As you can see, the accuracy is very high and only three isolated points are misclassified (in this case, we know their class, so we can use this term even if it's a clustering process). However, by performing a grid search, it's easy to find the best values that optimize the clustering process. It's important to tune up those parameters to avoid two common problems: few big clusters and many small ones. This problem can be easily avoided using the following method.

Spectral clustering

Spectral clustering is a more sophisticated approach based on a symmetric affinity matrix:

$$A = \begin{pmatrix} a_{00} & \cdots & a_{n0} \\ \vdots & \ddots & \vdots \\ a_{n0} & \cdots & a_{nn} \end{pmatrix}$$

Here, each element a_{ij} represents a measure of affinity between two samples. The most diffused measures (also supported by scikit-learn) are radial basis function and nearest neighbors. However, any kernel can be used if it produces measures that have the same features of a distance (non-negative, symmetric, and increasing).

The Laplacian matrix is computed and a standard clustering algorithm is applied to a subset of eigenvectors (this element is strictly related to each single strategy). scikit-learn implements the Shi-Malik algorithm (*Shi J., Malik J., Normalized Cuts and Image Segmentation, IEEE Transactions on Pattern Analysis and Machine Intelligence, Vol. 22, 08/2000*), also known as normalized-cuts, which partitions the samples into two sets (G_1 and G_2, which are formally graphs where each point is a vertex and the edges are derived from the normalized Laplacian matrix) so that the weights corresponding to the points inside a cluster are quite higher than the one belonging to the cut. A complete mathematical explanation is beyond the scope of this book; however, in *Von Luxburg U., A Tutorial on Spectral Clustering, 2007*, you can read a full explanation of many alternative spectral approaches.

Let's consider the previous half-moon example. In this case, the affinity (just like for DBSCAN) should be based on the nearest neighbors function; however, it's useful to compare different kernels. In the first experiment, we use an RBF kernel with different values for the gamma parameter:

```
from sklearn.cluster import SpectralClustering

>>> Yss = []
>>> gammas = np.linspace(0, 12, 4)

>>> for gamma in gammas:
        sc = SpectralClustering(n_clusters=2, affinity='rbf', gamma=gamma)
        Yss.append(sc.fit_predict(X))
```

In this algorithm, we need to specify how many clusters we want, so we set the value to 2. The resulting plots are shown in the following figure:

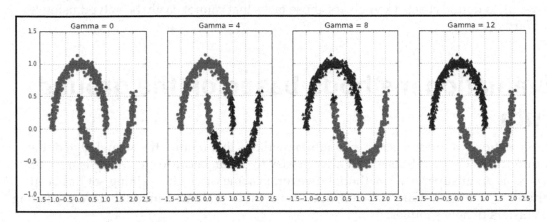

As you can see, when the scaling factor gamma is increased the separation becomes more accurate; however, considering the dataset, using the nearest neighbors kernel is not necessary in any search:

```
>>> sc = SpectralClustering(n_clusters=2, affinity='nearest_neighbors')
>>> Ys = sc.fit_predict(X)
```

The resulting plot is shown in the following figure:

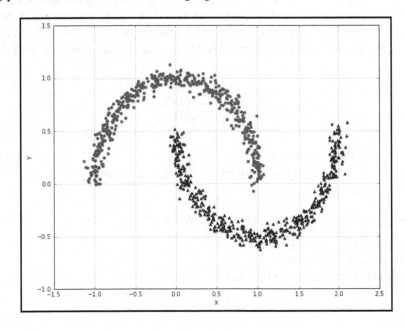

As for many other kernel-based methods, spectral clustering needs a previous analysis to detect which kernel can provide the best values for the affinity matrix. scikit-learn also allows us to define custom kernels for those tasks that cannot easily be solved using the standard ones.

Evaluation methods based on the ground truth

In this section, we present some evaluation methods that require the knowledge of the ground truth. This condition is not always easy to obtain because clustering is normally applied as an unsupervised method; however, in some cases, the training set has been manually (or automatically) labeled, and it's useful to evaluate a model before predicting the clusters of new samples.

Homogeneity

An important requirement for a clustering algorithm (given the ground truth) is that each cluster should contain only samples belonging to a single class. In Chapter 2, *Important Elements in Machine Learning*, we have defined the concepts of entropy $H(X)$ and conditional entropy $H(X|Y)$, which measures the uncertainty of X given the knowledge of Y. Therefore, if the class set is denoted as C and the cluster set as K, $H(C|K)$ is a measure of the uncertainty in determining the right class after having clustered the dataset. To have a homogeneity score, it's necessary to normalize this value considering the initial entropy of the class set $H(C)$:

$$h = 1 - \frac{H(C|K)}{H(C)}$$

In scikit-learn, there's the built-in function `homogeneity_score()` that can be used to compute this value. For this and the next few examples, we assume that we have a labeled dataset X (with true labels Y):

```
from sklearn.metrics import import homogeneity_score

>>> km = KMeans(n_clusters=4)
>>> Yp = km.fit_predict(X)
>>> print(homogeneity_score(Y, Yp))
0.806560739827
```

A value of 0.8 means that there's a residual uncertainty of about 20% because one or more clusters contain some points belonging to a secondary class. As with the other methods shown in the previous section, it's possible to use the homogeneity score to determine the optimal number of clusters.

Completeness

A complementary requirement is that each sample belonging to a class is assigned to the same cluster. This measure can be determined using the conditional entropy $H(K|C)$, which is the uncertainty in determining the right cluster given the knowledge of the class. Like for the homogeneity score, we need to normalize this using the entropy $H(K)$:

$$c = 1 - \frac{H(K|C)}{H(K)}$$

We can compute this score (on the same dataset) using the function `completeness_score()`:

```
from sklearn.metrics import completeness_score

>>> km = KMeans(n_clusters=4)
>>> Yp = km.fit_predict(X)
>>> print(completeness_score(Y, Yp))
0.807166746307
```

Also, in this case, the value is rather high, meaning that the majority of samples belonging to a class have been assigned to the same cluster. This value can be improved using a different number of clusters or changing the algorithm.

Adjusted rand index

The adjusted rand index measures the similarity between the original class partitioning (*Y*) and the clustering. Bearing in mind the same notation adopted in the previous scores, we can define:

- **a**: The number of pairs of elements belonging to the same partition in the class set *C* and to the same partition in the clustering set *K*
- **b**: The number of pairs of elements belonging to different partitions in the class set *C* and to different partitions in the clustering set *K*

If we total number of samples in the dataset is n, the rand index is defined as:

$$R = \frac{a + b}{\binom{n}{2}}$$

The *Corrected for Chance* version is the adjusted rand index, defined as follows:

$$AR = \frac{R - E[R]}{\max[R] - E[R]}$$

We can compute the adjusted rand score using the function `adjusted_rand_score()`:

```
from sklearn.metrics import adjusted_rand_score

>>> km = KMeans(n_clusters=4)
>>> Yp = km.fit_predict(X)
>>> print(adjusted_rand_score(Y, Yp))
0.831103137285
```

As the adjusted rand score is bounded between -1.0 and 1.0, with negative values representing a bad situation (the assignments are strongly uncorrelated), a score of 0.83 means that the clustering is quite similar to the ground truth. Also, in this case, it's possible to optimize this value by trying different numbers of clusters or clustering strategies.

References

- Karteeka Pavan K., Allam Appa Rao, Dattatreya Rao A. V., and Sridhar G.R., *Robust seed selection algorithm for k-means type algorithms*, International Journal of Computer Science and Information Technology 3, no. 5 (October 30, 2011)
- Shi J., Malik J., *Normalized Cuts and Image Segmentation, IEEE Transactions on Pattern Analysis and Machine Intelligence*, Vol. 22 (08/2000)
- Von Luxburg U., *A Tutorial on Spectral Clustering*, 2007
- Von Luxburg U., *Cluster stability: an overview*, arXiv 1007:1075v1, 7 July 2010

Summary

In this chapter, we introduced the k-means algorithm, which is based on the idea of defining (randomly or according to some criteria) k centroids that represent the clusters and optimize their position so that the sum of squared distances for every point in each cluster and the centroid is minimum. As the distance is a radial function, k-means assumes clusters to be convex and cannot solve problems where the shapes have deep concavities (like the half-moon problem).

In order to solve such situations, we presented two alternatives. The first one is called DBSCAN and is a simple algorithm that analyzes the difference between points surrounded by other samples and boundary samples. In this way, it can easily determine high-density areas (which become clusters) and low-density spaces among them. There are no assumptions about the shape or the number of clusters, so it's necessary to tune up the other parameters so as to generate the right number of clusters.

Spectral clustering is a family of algorithms based on a measure of affinity among samples. They use a classical method (such as k-means) on subspaces generated by the Laplacian of the affinity matrix. In this way, it's possible to exploit the power of many kernel functions to determine the affinity between points, which a simple distance cannot classify correctly. This kind of clustering is particularly efficient for image segmentation, but it can also be a good choice whenever the other methods fail to separate a dataset correctly.

In the next chapter, we're going to discuss another approach called hierarchical clustering. It allows us to segment data by splitting and merging clusters until a final configuration is reached.

10
Hierarchical Clustering

In this chapter, we're going to discuss a particular clustering technique called hierarchical clustering. Instead of working with the relationships existing in the whole dataset, this approach starts with a single entity containing all elements (divisive) or N separate elements (agglomerative), and proceeds by splitting or merging the clusters according to some specific criteria, which we're going to analyze and compare.

Hierarchical strategies

Hierarchical clustering is based on the general concept of finding a hierarchy of partial clusters, built using either a bottom-up or a top-down approach. More formally, they are called:

- **Agglomerative clustering**: The process starts from the bottom (each initial cluster is made up of a single element) and proceeds by merging the clusters until a stop criterion is reached. In general, the target has a sufficiently small number of clusters at the end of the process.
- **Divisive clustering**: In this case, the initial state is a single cluster with all samples and the process proceeds by splitting the intermediate cluster until all elements are separated. At this point, the process continues with an aggregation criterion based on the dissimilarity between elements. A famous approach (which is beyond the scope of this book) called **DIANA** is described in Kaufman L., Roussew P.J., *Finding Groups In Data: An Introduction To Cluster Analysis*, Wiley.

scikit-learn implements only the agglomerative clustering. However, this is not a real limitation because the complexity of divisive clustering is higher and the performances of agglomerative clustering are quite similar to the ones achieved by the divisive approach.

Agglomerative clustering

Let's consider the following dataset:

$$X = \{\bar{x}_1, \bar{x}_2, \ldots, \bar{x}_n\} \text{ where } \bar{x}_i \in \mathbb{R}^m$$

We define **affinity**, a metric function of two arguments with the same dimensionality m. The most common metrics (also supported by scikit-learn) are:

- **Euclidean** or *L2*:

$$d_{Euclidean}(\bar{x}_1, \bar{x}_2) = \|\bar{x}_1 - \bar{x}_2\|_2 = \sqrt{\sum_i (x_1^i - x_2^i)^2}$$

- **Manhattan** (also known as City Block) or *L1*:

$$d_{Manhattan}(\bar{x}_1, \bar{x}_2) = \|\bar{x}_1 - \bar{x}_2\|_1 = \sum_i |x_1^i - x_2^i|$$

- **Cosine distance**:

$$d_{Cosine}(\bar{x}_1, \bar{x}_2) = 1 - \frac{\bar{x}_1 \cdot \bar{x}_2}{\|\bar{x}_1\|_2 \|\bar{x}_2\|_2}$$

The Euclidean distance is normally a good choice, but sometimes it's useful to a have a metric whose difference with the Euclidean one gets larger and larger. The Manhattan metric has this property; to show it, in the following figure there's a plot representing the distances from the origin of points belonging to the line $y = x$:

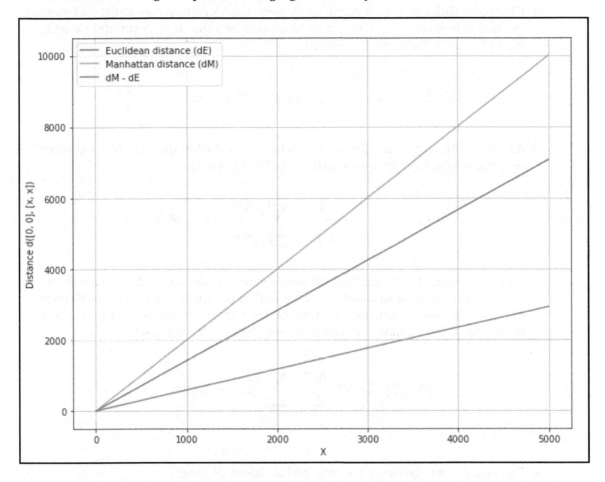

The cosine distance, instead, is useful when we need a distance proportional to the angle between two vectors. If the direction is the same, the distance is null, while it is maximum when the angle is equal to 180° (meaning opposite directions). This distance can be employed when the clustering must not consider the $L2$ norm of each point. For example, a dataset could contain bidimensional points with different scales and we need to group them into clusters corresponding to circular sectors. Alternatively, we could be interested in their position according to the four quadrants because we have assigned a specific meaning (invariant to the distance between a point and the origin) to each of them.

Once a metric has been chosen (let's simply call it $d(x,y)$), the next step is defining a strategy (called **linkage**) to aggregate different clusters. There are many possible methods, but scikit-learn supports the three most common ones:

- **Complete linkage**: For each pair of clusters, the algorithm computes and merges them to minimize the maximum distance between the clusters (in other words, the distance of the farthest elements):

$$\forall\, C_i, C_j\ \ L_{ij} = max\{d(x_a, x_b)\, \forall\, x_a \in C_i\ and\ x_b \in C_j\}$$

- **Average linkage**: It's similar to complete linkage, but in this case the algorithm uses the average distance between the pairs of clusters:

$$\forall\, C_i, C_j\ \ L_{ij} = \frac{1}{|C_i||C_j|} \sum_{x_a \in C_i} \sum_{x_b \in C_j} d(x_a, x_b)$$

- **Ward's linkage**: In this method, all clusters are considered and the algorithm computes the sum of squared distances within the clusters and merges them to minimize it. From a statistical viewpoint, the process of agglomeration leads to a reduction in the variance of each resulting cluster. The measure is:

$$\forall\, C_i, C_j\ \ L_{ij} = \sum_{x_a \in C_i} \sum_{x_b \in C_j} \|x_a - x_b\|^2$$

- The Ward's linkage supports only the Euclidean distance.

Dendrograms

To better understand the agglomeration process, it's useful to introduce a graphical method called a **dendrogram**, which shows in a static way how the aggregations are performed, starting from the bottom (where all samples are separated) till the top (where the linkage is complete). Unfortunately, scikit-learn doesn't support them. However, SciPy (which is a mandatory requirement for it) provides some useful built-in functions.

Let's start by creating a dummy dataset:

```
from sklearn.datasets import make_blobs

>>> nb_samples = 25
>>> X, Y = make_blobs(n_samples=nb_samples, n_features=2, centers=3,
cluster_std=1.5)
```

To avoid excessive complexity in the resulting plot, the number of samples has been kept very low. In the following figure, there's a representation of the dataset:

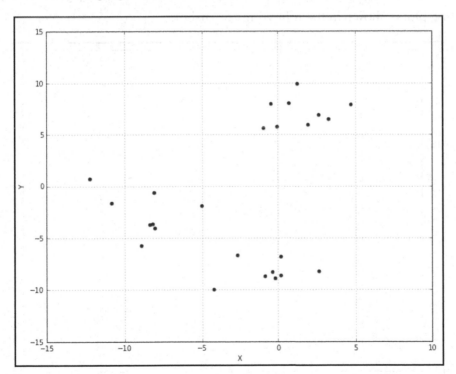

Now we can compute the dendrogram. The first step is computing a distance matrix:

```
from scipy.spatial.distance import pdist

>>> Xdist = pdist(X, metric='euclidean')
```

We have chosen a Euclidean metric, which is the most suitable in this case. At this point, it's necessary to decide which linkage we want. Let's take Ward; however, all known methods are supported:

```
from scipy.cluster.hierarchy import linkage

>>> Xl = linkage(Xdist, method='ward')
```

Now, it's possible to create and visualize a dendrogram:

```
from scipy.cluster.hierarchy import dendrogram

>>> Xd = dendrogram(Xl)
```

The resulting plot is shown in the following screenshot:

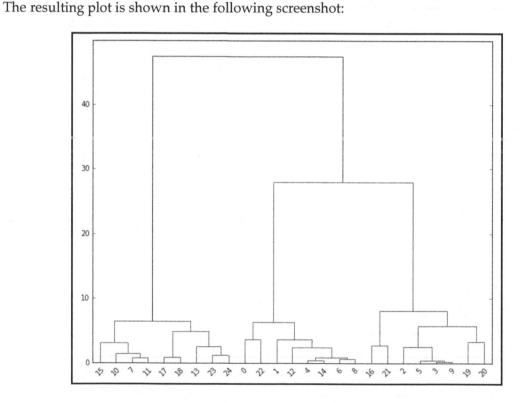

In the *x* axis, there are the samples (numbered progressively), while the *y* axis represents the distance. Every arch connects two clusters that are merged together by the algorithm. For example, 23 and 24 are single elements merged together. The element 13 is then aggregated to the resulting cluster, and so the process continues.

As you can see, if we decide to cut the graph at the distance of 10, we get two separate clusters: the first one from 15 to 24 and the other one from 0 to 20. Looking at the previous dataset plot, all the points with $Y < 10$ are considered to be part of the first cluster, while the others belong to the second cluster. If we increase the distance, the linkage becomes very aggressive (particularly in this example with only a few samples) and with values greater than 27, only one cluster is generated (even if the internal variance is quite high!).

Agglomerative clustering in scikit-learn

Let's consider a more complex dummy dataset with 8 centers:

```
>>> nb_samples = 3000
>>> X, _ = make_blobs(n_samples=nb_samples, n_features=2, centers=8,
cluster_std=2.0)
```

A graphical representation is shown in the following figure:

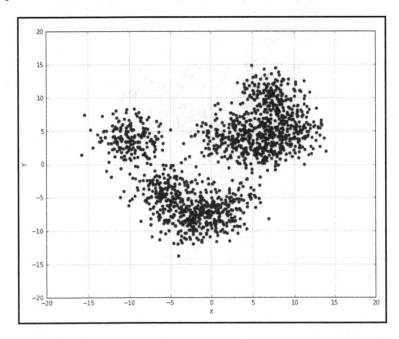

We can now perform an agglomerative clustering with different linkages (always keeping the Euclidean distance) and compare the results. Let's start with a complete linkage (AgglomerativeClustering uses the method fit_predict() to train the model and transform the original dataset):

```
from sklearn.cluster import AgglomerativeClustering

>>> ac = AgglomerativeClustering(n_clusters=8, linkage='complete')
>>> Y = ac.fit_predict(X)
```

A plot of the result (using both different markers and colors) is shown in the following figure:

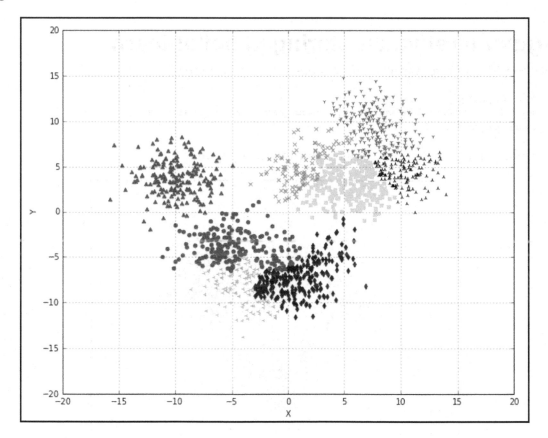

The result is totally bad. This approach penalizes the inter-variance and merges cluster, which in most cases should be different. In the previous plot, the three clusters in the middle are quite fuzzy, and the probability of wrong placement is very high considering the variance of the cluster represented by dots. Let's now consider the average linkage:

```
>>> ac = AgglomerativeClustering(n_clusters=8, linkage='average')
>>> Y = ac.fit_predict(X)
```

The result is shown in the following screenshot:

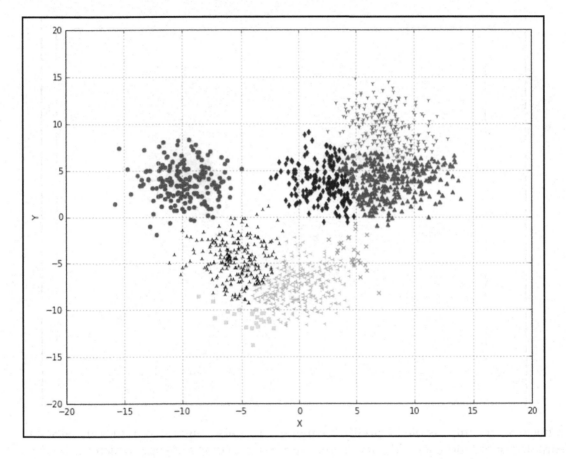

In this case, the clusters are better defined, even if some of them could have become really small. It can also be useful to try other metrics (in particular *L1*) and compare the results. The last method, which is often the best (it's the default one), is Ward's linkage, that can be used only with a Euclidean metric (also the default one):

```
>>> ac = AgglomerativeClustering(n_clusters=8)
>>> Y = ac.fit_predict(X)
```

The resulting plot is shown in the following figure:

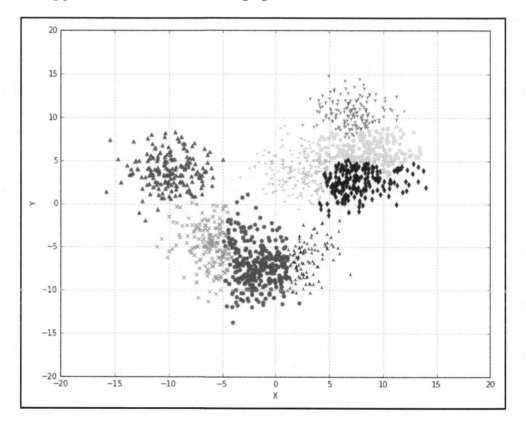

In this case, it's impossible to modify the metric so, as also suggested in the official scikit-learn documentation, a valid alternative could be the average linkage, which can be used with any affinity.

Connectivity constraints

scikit-learn also allows specifying a connectivity matrix, which can be used as a constraint when finding the clusters to merge. In this way, clusters which are far from each other (non-adjacent in the connectivity matrix) are skipped. A very common method for creating such a matrix involves using the k-nearest neighbors graph function (implemented as `kneighbors_graph()`), that is based on the number of neighbors a sample has (according to a specific metric). In the following example, we consider a circular dummy dataset (often used in the official documentation also):

```
from sklearn.datasets import make_circles

>>> nb_samples = 3000
>>> X, _ = make_circles(n_samples=nb_samples, noise=0.05)
```

A graphical representation is shown in the following figure:

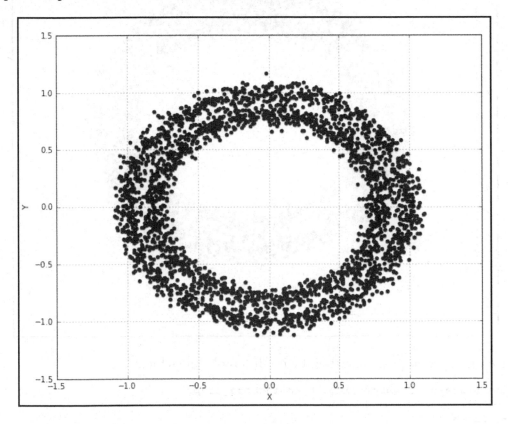

We start with unstructured agglomerative clustering based on average linkage and impose 20 clusters:

```
>>> ac = AgglomerativeClustering(n_clusters=20, linkage='average')
>>> ac.fit(X)
```

In this case, we have used the method `fit()` because the class `AgglomerativeClustering`, after being trained, exposes the labels (cluster number) through the instance variable `labels_` and it's easier to use this variable when the number of clusters is very high. A graphical plot of the result is shown in the following figure:

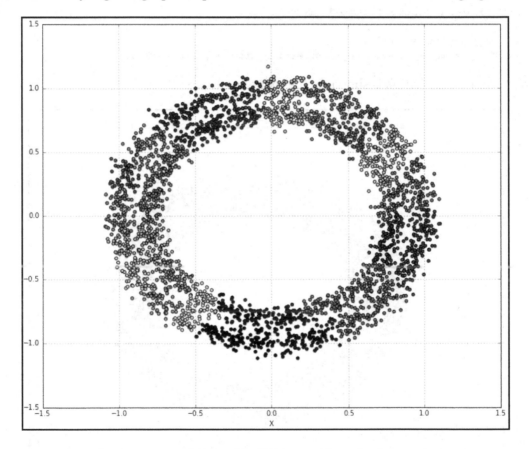

Now we can try to impose a constraint with different values for k:

```
from sklearn.neighbors import kneighbors_graph

>>> acc = []
>>> k = [50, 100, 200, 500]
```

```
>>> for i in range(4):
>>>     kng = kneighbors_graph(X, k[i])
>>>     ac1 = AgglomerativeClustering(n_clusters=20, connectivity=kng,
linkage='average')
>>>     ac1.fit(X)
>>>     acc.append(ac1)
```

The resulting plots are shown in the following screenshot:

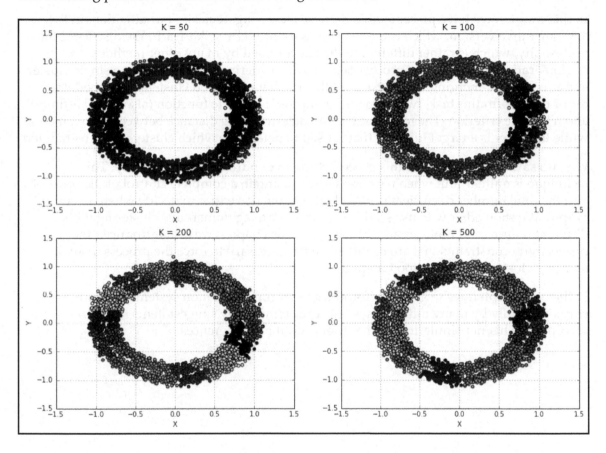

As you can see, imposing a constraint (in this case, based on k-nearest neighbors) allows controlling how the agglomeration creates new clusters and can be a powerful tool for tuning the models, or for avoiding elements whose distance is large in the original space could be taken into account during the merging phase (this is particularly useful when clustering images).

References

Kaufman L., Roussew P.J., *Finding Groups In Data: An Introduction To Cluster Analysis*, Wiley

Summary

In this chapter, we have presented hierarchical clustering, focusing our attention on the agglomerative version, which is the only one supported by scikit-learn. We discussed the philosophy, which is rather different to the one adopted by many other methods. In agglomerative clustering, the process begins by considering each sample as a single cluster and proceeds by merging the blocks until the number of desired clusters is reached. In order to perform this task, two elements are needed: a metric function (also called affinity) and a linkage criterion. The former is used to determine the distance between the elements, while the latter is a target function that is used to determine which clusters must be merged.

We also saw how to visualize this process through dendrograms using SciPy. This technique is quite useful when it's necessary to maintain a complete control of the process and the final number of clusters is initially unknown (it's easier to decide where to cut the graph). We showed how to use scikit-learn to perform agglomerative clustering with different metrics and linkages and, at the end of the chapter, we also introduced the connectivity constraints that are useful when it's necessary to force the process to avoid merging clusters which are too far apart.

In the next chapter, we're going to introduce the recommendation systems, that are employed daily by many different systems to automatically suggest items to a user, according to his/her similarity to other users and their preferences.

11
Introduction to Recommendation Systems

Imagine an online shop with thousands of articles. If you're not a registered user, you'll probably see a homepage with some highlights, but if you've already bought some items, it would be interesting if the website showed products that you would probably buy, instead of a random selection. This is the purpose of a recommender system, and in this chapter, we're going to discuss the most common techniques to create such a system.

The basic concepts are users, items, and ratings (or an implicit feedback about the products, like the fact of having bought them). Every model must work with known data (like in a supervised scenario), to be able to suggest the most suitable items or to predict the ratings for all the items not evaluated yet.

We're going to discuss two different kinds of strategies:

- User or content based
- Collaborative filtering

The first approach is based on the information we have about users or products and its target is to associate a new user with an existing group of peers to suggest all the items positively rated by the other members, or to cluster the products according to their features and propose a subset of items similar to the one taken into account. The second approach, which is a little bit more sophisticated, works with explicit ratings and its purpose is to predict this value for every item and every user. Even if collaborative filtering needs more computational power as, nowadays, the great availability of cheap resources, allows using this algorithm with millions of users and products to provide the most accurate recommendations in real-time. The model can also be retrained or updated every day.

Naive user-based systems

In this first scenario, we assume that we have a set of users represented by feature vectors:

$$U = \{\bar{u}_1, \bar{u}_2, \ldots, \bar{u}_n\} \, where \, \bar{u}_n \in \mathbb{R}^n$$

Typical features are age, gender, interests, and so on. All of them must be encoded using one of the techniques discussed in the previous chapters (for example, they can be binarized). Moreover, we have a set of items:

$$I = \{i_1, i_2, \ldots, i_m\}$$

Let's assume also that there is a relation which associates each user with a subset of items (bought or positively reviewed), items for which an explicit action or feedback has been performed:

$$g(\bar{u}) \rightarrow \{i_1, i_2, \ldots, i_k\} \, where \, k \in (0, m)$$

In a user-based system, the users are periodically clustered (normally using a **k-nearest neighbors** approach), and therefore, considering a generic user u (also new), we can immediately determine the ball containing all the users who are similar (therefore neighbors) to our sample:

$$B_R(\bar{u}) = \{\bar{u}_1, \bar{u}_2, \ldots, \bar{u}_k\}$$

At this point, we can create the set of suggested items using the relation previously introduced:

$$I_{Suggested}(\bar{u}) = \left\{ \bigcup_i g(\bar{u}_i) \, where \, \bar{u}_i \in B_R(\bar{u}) \right\}$$

In other words, the set contains all the unique products positively rated or bought by the neighborhood. I've used the adjective naive because there's a similar alternative that we're going to discuss in the section dedicated to collaborative filtering.

User-based system implementation with scikit-learn

For our purposes, we need to create a dummy dataset of users and products:

```python
import numpy as np

>>> nb_users = 1000
>>> users = np.zeros(shape=(nb_users, 4))

>>> for i in range(nb_users):
>>>     users[i, 0] = np.random.randint(0, 4)
>>>     users[i, 1] = np.random.randint(0, 2)
>>>     users[i, 2] = np.random.randint(0, 5)
>>>     users[i, 3] = np.random.randint(0, 5)
```

We assume that we have 1,000 users with four features represented by integer numbers bounded between 0 and 4 or 5. It doesn't matter what they mean; their role is to characterize a user and allow for clustering of the set.

For the products, we also need to create the association:

```python
>>> nb_product = 20
>>> user_products = np.random.randint(0, nb_product, size=(nb_users, 5))
```

We assume that we have 20 different items (from 1 to 20; 0 means that a user didn't buy anything) and an association matrix where each user is linked to a number of products bounded between 0 and 5 (maximum). For example:

$$
M_{UxI} = \begin{pmatrix} i_1 & i_2 & 0 & 0 & 0 \\ i_{15} & i_3 & i_{12} & 0 & 0 \\ \vdots & \vdots & \vdots & \vdots & \vdots \\ i_4 & i_8 & i_{11} & i_2 & i_5 \\ i_8 & 0 & 0 & 0 & 0 \end{pmatrix}
$$

At this point, we need to cluster the users using the `NearestNeighbors` implementation provided by scikit-learn:

```
from sklearn.neighbors import NearestNeighbors

>>> nn = NearestNeighbors(n_neighbors=20, radius=2.0)
>>> nn.fit(users)
NearestNeighbors(algorithm='auto', leaf_size=30, metric='minkowski',
        metric_params=None, n_jobs=1, n_neighbors=20, p=2, radius=2.0)
```

We have selected to have 20 neighbors and a Euclidean radius equal to 2. This parameter is used when we want to query the model to know which items are contained in the ball whose center is a sample and with a fixed radius. In our case, we are going to query the model to get all the neighbors of a test user:

```
>>> test_user = np.array([2, 0, 3, 2])
>>> d, neighbors = nn.kneighbors(test_user.reshape(1, -1))

>>> print(neighbors)
array([[933,  67, 901, 208,  23, 720, 121, 156, 167,  60, 337, 549,  93,
        563, 326, 944, 163, 436, 174,  22]], dtype=int64)
```

Now we need to build the recommendation list using the association matrix:

```
>>> suggested_products = []

>>> for n in neighbors:
>>>     for products in user_products[n]:
>>>         for product in products:
>>>             if product != 0 and product not in suggested_products:
>>>                 suggested_products.append(product)

>>> print(suggested_products)
[14, 5, 13, 4, 8, 9, 16, 18, 10, 7, 1, 19, 12, 11, 6, 17, 15, 3, 2]
```

For each neighbor, we retrieve the products he/she bought and perform a union, avoiding the inclusion of items with zero value (meaning no product) and double elements. The result is a list (not sorted) of suggestions that can be obtained almost in real time for many different systems. In some cases, when the number of users or items is too huge, it's possible to limit the list to a fixed number of elements and to reduce the number of neighbors. This approach is also naive because it doesn't consider the actual distance (or similarity) between users to weigh the suggestions. It's possible to consider the distance as a weighing factor, but it's simpler to adopt the collaborative filtering approach which provides a more robust solution.

Content-based systems

This is probably the simplest method and it's based only on the products, modeled as feature vectors:

$$I = \{\bar{\imath}_1, \bar{\imath}_2, \dots, \bar{\imath}_n\} \; where \; \bar{\imath}_n \in \mathbb{R}^n$$

Just like the users, the features can also be categorical (indeed, for products it's easier), for example, the genre of a book or a movie, and they can be used together with numerical values (like price, length, number of positive reviews, and so on) after encoding them.

Then a clustering strategy is adopted, even if the most used is **k-nearest neighbors** as it allows controlling the size of each neighborhood to determine, given a sample product, the quality and the number of suggestions.

Using scikit-learn, first of all we create a dummy product dataset:

```
>>> nb_items = 1000
>>> items = np.zeros(shape=(nb_items, 4))

>>> for i in range(nb_items):
>>>     items[i, 0] = np.random.randint(0, 100)
>>>     items[i, 1] = np.random.randint(0, 100)
>>>     items[i, 2] = np.random.randint(0, 100)
>>>     items[i, 3] = np.random.randint(0, 100)
```

In this case, we have 1000 samples with four integer features bounded between 0 and 100. Then we proceed, as in the previous example, towards clustering them:

```
>>> nn = NearestNeighbors(n_neighbors=10, radius=5.0)
>>> nn.fit(items)
```

At this point, it's possible to query our model with the method `radius_neighbors()`, which allows us to restrict our research only to a limited subset. The default radius (set through the parameter `radius`) is 5.0, but we can change it dynamically:

```
>>> test_product = np.array([15, 60, 28, 73])
>>> d, suggestions = nn.radius_neighbors(test_product.reshape(1, -1),
radius=20)

>>> print(suggestions)
[array([657, 784, 839, 342, 446, 196], dtype=int64)]
```

```
>>> d, suggestions = nn.radius_neighbors(test_product.reshape(1, -1),
radius=30)

>>> print(suggestions)
[ array([844, 340, 657, 943, 461, 799, 715, 863, 979, 784, 54, 148, 806,
  465, 585, 710, 839, 695, 342, 881, 864, 446, 196, 73, 663, 580, 216],
dtype=int64)]
```

Of course, when trying these examples, the number of suggestions can be different, as we are using random datasets, so I suggest trying different values for the radius (in particular when using different metrics).

When clustering with **k-nearest neighbors**, it's important to consider the metric adopted for determining the distance between the samples. The default for scikit-learn is the Minkowski distance, which is a generalization of Euclidean and Manhattan distance, and is defined as:

$$d_{Minkowsky} = \left(\sum_i |a_i - b_i|^p \right)^{\frac{1}{p}}$$

The parameter p controls the type of distance and the default value is 2, so that the resulting metric is a classical Euclidean distance. Other distances are offered by SciPy (in the package `scipy.spatial.distance`) and include, for example, the **Hamming** and **Jaccard** distances. The former is defined as the disagree proportion between two vectors (if they are binary this is the normalized number of different bits). For example:

```
from scipy.spatial.distance import hamming

>>> a = np.array([0, 1, 0, 0, 1, 0, 1, 1, 0, 0])
>>> b = np.array([1, 1, 0, 0, 0, 1, 1, 1, 1, 0])
>>> d = hamming(a, b)

>>> print(d)
0.40000000000000002
```

It means there's a disagree proportion of 40 percent, or, considering that both vectors are binary, there 4 different bits (out of 10). This measure can be useful when it's necessary to emphasize the presence/absence of a particular feature.

The Jaccard distance is defined as:

$$d_{Jaccard} = 1 - J(A, B) = 1 - \frac{|A \cap B|}{|A \cup B|}$$

It's particularly useful to measure the dissimilarity between two different sets (A and B) of items. If our feature vectors are binary, it's immediate to apply this distance using Boolean logic. Using the previous test values, we get:

```
from scipy.spatial.distance import jaccard

>>> d = jaccard(a, b)
>>> print(d)
0.5714285714285714
```

This measure is bounded between 0 (equal vectors) and 1 (total dissimilarity).

As for the Hamming distance, it can be very useful when it's necessary to compare items where their representation is made up of binary states (like present/absent, yes/no, and so forth). If you want to adopt a different metric for **k-nearest neighbors**, it's possible to specify it directly using the metric parameter:

```
>>> nn = NearestNeighbors(n_neighbors=10, radius=5.0, metric='hamming')
>>> nn.fit(items)

>>> nn = NearestNeighbors(n_neighbors=10, radius=5.0, metric='jaccard')
>>> nn.fit(items)
```

Model-free (or memory-based) collaborative filtering

As with the user-based approach, let's consider having two sets of elements: users and items. However, in this case, we don't assume that they have explicit features. Instead, we try to model a user-item matrix based on the preferences of each user (rows) for each item (columns). For example:

$$M_{UxI} = \begin{pmatrix} 0 & 1 & 4 & 3 & 0 & 4 & 3 & ... & 5 \\ 2 & 1 & 2 & 3 & 0 & 0 & 4 & ... & 1 \\ 0 & 2 & 0 & 3 & 1 & 2 & 4 & ... & 2 \\ 5 & 0 & 0 & 1 & 2 & 1 & 3 & ... & 1 \\ 3 & 0 & 0 & 3 & 0 & 1 & 0 & ... & 4 \\ 1 & 4 & 1 & 0 & 3 & 5 & 0 & ... & 3 \\ \vdots & \vdots & \vdots & \vdots & \vdots & \vdots & \vdots & \vdots & \vdots \\ 0 & 2 & 3 & 1 & 2 & 4 & 4 & ... & 0 \\ 1 & 3 & 2 & 0 & 0 & 2 & 2 & ... & 1 \end{pmatrix}$$

In this case, the ratings are bounded between 1 and 5 (0 means no rating), and our goal is to cluster the users according to their rating vector (which is, indeed, an internal representation based on a particular kind of feature). This allows producing recommendations even when there are no explicit pieces of information about the user. However, it has a drawback, called **cold-startup**, which means that when a new user has no ratings, it's impossible to find the right neighborhood, because he/she can belong to virtually any cluster.

Once the clustering is done, it's easy to check which products (not rated yet) have the higher rating for a given user and therefore are more likely to be bought. It's possible to implement a solution in scikit-learn as we've done before, but I'd like to introduce a small framework called **Crab** (see the box at the end of this section) that simplifies this process.

In order to build the model, we first need to define the user-item matrix as a Python dictionary with the structure:

```
{ user_1: { item1: rating, item2: rating, ... }, ..., user_n: ... }
```

A missing value in a user internal dictionary means no rating. In our example, we consider 5 users with 5 items:

```
from scikits.crab.models import MatrixPreferenceDataModel

>>> user_item_matrix = {
        1: {1: 2, 2: 5, 3: 3},
        2: {1: 5, 4: 2},
        3: {2: 3, 4: 5, 3: 2},
        4: {3: 5, 5: 1},
        5: {1: 3, 2: 3, 4: 1, 5: 3}
    }

>>> model = MatrixPreferenceDataModel(user_item_matrix)
```

Once the user-item matrix has been defined, we need to pick a metric and therefore, a distance function $d(u_i, u_j)$, to build a similarity matrix:

$$S = \begin{pmatrix} d(\bar{u}_1, \bar{u}_1) & \cdots & d(\bar{u}_n, \bar{u}_1) \\ \vdots & \ddots & \vdots \\ d(\bar{u}_1, \bar{u}_n) & \cdots & d(\bar{u}_n, \bar{u}_n) \end{pmatrix}$$

Using Crab, we do this in the following way (using a Euclidean metric):

```
from scikits.crab.similarities import UserSimilarity
from scikits.crab.metrics import euclidean_distances

>>> similarity_matrix = UserSimilarity(model, euclidean_distances)
```

There are many metrics, like Pearson or Jaccard, so I suggest visiting the website (http://muricoca.github.io/crab) to retrieve further information. At this point, it's possible to build the recommendation system (based on the k-nearest neighbors clustering method) and test it:

```
from scikits.crab.recommenders.knn import UserBasedRecommender

>>> recommender = UserBasedRecommender(model, similarity_matrix,
with_preference=True)

>>> print(recommender.recommend(2))
[(2, 3.6180339887498949), (5, 3.0), (3, 2.5527864045000417)]
```

So the recommender suggests the following predicted rating for user 2:

- **Item 2**: 3.6 (which can be rounded to 4.0)
- **Item 5**: 3
- **Item 3**: 2.5 (which can be rounded to 3.0)

When running the code, it's possible to see some warnings (Crab is still under development); however, they don't condition the functionality. If you want to avoid them, you can use the `catch_warnings()` context manager:

```
import warnings

>>> with warnings.catch_warnings():
>>>     warnings.simplefilter("ignore")
>>>     print(recommender.recommend(2))
```

It's possible to suggest all the items, or limit the list to the higher ratings (so, for example, avoiding the item 3). This approach is quite similar to the user-based model. However, it's faster (very big matrices can be processed in parallel) and it doesn't take care of details that can produce misleading results. Only the ratings are considered as useful features to define a user. Like model-based collaborative filtering, the cold-startup problem can be addressed in two ways:

- Asking the user to rate some items (this approach is often adopted because it's easy to show some movie/book covers, asking the user to select what they like and what they don't).
- Placing the user in an average neighborhood by randomly assigning some mean ratings. In this approach, it's possible to start using the recommendation system immediately. However, it's necessary to accept a certain degree of error at the beginning and to correct the dummy ratings when the real ones are produced.

Crab is an open-source framework for building collaborative filtering systems. It's still under development and therefore, doesn't implement all possible features. However, it's very easy to use and is quite powerful for many tasks. The home page with installation instructions and documentation is: `http://muricoca.github.io/crab/index.html`. Crab depends on scikits.learn, which still has some issues with Python 3. Therefore, I recommend using Python 2.7 for this example. It's possible to install both packages using pip: `pip install -U scikits.learn` and `pip install -U crab`.

Model-based collaborative filtering

This is currently one of the most advanced approaches and is an extension of what was already seen in the previous section. The starting point is always a rating-based user-item matrix:

$$M_{UxI} = \begin{pmatrix} r_{11} & \cdots & r_{1n} \\ \vdots & \ddots & \vdots \\ r_{m1} & \cdots & r_{mn} \end{pmatrix}$$

However, in this case, we assume the presence of **latent factors** for both the users and the items. In other words, we define a generic user as:

$$\bar{p}_i = (p_{i1}, p_{i2}, \dots, p_{ik}) \ where \ p_{ij} \in \mathbb{R}$$

A generic item is defined as:

$$\bar{q}_j = \left(q_{j1}, q_{j2}, \dots, q_{jk}\right) \ where \ q_{jt} \in \mathbb{R}$$

We don't know the value of each vector component (for this reason they are called latent), but we assume that a ranking is obtained as:

$$r_{ij} = \bar{p}_i \cdot \bar{q}_j{}^T$$

So we can say that a ranking is obtained from a latent space of rank k, where k is the number of latent variables we want to consider in our model. In general, there are rules to determine the right value for k, so the best approach is to check different values and test the model with a subset of known ratings. However, there's still a big problem to solve: finding the latent variables. There are several strategies, but before discussing them, it's important to understand the dimensionality of our problem. If we have 1000 users and 500 products, M has 500,000 elements. If we decide to have rank equal to 10, it means that we need to find 5000000 variables constrained by the known ratings. As you can imagine, this problem can easily become impossible to solve with standard approaches and parallel solutions must be employed.

Singular Value Decomposition strategy

The first approach is based on the **Singular Value Decomposition (SVD)** of the user-item matrix. This technique allows transforming a matrix through a low-rank factorization and can also be used in an incremental way as described in Sarwar B., Karypis G., Konstan J., Riedl J., *Incremental Singular Value Decomposition Algorithms for Highly Scalable Recommender Systems*, 2002. In particular, if the user-item matrix has m rows and n columns:

$$M_{UxI} = U\Sigma V^T \text{ where } U \in \mathbb{R}^{m \times t}, \Sigma \in \mathbb{R}^{t \times t} \text{ and } V \in \mathbb{R}^{n \times n}$$

We have assumed that we have real matrices (which is often true in our case), but, in general, they are complex. U and V are unitary, while sigma is diagonal. The columns of U contain the left singular vectors, the rows of transposed V contain the right singular vectors, while the diagonal matrix Sigma contains the singular values. Selecting k latent factors means taking the first k singular values and, therefore, the corresponding k left and right singular vectors:

$$M_k = U_k \Sigma_k V_k^T$$

This technique has the advantage of minimizing the Frobenius norm of the difference between M and M_k for any value of k, and therefore, it's an optimal choice to approximate the full decomposition. Before moving to the prediction stage, let's create an example using SciPy. The first thing to do is to create a dummy user-item matrix:

```
>>> M = np.random.randint(0, 6, size=(20, 10))

>>> print(M)
array([[0, 4, 5, 0, 1, 4, 3, 3, 1, 3],
       [1, 4, 2, 5, 3, 3, 4, 3, 1],
       [1, 1, 2, 2, 1, 5, 1, 4, 2, 5],
       [0, 4, 1, 2, 2, 5, 1, 1, 5, 5],
       [2, 5, 3, 1, 1, 2, 2, 4, 1, 1],
       [1, 4, 3, 3, 0, 0, 2, 3, 3, 5],
       [3, 5, 2, 1, 5, 3, 4, 1, 0, 2],
       [5, 2, 2, 0, 1, 0, 4, 4, 1, 0],
       [0, 2, 4, 1, 3, 1, 3, 0, 5, 4],
       [2, 5, 1, 5, 3, 0, 1, 4, 5, 2],
       [1, 0, 0, 5, 1, 3, 2, 0, 3, 5],
       [5, 3, 1, 5, 0, 0, 4, 2, 2, 2],
       [5, 3, 2, 4, 2, 0, 4, 4, 0, 3],
```

```
       [3,  2,  5,  1,  1,  2,  1,  1,  3,  0],
       [1,  5,  5,  2,  5,  2,  4,  5,  1,  4],
       [4,  0,  2,  2,  1,  0,  4,  4,  3,  3],
       [4,  2,  2,  3,  3,  4,  5,  3,  5,  1],
       [5,  0,  5,  3,  0,  0,  3,  5,  2,  2],
       [1,  3,  2,  2,  3,  0,  5,  4,  1,  0],
       [1,  3,  1,  4,  1,  5,  4,  4,  2,  1]])
```

We're assuming that we have 20 users and 10 products. The ratings are bounded between 1 and 5, and 0 means no rating. Now we can decompose *M*:

```
from scipy.linalg import svd

import numpy as np

>>> U, s, V = svd(M, full_matrices=True)
>>> S = np.diag(s)

>>> print(U.shape)
(20L, 20L)

>>> print(S.shape)
(10L, 10L)

>>> print(V.shape)
(10L, 10L)
```

Now let's consider only the first eight singular values, which will have eight latent factors for both the users and items:

```
>>> Uk = U[:, 0:8]
>>> Sk = S[0:8, 0:8]
>>> Vk = V[0:8, :]
```

Bear in mind that in SciPy SVD implementation, *V* is already transposed. According to Sarwar B., Karypis G., Konstan J., Riedl J., *Incremental Singular Value Decomposition Algorithms for Highly Scalable Recommender Systems*, 2002, we can easily get a prediction considering the cosine similarity (which is proportional to the dot product) between customers and products. The two latent factor matrices are:

$$\begin{cases} S_U = U_k \cdot \sqrt{\Sigma_k}^T \\ S_I = \sqrt{\Sigma_k} \cdot V_k^T \end{cases}$$

In order to take into account the loss of precision, it's useful also to consider the average rating per user (which corresponds to the mean row value of the user-item matrix), so that the result rating prediction for the user i and the item j becomes:

$$\tilde{r}_{ij} = E[r_i] + S_U(i) \cdot S_I(j)$$

Here $S_u(i)$ and $S_i(j)$ are the user and product vectors respectively. Continuing with our example, let's determine the rating prediction for user 5 and item 2:

```
>>> Su = Uk.dot(np.sqrt(Sk).T)
>>> Si = np.sqrt(Sk).dot(Vk).T
>>> Er = np.mean(M, axis=1)

>>> r5_2 = Er[5] + Su[5].dot(Si[2])
>>> print(r5_2)
2.38848720112
```

This approach has medium complexity. In particular, the SVD is $O(m^3)$ and an incremental strategy (as described in Sarwar B., Karypis G., Konstan J., Riedl J., *Incremental Singular Value Decomposition Algorithms for Highly Scalable Recommender Systems*, 2002) must be employed when new users or items are added; however, it can be effective when the number of elements is not too big. In all the other cases, the next strategy (together with a parallel architecture) can be adopted.

Alternating least squares strategy

The problem of finding the latent factors can be easily expressed as a least square optimization problem by defining the following loss function:

$$L = \sum_{(i,j)} (r_{ij} - \bar{p}_i \cdot \bar{q}_j{}^T)^2 + \alpha(\|\bar{p}_i\|^2 + \|\bar{q}_j\|^2)$$

L is limited only to known samples (user, item). The second term works as a regularization factor and the whole problem can easily be solved with any optimization method. However, there's an additional issue: we have two different sets of variables to determine (user and item factors). We can solve this problem with an approach called **alternating least squares**, described in Koren Y., Bell R., Volinsky C., *Matrix Factorization Techniques for Recommender Systems*, IEEE Computer Magazine, 08/2009. The algorithm is very easy to describe and can be summarized in two main iterating steps:

- p_i is fixed and q_j is optimized
- q_j is fixed and p_i is optimized

The algorithm stops when a predefined precision has been achieved. It can be easily implemented with parallel strategies to be able to process huge matrices in a short time. Moreover, considering the price of virtual clusters, it's also possible to retrain the model periodically, to immediately (with an acceptable delay) include new products and users.

Alternating least squares with Apache Spark MLlib

Apache Spark is beyond the scope of this book, so if you want to know more about this powerful framework, I suggest you read the online documentation or one the many books available. In Pentreath N., *Machine Learning with Spark*, Packt, there's an interesting introduction on the library MLlib and how to implement most of the algorithms discussed in this book.

Spark is a parallel computational engine that is now part of the Hadoop project (even if it doesn't use its code), that can run in local mode or on very large clusters (with thousands of nodes), to execute complex tasks using huge amounts of data. It's mainly based on Scala, though there are interfaces for Java, Python, and R. In this example, we're going to use PySpark, which is the built-in shell for running Spark with Python code.

After launching PySpark in local mode, we get a standard Python prompt and we can start working, just like with any other standard Python environment:

```
# Linux
>>> ./pyspark

# Mac OS X
>>> pyspark

# Windows
>>> pyspark

Python 2.7.12 |Anaconda 4.0.0 (64-bit)| (default, Jun 29 2016, 11:07:13)
[MSC v.1500 64 bit (AMD64)] on win32
Type "help", "copyright", "credits" or "license" for more information.
Anaconda is brought to you by Continuum Analytics.
Please check out: http://continuum.io/thanks and https://anaconda.org
Using Spark's default log4j profile: org/apache/spark/log4j-
defaults.properties
Setting default log level to "WARN".
To adjust logging level use sc.setLogLevewl(newLevel).
Welcome to
      ____              __
     / __/__  ___ _____/ /__
    _\ \/ _ \/ _ `/ __/  '_/
   /__ / .__/\_,_/_/ /_/\_\   version 2.0.2
      /_/

Using Python version 2.7.12 (default, Jun 29 2016 11:07:13)
SparkSession available as 'spark'.
>>>
```

Spark MLlib implements the ALS algorithm through a very simple mechanism. The class Rating is a wrapper for the tuple (user, product, rating), so we can easily define a dummy dataset (which must be considered only as an example, because it's very limited):

```
from pyspark.mllib.recommendation import Rating

import numpy as np

>>> nb_users = 200
>>> nb_products = 100

>>> ratings = []

>>> for _ in range(10):
>>>     for i in range(nb_users):
>>>         rating = Rating(user=i,
```

```
>>>                         product=np.random.randint(1, nb_products),
>>>                         rating=np.random.randint(0, 5))
>>>         ratings.append(rating)

>>> ratings = sc.parallelize(ratings)
```

We assumed that we have 200 users and 100 products and we have populated a list of ratings by iterating 10 times the main loop which assigns a rating to a random product. We're not controlling repetitions or other uncommon situations. The last command `sc.parallelize()` is a way to ask Spark to transform our list into a structure called **resilient distributed dataset** (RDD), which will be used for the remaining operations. There are no actual limits to the size of these structures, because they are distributed across different executors (if in clustered mode) and can work with petabytes datasets just like we work with kilobytes ones.

At this point, we can train an `ALS` model (which is formally `MatrixFactorizationModel`) and use it to make some predictions:

```
from pyspark.mllib.recommendation import ALS

>>> model = ALS.train(ratings, rank=5, iterations=10)
```

We want 5 latent factors and 10 optimization iterations. As discussed before, it's not very easy to determine the right rank for each model, so, after a training phase, there should always be a validation phase with known data. The mean squared error is a good measure to understand how the model is working. We can do it using the same training data set. The first thing to do is to remove the ratings (because we need only the tuple made up of user and product):

```
>>> test = ratings.map(lambda rating: (rating.user, rating.product))
```

If you're not familiar with the MapReduce paradigm, you only need to know that `map()` applies the same function (in this case, a lambda) to all the elements. Now we can massively predict the ratings:

```
>>> predictions = model.predictAll(test)
```

However, in order to compute the error, we also need to add the user and product, to have tuples that can be compared:

```
>>> full_predictions = predictions.map(lambda pred: ((pred.user,
pred.product), pred.rating))
```

The result is a sequence of rows with a structure `((user, item), rating)`, just like a standard dictionary entry `(key, value)`. This is useful because, using Spark, we can join two RDDs by using their keys. We do the same thing for the original dataset also, and then we proceed by joining the training values with the predictions:

```
>>> split_ratings = ratings.map(lambda rating: ((rating.user,
rating.product), rating.rating))
>>> joined_predictions = split_ratings.join(full_predictions)
```

Now for each key `(user, product)`, we have two values: target and prediction. Therefore, we can compute the mean squared error:

```
>>> mse = joined_predictions.map(lambda x: (x[1][0] - x[1][1]) ** 2).mean()
```

The first map transforms each row into the squared difference between the target and prediction, while the `mean()` function computes the average value. At this point, let's check our error and produce a prediction:

```
>>> print('MSE: %.3f' % mse)
MSE: 0.580

>>> prediction = model.predict(10, 20)
>>> print('Prediction: %3.f' % prediction)
Prediction: 2.810
```

So, our error is quite low but it can be improved by changing the rank or the number of iterations. The prediction for the rating of the product 20 by the user 10 is about 2.8 (that can be rounded to 3). If you run the code, these values can be different as we're using a random user-item matrix. Moreover, if you don't want to use the shell and run the code directly, you need to declare a `SparkContext` explicitly at the beginning of your file:

```
from pyspark import SparkContext, SparkConf

>>> conf = SparkConf().setAppName('ALS').setMaster('local[*]')
>>> sc = SparkContext(conf=conf)
```

We have created a configuration through the `SparkConf` class and specified both an application name and a master (in local mode with all cores available). This is enough to run our code. However, if you need further information, visit the page mentioned in the information box at the end of the chapter. To run the application (since Spark 2.0), you must execute the following command:

```
# Linux, Mac OSx
./spark-submit als_spark.py

# Windows
spark-submit als_spark.py
```

When running a script using `spark-submit`, you will see hundreds of log lines that inform you about all the operations that are being performed. Among them, at the end of the computation, you'll also see the print function messages (`stdout`).

Of course, this is only an introduction to Spark ALS, but I hope it was useful to understand how easy this process can be and, at the same time, how the dimensional limitations can be effectively addressed.

If you don't know how to set up the environment and launch PySpark, I suggest reading the online quick-start guide (`https://spark.apache.org/docs/2.1.0/quick-start.html`) that can be useful even if you don't know all the details and configuration parameters.

References

- Sarwar B., Karypis G., Konstan J., Riedl J., *Incremental Singular Value Decomposition Algorithms for Highly Scalable Recommender Systems*, 2002
- Koren Y., Bell R., Volinsky C., *Matrix Factorization Techniques For Recommender Systems*, IEEE Computer Magazine, 08/2009
- Pentreath N., *Machine Learning with Spark*, Packt

Summary

In this chapter, we discussed the main techniques for building a recommender system. In a user-based scenario, we assume that we have enough pieces of information about the users to be able to cluster them, and moreover, we implicitly assume that similar users would like the same products. In this way, it's immediate to determine the neighborhood of every new user and to suggest the products positively rated by his/her peers. In a similar way, a content-based scenario is based on the clustering of products according to their peculiar features. In this case, the assumption is weaker, because it's more probable that a user who bought an item or rated it positively will do the same with similar products.

Then we introduced collaborative filtering, which is a technique based on explicit ratings, used to predict all missing values for all users and products. In the memory-based variant, we don't train a model but we try to work directly with a user-product matrix, looking for the k-nearest neighbors of a test user, and computing the ranking through an average. This approach is very similar to the user-based scenario and has the same limitations; in particular, it's very difficult to manage large matrices. On the other hand, the model-based approach is more complex, but, after training the model, it can predict the ratings in real time. Moreover, there are parallel frameworks like Spark, which can be employed to process a huge amount of data using a cluster of cheap servers.

In the next chapter, we're going to introduce some natural language processing techniques, which are very important when automatically classifying texts or working with machine translation systems.

12
Introduction to Natural Language Processing

Natural language processing is a set of machine learning techniques that allows working with text documents, considering their internal structure and the distribution of words. In this chapter, we're going to discuss all common methods to collect texts, split them into atoms, and transform them into numerical vectors. In particular, we'll compare different methods to tokenize documents (separate each word), to filter them, to apply special transformations to avoid inflected or conjugated forms, and finally to build a common vocabulary. Using the vocabulary, it will be possible to apply different vectorization approaches to build feature vectors that can easily be used for classification or clustering purposes. To show how to implement the whole pipeline, at the end of the chapter, we're going to set up a simple classifier for news lines.

NLTK and built-in corpora

Natural Language Toolkit (NLTK) is a very powerful Python framework that implements most NLP algorithms and will be adopted in this chapter together with scikit-learn. Moreover, NLTK provides some built-in corpora that can be used to test algorithms. Before starting to work with NLTK, it's normally necessary to download all the additional elements (corpora, dictionaries, and so on) using a specific graphical interface. This can be done in the following way:

```
import nltk

>>> nltk.download()
```

This command will launch the user interface, as shown in the following figure:

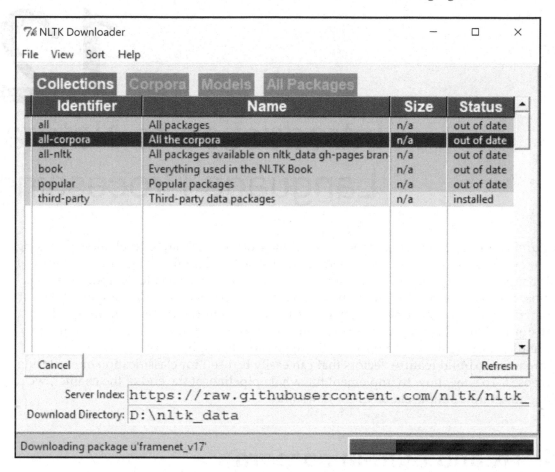

It's possible to select every single feature or download all elements (I suggest this option if you have enough free space) to immediately exploit all NLTK functionalities.

 NLTK can be installed using pip (`pip install -U nltk`) or with one of the binary distributions available at `http://www.nltk.org`. On the same website, there's complete documentation that can be useful for going deeper into each topic.

Corpora examples

A subset of the Gutenberg project is provided and can be freely accessed in this way:

```
from nltk.corpus import gutenberg
```

```
>>> print(gutenberg.fileids())
[u'austen-emma.txt', u'austen-persuasion.txt', u'austen-sense.txt',
u'bible-kjv.txt', u'blake-poems.txt', u'bryant-stories.txt', u'burgess-
busterbrown.txt', u'carroll-alice.txt', u'chesterton-ball.txt',
u'chesterton-brown.txt', u'chesterton-thursday.txt', u'edgeworth-
parents.txt', u'melville-moby_dick.txt', u'milton-paradise.txt',
u'shakespeare-caesar.txt', u'shakespeare-hamlet.txt', u'shakespeare-
macbeth.txt', u'whitman-leaves.txt']
```

A single document can be accessed as a raw version or split into sentences or words:

```
>>> print(gutenberg.raw('milton-paradise.txt'))
[Paradise Lost by John Milton 1667]


Book I


Of Man's first disobedience, and the fruit
Of that forbidden tree whose mortal taste
Brought death into the World, and all our woe,
With loss of Eden, till one greater Man
Restore us, and regain the blissful seat,
Sing, Heavenly Muse, that, on the secret top...

>>> print(gutenberg.sents('milton-paradise.txt')[0:2])
[[u'[', u'Paradise', u'Lost', u'by', u'John', u'Milton', u'1667', u']'],
[u'Book', u'I']]

>>> print(gutenberg.words('milton-paradise.txt')[0:20])
[u'[', u'Paradise', u'Lost', u'by', u'John', u'Milton', u'1667', u']',
u'Book', u'I', u'Of', u'Man', u"'", u's', u'first', u'disobedience', u',',
u'and', u'the', u'fruit']
```

As we're going to discuss, in many cases, it can be useful to have the raw text so as to split it into words using a custom strategy. In many other situations, accessing sentences directly allows working with the original structural subdivision. Other corpora include web texts, Reuters news lines, the Brown corpus, and many more. For example, the Brown corpus is a famous collection of documents divided by genre:

```
from nltk.corpus import brown

>>> print(brown.categories())
[u'adventure', u'belles_lettres', u'editorial', u'fiction', u'government',
u'hobbies', u'humor', u'learned', u'lore', u'mystery', u'news',
u'religion', u'reviews', u'romance', u'science_fiction']

>>> print(brown.sents(categories='editorial')[0:100])
[[u'Assembly', u'session', u'brought', u'much', u'good'], [u'The',
u'General', u'Assembly', u',', u'which', u'adjourns', u'today', u',',
u'has', u'performed', u'in', u'an', u'atmosphere', u'of', u'crisis',
u'and', u'struggle', u'from', u'the', u'day', u'it', u'convened', u'.'],
...]
```

 Further information about corpora can be found at http://www.nltk.org/book/ch02.html.

The bag-of-words strategy

In NLP, a very common pipeline can be subdivided into the following steps:

1. Collecting a document into a corpus.
2. Tokenizing, stopword (articles, prepositions and so on) removal, and stemming (reduction to radix-form).
3. Building a common vocabulary.
4. Vectorizing the documents.
5. Classifying or clustering the documents.

The pipeline is called **bag-of-words** and will be discussed in this chapter. A fundamental assumption is that the order of each single word in a sentence is not important. In fact, when defining a feature vector, as we're going to see, the measures taken into account are always related to frequencies and therefore they are insensitive to the local positioning of all elements. From some viewpoints, this is a limitation because in a natural language the internal order of a sentence is necessary to preserve the meaning; however, there are many models that can work efficiently with texts without the complication of local sorting. When it's absolutely necessary to consider small sequences, it will be done by adopting groups of tokens (called n-grams) but considering them as a single atomic element during the vectorization step.

In the following figure, there's a schematic representation of this process (without the fifth step) for a sample document (sentence):

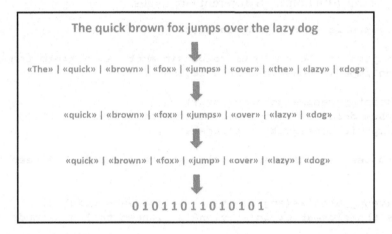

There are many different methods used to carry out each step and some of them are context-specific. However, the goal is always the same: maximizing the information of a document and reducing the size of the common vocabulary by removing terms that are too frequent or derived from the same radix (such as verbs). The information content of a document is in fact determined by the presence of specific terms (or group of terms) whose frequency in the corpus is limited. In the example shown in the previous figure, **fox** and **dog** are important terms, while **the** is useless (often called a **stopword**). Moreover, **jumps** can be converted to the standard form **jump**, which expresses a specific action when present in different forms (like jumping or jumped). The last step is transforming into a numerical vector, because our algorithms work with numbers, and it's important to limit the length of the vectors so as to improve the learning speed and the memory consumption. In the following sections, we're going to discuss each step in detail, and at the end, we're going to build a sample classifier for news lines.

Tokenizing

The first step in processing a piece of text or a corpus is splitting it into atoms (sentences, words, or parts of words), normally defined as **tokens**. Such a process is quite simple; however, there can be different strategies to solve particular problems.

Sentence tokenizing

In many cases, it's useful to split large text into sentences, which are normally delimited by a full stop or another equivalent mark. As every language has its own orthographic rules, NLTK offers a method called `sent_tokenize()` that accepts a language (the default is English) and splits the text according to the specific rules. In the following example, we show the usage of this function with different languages:

```
from nltk.tokenize import sent_tokenize

>>> generic_text = 'Lorem ipsum dolor sit amet, amet minim temporibus in
sit. Vel ne impedit consequat intellegebat.'

>>> print(sent_tokenize(generic_text))
['Lorem ipsum dolor sit amet, amet minim temporibus in sit.',
 'Vel ne impedit consequat intellegebat.']

>>> english_text = 'Where is the closest train station? I need to reach
London'

>>> print(sent_tokenize(english_text, language='english'))
['Where is the closest train station?', 'I need to reach London']

>>> spanish_text = u'¿Dónde está la estación más cercana? Inmediatamente me
tengo que ir a Barcelona.'

>>> for sentence in sent_tokenize(spanish_text, language='spanish'):
>>>     print(sentence)
¿Dónde está la estación más cercana?
Inmediatamente me tengo que ir a Barcelona.
```

Word tokenizing

The simplest way to tokenize a sentence into words is provided by the class
`TreebankWordTokenizer`, which, however, has some limitations:

```
from nltk.tokenize import TreebankWordTokenizer

>>> simple_text = 'This is a simple text.'

>>> tbwt = TreebankWordTokenizer()

>>> print(tbwt.tokenize(simple_text))
['This', 'is', 'a', 'simple', 'text', '.']

>>> complex_text = 'This isn\'t a simple text'

>>> print(tbwt.tokenize(complex_text))
['This', 'is', "n't", 'a', 'simple', 'text']
```

As you can see, in the first case the sentence has been correctly split into words, keeping the
punctuation separate (this is not a real issue because it can be removed in a second step).
However, in the complex example, the contraction `isn't` has been split into `is` and `n't`.
Unfortunately, without a further processing step, it's not so easy converting a token with a
contraction into its normal form (like `not`), therefore, another strategy must be employed.
A good way to solve the problem of separate punctuation is provided by the class
`RegexpTokenizer`, which offers a flexible way to split words according to a regular
expression:

```
from nltk.tokenize import RegexpTokenizer

>>> complex_text = 'This isn\'t a simple text.'

>>> ret = RegexpTokenizer('[a-zA-Z0-9\'\.]+')
>>> print(ret.tokenize(complex_text))
['This', "isn't", 'a', 'simple', 'text.']
```

Most of the common problems can be easily solved using this class, so I suggest you learn
how to write simple regular expressions that can match specific patterns. For example, we
can remove all numbers, commas, and other punctuation marks from a sentence:

```
>>> complex_text = 'This isn\'t a simple text. Count 1, 2, 3 and then go!'

>>> ret = RegexpTokenizer('[a-zA-Z\']+')
>>> print(ret.tokenize(complex_text))
['This', "isn't", 'a', 'simple', 'text', 'Count', 'and', 'the', 'go']
```

Even if there are other classes provided by NLTK, they can always be implemented using a customized `RegexpTokenizer`, which is powerful enough to solve almost every particular problem; so I prefer not to go deeper in this discussion.

Stopword removal

Stopwords are part of a normal speech (articles, conjunctions, and so on), but their occurrence frequency is very high and they don't provide any useful semantic information. For these reasons, it's a good practice to filter sentences and corpora by removing them all. NLTK provides lists of stopwords for the most common languages and their usage is immediate:

```
from nltk.corpus import stopwords

>>> sw = set(stopwords.words('english'))
```

A subset of English stopwords is shown in the following snippet:

```
>>> print(sw)
{u'a',
 u'about',
 u'above',
 u'after',
 u'again',
 u'against',
 u'ain',
 u'all',
 u'am',
 u'an',
 u'and',
 u'any',
 u'are',
 u'aren',
 u'as',
 u'at',
 u'be', ...
```

To filter a sentence, it's possible to adopt a functional approach:

```
>>> complex_text = 'This isn\'t a simple text. Count 1, 2, 3 and then go!'

>>> ret = RegexpTokenizer('[a-zA-Z\']+')
>>> tokens = ret.tokenize(complex_text)
>>> clean_tokens = [t for t in tokens if t not in sw]
>>> print(clean_tokens)
['This', "isn't", 'simple', 'text', 'Count', 'go']
```

Language detection

Stopwords, like other important features, are strictly related to a specific language, so it's often necessary to detect the language before moving on to any other step. A simple, free, and reliable solution is provided by the `langdetect` library, which has been ported from Google's language detection system. Its usage is immediate:

```
from langdetect import detect

>>> print(detect('This is English'))
en

>>> print(detect('Dies ist Deutsch'))
de
```

The function returns the ISO 639-1 codes (`https://en.wikipedia.org/wiki/List_of_ISO_639-1_codes`), which can be used as keys in a dictionary to get the complete language name. Where the text is more complex, the detection can more difficult and it's useful to know whether there are any ambiguities. It's possible to get the probabilities for the expected languages through the `detect_langs()` method:

```
from langdetect import detect_langs

>>> print(detect_langs('I really love you mon doux amour!'))
[fr:0.714281321163, en:0.285716747181]
```

 langdetect can be installed using pip (`pip install --upgrade langdetect`). Further information is available at `https://pypi.python.org/pypi/langdetect`.

Stemming

Stemming is a process that is used to transform particular words (such as verbs or plurals) into their radical form so as to preserve the semantics without increasing the number of unique tokens. For example, if we consider the three expressions I run, He runs, and Running, they can be reduced into a useful (though grammatically incorrect) form: I run, He run, Run. In this way, we have a single token that defines the same concept (run), which, for clustering or classification purposes, can be used without any precision loss. There are many stemmer implementations provided by NLTK. The most common (and flexible) is SnowballStemmer, based on a multilingual algorithm:

```
from nltk.stem.snowball import SnowballStemmer

>>> ess = SnowballStemmer('english', ignore_stopwords=True)
>>> print(ess.stem('flies'))
fli

>>> fss = SnowballStemmer('french', ignore_stopwords=True)
>>> print(fss.stem('courais'))
cour
```

The ignore_stopwords parameter informs the stemmer not to process the stopwords. Other implementations are PorterStemmer and LancasterStemmer. Very often the result is the same, but in some cases, a stemmer can implement more selective rules. For example:

```
from nltk.stem.snowball import PorterStemmer
from nltk.stem.lancaster import LancasterStemmer

>>> print(ess.stem('teeth'))
teeth

>>> ps = PorterStemmer()
>>> print(ps.stem('teeth'))
teeth

>>> ls = LancasterStemmer()
>>> print(ls.stem('teeth'))
tee
```

As you can see, Snowball and Porter algorithms keep the word unchanged, while Lancaster extracts a radix (which is meaningless). On the other hand, the latter algorithm implements many specific English rules, which can really reduce the number of unique tokens:

```
>>> print(ps.stem('teen'))
teen

>>> print(ps.stem('teenager'))
teenag

>>> print(ls.stem('teen'))
teen

>>> print(ls.stem('teenager'))
teen
```

Unfortunately, both Porter and Lancaster stemmers are available in NLTK only in English; so the default choice is often Snowball, which is available in many languages and can be used in conjunction with an appropriate stopword set.

Vectorizing

This is the last step of the bag-of-words pipeline and it is necessary for transforming text tokens into numerical vectors. The most common techniques are based on a count or frequency computation, and they are both available in scikit-learn with sparse matrix representations (this is a choice that can save a lot of space considering that many tokens appear only a few times while the vectors must have the same length).

Count vectorizing

The algorithm is very simple and it's based on representing a token considering how many times it appears in a document. Of course, the whole corpus must be processed in order to determine how many unique tokens are present and their frequencies. Let's see an example of the CountVectorizer class on a simple corpus:

```
from sklearn.feature_extraction.text import CountVectorizer

>>> corpus = [
        'This is a simple test corpus',
        'A corpus is a set of text documents',
        'We want to analyze the corpus and the documents',
        'Documents can be automatically tokenized'
]
```

```
>>> cv = CountVectorizer()
>>> vectorized_corpus = cv.fit_transform(corpus)
>>> print(vectorized_corpus.todense())
[[0 0 0 0 0 1 0 1 0 0 1 1 0 0 1 0 0 0 0]
 [0 0 0 0 0 1 1 1 1 0 0 1 0 0 0 0 0 0 0]
 [1 1 0 0 0 1 1 0 0 0 0 0 0 2 0 1 0 1 1]
 [0 0 1 1 1 0 1 0 0 0 0 0 0 0 0 1 0 0]]
```

As you can see, each document has been transformed into a fixed-length vector, where 0 means that the corresponding token is not present, while a positive number represents the occurrences. If we need to exclude all tokens whose document frequency is less than a predefined value, we can set it through the parameter `min_df` (the default value is 1). Sometimes it can be useful to avoid terms that are very common; however, the next strategy will manage this problem in a more reliable and complete way.

The vocabulary can be accessed through the instance variable `vocabulary_`:

```
>>> print(cv.vocabulary_)
{u'and': 1, u'be': 3, u'we': 18, u'set': 9, u'simple': 10, u'text': 12,
u'is': 7, u'tokenized': 16, u'want': 17, u'the': 13, u'documents': 6,
u'this': 14, u'of': 8, u'to': 15, u'can': 4, u'test': 11, u'corpus': 5,
u'analyze': 0, u'automatically': 2}
```

Given a generic vector, it's possible to retrieve the corresponding list of tokens with an inverse transformation:

```
>>> vector = [0, 0, 0, 0, 0, 1, 0, 1, 0, 0, 1, 1, 0, 0, 1, 0, 0, 1, 1]
>>> print(cv.inverse_transform(vector))
[array([u'corpus', u'is', u'simple', u'test', u'this', u'want', u'we'],
       dtype='<U13')]
```

Both this and the following method can also use an external tokenizer (through the parameter `tokenizer`), it can be customized using the techniques discussed in previous sections:

```
>>> ret = RegexpTokenizer('[a-zA-Z0-9\']+')
>>> sw = set(stopwords.words('english'))
>>> ess = SnowballStemmer('english', ignore_stopwords=True)

>>> def tokenizer(sentence):
>>>     tokens = ret.tokenize(sentence)
>>>     return [ess.stem(t) for t in tokens if t not in sw]

>>> cv = CountVectorizer(tokenizer=tokenizer)
>>> vectorized_corpus = cv.fit_transform(corpus)
>>> print(vectorized_corpus.todense())
[[0 0 1 0 0 1 1 0 0 0]
```

```
[0 0 1 1 1 0 0 1 0 0]
[1 0 1 1 0 0 0 0 0 1]
[0 1 0 1 0 0 0 0 1 0]]
```

With our tokenizer (using stopwords and stemming), the vocabulary is shorter and so are the vectors.

N-grams

So far, we have considered only single tokens (also called unigrams), but in many contexts, it's useful to consider short sequences of words (bigrams or trigrams) as atoms for our classifiers, just like all the other tokens. For example, if we are analyzing the sentiment of some texts, it could be a good idea to consider bigrams such as pretty good, very bad, and so on. From a semantic viewpoint, in fact, it's important to consider not just the adverbs but the whole compound form. It's possible to inform our vectorizers about the range of n-grams we want to consider. For example, if we need unigrams and bigrams, we can use this snippet:

```
>>> cv = CountVectorizer(tokenizer=tokenizer, ngram_range=(1, 2))
>>> vectorized_corpus = cv.fit_transform(corpus)
>>> print(vectorized_corpus.todense())
[[0 0 0 0 0 1 0 1 0 0 1 1 0 0 1 0 0 0 0]
 [0 0 0 0 0 1 1 1 1 0 0 1 0 0 0 0 0 0]
 [1 1 0 0 0 1 1 0 0 0 0 0 2 0 1 0 1 1]
 [0 0 1 1 1 0 1 0 0 0 0 0 0 0 0 1 0 0]]

>>> print(cv.vocabulary_)
{u'and': 1, u'be': 3, u'we': 18, u'set': 9, u'simple': 10, u'text': 12,
u'is': 7, u'tokenized': 16, u'want': 17, u'the': 13, u'documents': 6,
u'this': 14, u'of': 8, u'to': 15, u'can': 4, u'test': 11, u'corpus': 5,
u'analyze': 0, u'automatically': 2}
```

As you can see, the vocabulary now contains the bigrams, and the vectors include their relative frequencies.

Tf-idf vectorizing

The most common limitation of count vectorizing is that the algorithm doesn't consider the whole corpus while considering the frequency of each token. The goal of vectorizing is normally preparing the data for a classifier; therefore it's necessary to avoid features that are present very often, because their information decreases when the number of global occurrences increases. For example, in a corpus about a sport, the word `match` could be present in a huge number of documents; therefore it's almost useless as a classification feature. To address this issue, we need a different approach. If we have a corpus C with n documents, we define **term-frequency**, the number of times a token occurs in a document, as:

$$t_f(t, d) \; \forall \, d \in C \; and \; \forall \, t \in d$$

We define **inverse-document-frequency**, as the following measure:

$$idf(t, C) = log \frac{n}{1 + count(D, t)} \; where \; count(D, t) = \sum_i 1(t \in D)$$

In other words, `idf(t,C)` measures how much information is provided by every single term. In fact, if `count(D,t)` = n, it means that a token is always present and *idf(t, C)* comes close to 0, and vice-versa. The term 1 in the denominator is a correction factor, which avoids null idf for `count(D,t)` = n. So, instead of considering only the term frequency, we weigh each token by defining a new measure:

$$t_f \cdot idf(t, d, C) = t_f(t, d) \, idf(t, C)$$

scikit-learn provides the `TfIdfVectorizer` class, which we can apply to the same toy corpus used in the previous paragraph:

```
>>> from sklearn.feature_extraction.text import TfidfVectorizer

>>> tfidfv = TfidfVectorizer()
>>> vectorized_corpus = tfidfv.fit_transform(corpus)
>>> print(vectorized_corpus.todense())
[[ 0.          0.          0.          0.          0.          0.31799276
   0.          0.39278432  0.          0.          0.49819711  0.49819711
   0.          0.          0.49819711  0.          0.          0.
   0.          ]
 [ 0.          0.          0.          0.          0.          0.30304005
```

```
     0.30304005   0.37431475   0.4747708    0.4747708    0.           0.
     0.4747708    0.           0.           0.           0.           0.
 0.          ]
   [ 0.31919701   0.31919701   0.           0.           0.           0.20373932
     0.20373932   0.           0.           0.           0.           0.
 0.
     0.63839402   0.           0.31919701   0.           0.31919701   0.31919701]
   [ 0.           0.           0.47633035   0.47633035   0.47633035   0.
     0.30403549   0.           0.           0.           0.           0.
 0.
     0.           0.           0.           0.47633035   0.           0.          ]]
```

Let's now check the vocabulary to make a comparison with simple count vectorizing:

```
>>> print(tfidfv.vocabulary_)
{u'and': 1, u'be': 3, u'we': 18, u'set': 9, u'simple': 10, u'text': 12,
u'is': 7, u'tokenized': 16, u'want': 17, u'the': 13, u'documents': 6,
u'this': 14, u'of': 8, u'to': 15, u'can': 4, u'test': 11, u'corpus': 5,
u'analyze': 0, u'automatically': 2}
```

The term documents is the sixth feature in both vectorizers and appears in the last three documents. As you can see, it's weight is about 0.3, while the term the is present twice only in the third document and its weight is about 0.64. The general rule is: if a term is representative of a document, its weight becomes close to 1.0, while it decreases if finding it in a sample document doesn't allow us to easily determine its category.

Also in this case, it's possible to use an external tokenizer and specify the desired n-gram range. Moreover, it's possible to normalize the vectors (through the parameter norm) and decide whether to include or exclude the addend 1 to the denominator of idf (through the parameter smooth_idf). It's also possible to define the range of accepted document frequencies using the parameters min_df and max_df so as to exclude tokens whose occurrences are below or beyond a minimum/maximum threshold. They accept both integers (number of occurrences) or floats in the range of [0.0, 1.0] (proportion of documents). In the next example, we use some of these parameters:

```
>>> tfidfv = TfidfVectorizer(tokenizer=tokenizer, ngram_range=(1, 2),
norm='12')
>>> vectorized_corpus = tfidfv.fit_transform(corpus)
>>> print(vectorized_corpus.todense())
[[ 0.           0.           0.           0.           0.30403549   0.
 0.
     0.           0.           0.           0.           0.47633035   0.47633035
     0.47633035   0.47633035   0.           0.           0.           0.
 0.          ]
   [ 0.           0.           0.           0.           0.2646963    0.
     0.4146979    0.2646963    0.           0.4146979    0.4146979    0.
```

```
0.
   0.           0.           0.4146979   0.4146979   0.          0.
0.        ]
  [ 0.4146979   0.4146979   0.          0.          0.2646963   0.4146979
   0.           0.2646963   0.          0.          0.          0.
0.
   0.           0.           0.          0.          0.          0.4146979
   0.4146979 ]
  [ 0.          0.           0.47633035  0.47633035  0.          0.
0.
   0.30403549  0.47633035  0.          0.          0.          0.
0.
   0.           0.           0.          0.47633035  0.          0.         ]]
```

```
>>> print(tfidfv.vocabulary_)
{u'analyz corpus': 1, u'set': 9, u'simpl test': 12, u'want analyz': 19,
u'automat': 2, u'want': 18, u'test corpus': 14, u'set text': 10, u'corpus
set': 6, u'automat token': 3, u'corpus document': 5, u'text document': 16,
u'token': 17, u'document automat': 8, u'text': 15, u'test': 13, u'corpus':
4, u'document': 7, u'simpl': 11, u'analyz': 0}
```

In particular, normalizing vectors is always a good choice if they must be used as input for a classifier, as we'll see in the next chapter.

A sample text classifier based on the Reuters corpus

We are going to build a sample text classifier based on the NLTK Reuters corpus. This one is made of up thousands of news lines divided into 90 categories:

```
from nltk.corpus import reuters
```

```
>>> print(reuters.categories())
[u'acq', u'alum', u'barley', u'bop', u'carcass', u'castor-oil', u'cocoa',
u'coconut', u'coconut-oil', u'coffee', u'copper', u'copra-cake', u'corn',
u'cotton', u'cotton-oil', u'cpi', u'cpu', u'crude', u'dfl', u'dlr', u'dmk',
u'earn', u'fuel', u'gas', u'gnp', u'gold', u'grain', u'groundnut',
u'groundnut-oil', u'heat', u'hog', u'housing', u'income', u'instal-debt',
u'interest', u'ipi', u'iron-steel', u'jet', u'jobs', u'l-cattle', u'lead',
u'lei', u'lin-oil', u'livestock', u'lumber', u'meal-feed', u'money-fx',
u'money-supply', u'naphtha', u'nat-gas', u'nickel', u'nkr', u'nzdlr',
u'oat', u'oilseed', u'orange', u'palladium', u'palm-oil', u'palmkernel',
u'pet-chem', u'platinum', u'potato', u'propane', u'rand', u'rape-oil',
u'rapeseed', u'reserves', u'retail', u'rice', u'rubber', u'rye', u'ship',
u'silver', u'sorghum', u'soy-meal', u'soy-oil', u'soybean', u'strategic-
```

```
metal', u'sugar', u'sun-meal', u'sun-oil', u'sunseed', u'tea', u'tin',
u'trade', u'veg-oil', u'wheat', u'wpi', u'yen', u'zinc']
```

To simplify the process, we'll take only two categories, which have a similar number of documents:

```
import numpy as np

>>> Xr = np.array(reuters.sents(categories=['rubber']))
>>> Xc = np.array(reuters.sents(categories=['cotton']))
>>> Xw = np.concatenate((Xr, Xc))
```

As each document is already split into tokens and we want to apply our custom tokenizer (with stopword removal and stemming), we need to rebuild the full sentences:

```
>>> X = []

>>> for document in Xw:
>>>     X.append(' '.join(document).strip().lower())
```

Now we need to prepare the label vector, by assigning 0 to rubber and 1 to cotton:

```
>>> Yr = np.zeros(shape=Xr.shape)
>>> Yc = np.ones(shape=Xc.shape)
>>> Y = np.concatenate((Yr, Yc))
```

At this point, we can vectorize our corpus:

```
>>> tfidfv = TfidfVectorizer(tokenizer=tokenizer, ngram_range=(1, 2),
norm='12')
>>> Xv = tfidfv.fit_transform(X)
```

Now the dataset is ready, and we can proceed by splitting it into train and test subsets and finally train our classifier. I've decided to adopt a random forest because it's particularly efficient for this kind of task, but the reader can try different classifiers and compare the results:

```
from sklearn.model_selection import train_test_split
from sklearn.ensemble import RandomForestClassifier

>>> X_train, X_test, Y_train, Y_test = train_test_split(Xv, Y,
test_size=0.25)

>>> rf = RandomForestClassifier(n_estimators=25)
>>> rf.fit(X_train, Y_train)
>>> score = rf.score(X_test, Y_test)
>>> print('Score: %.3f' % score)
Score: 0.874
```

The score is about 88%, which is a quite good result, but let's try a prediction with a fake news line:

```
>>> test_newsline = ['Trading tobacco is reducing the amount of requests
for cotton and this has a negative impact on our economy']

>>> yvt = tfidfv.transform(test_newsline)
>>> category = rf.predict(yvt)
>>> print('Predicted category: %d' % int(category[0]))
Predicted category: 1
```

The classification result is correct; however, by adopting some techniques that we're going to discuss in the next chapter, it's also possible to get better performance in more complex real-life problems.

References

1. Perkins J., Python 3 Text Processing with NLTK 3 Cookbook, Packt.
2. Hardeniya N., NLTK Essentials, Packt
3. Bonaccorso G., BBC News classification algorithm comparison, `https://github.com/giuseppebonaccorso/bbc_news_classification_comparison`.

Summary

In this chapter, we discussed all the basic NLP techniques, starting from the definition of a corpus up to the final transformation into feature vectors. We analyzed different tokenizing methods to address particular problems or situations of splitting a document into words. Then we introduced some filtering techniques that are necessary to remove all useless elements (also called stopwords) and to convert the inflected forms into standard tokens.

These steps are important in order to increase the information content by removing frequently used terms. When the documents have been successfully cleaned, it is possible to vectorize them using a simple approach such as the one implemented by the count-vectorizer, or a more complex one that takes into account the global distribution of terms, such as tf-idf. The latter was introduced to complete the work done by the stemming phase; in fact, it's purpose is to define vectors where each component will be close to 1 when the amount of information is high and vice-versa. Normally a word that is present in many documents isn't a good marker for a classifier; therefore, if not already removed by the previous steps, tf-idf will automatically reduce its weight. At the end of the chapter, we built a simple text classifier that implements the whole bag-of-words pipeline and uses a random forest to classify news lines.

In the next chapter, we're going to complete this introduction with a brief discussion of advanced techniques such as topic modeling, latent semantic analysis, and sentiment analysis.

13
Topic Modeling and Sentiment Analysis in NLP

In this chapter, we're going to introduce some common topic modeling methods, discussing some applications. Topic modeling is a very important NLP section and its purpose is to extract semantic pieces of information out of a corpus of documents. We're going to discuss **latent semantic analysis**, one of most famous methods; it's based on the same philosophy already discussed for model-based recommendation systems. We'll also discuss its probabilistic variant, PLSA, which is aimed at building a latent factor probability model without any assumption of prior distributions. On the other hand, the **Latent Dirichlet Allocation** is a similar approach that assumes a prior Dirichlet distribution for latent variables. In the last section, we're going to discuss sentiment analysis with a concrete example based on a Twitter dataset.

Topic modeling

The main goal of topic modeling in natural language processing is to analyze a corpus in order to identify common topics among documents. In this context, even if we talk about semantics, this concept has a particular meaning, driven by a very important assumption. A topic derives from the usage of particular terms in the same document and it is confirmed by the multiplicity of different documents where the first condition is true.

In other words, we don't consider a human-oriented semantics but a statistical modeling that works with meaningful documents (this guarantees that the usage of terms is aimed to express a particular concept and, therefore, there's a human semantic purpose behind them). For this reason, the starting point of all our methods is an occurrence matrix, normally defined as a document-term matrix (we have already discussed count vectorizing and tf-idf in `Chapter 12`, *Introduction to NLP*):

$$M_{dw} = \begin{pmatrix} f(d_1, w_1) & \dots & f(d_1, w_n) \\ \vdots & \ddots & \vdots \\ f(d_m, w_1) & \dots & f(d_m, w_n) \end{pmatrix} \ where \ f(d_i, w_j) \ is \ a \ frequency \ measure$$

In many papers, this matrix is transposed (it's a term-document one); however, scikit-learn produces document-term matrices, and, to avoid confusion, we are going to consider this structure.

Latent semantic analysis

The idea behind latent semantic analysis is factorizing M_{dw} so as to extract a set of latent variables (this means that we can assume their existence but they cannot be observed directly) that work as connectors between the document and terms. As discussed in `Chapter 11`, *Introduction to Recommendation Systems*, a very common decomposition method is SVD:

$$M_{UxI} = U\Sigma V^T \ where \ U \in \mathbb{R}^{m \times t}, \Sigma \in \mathbb{R}^{t \times t} \ and \ V \in \mathbb{R}^{n \times n}$$

However, we're not interested in a full decomposition; we are interested only in the subspace defined by the top k singular values:

$$M_k = U_k \Sigma_k V_k^T$$

This approximation has the reputation of being the best one considering the Frobenius norm, so it guarantees a very high level of accuracy. When applying it to a document-term matrix, we obtain the following decomposition:

$$M_{dwk} = \begin{pmatrix} g(d_1, t_1) & \cdots & g(d_1, t_k) \\ \vdots & \ddots & \vdots \\ g(d_m, t_1) & \cdots & g(d_m, t_k) \end{pmatrix} \cdot \begin{pmatrix} h(t_1, w_1) & \cdots & h(t_1, w_n) \\ \vdots & \ddots & \vdots \\ h(t_k, w_1) & \cdots & h(t_k, w_n) \end{pmatrix}$$

Or, in a more compact way:

$$M_{dwk} = M_{dtk} \cdot M_{twk}$$

Here, the first matrix defines a relationship among documents and k latent variables, and the second a relationship among k latent variables and words. Considering the structure of the original matrix and what is explained at the beginning of this chapter, we can consider the latent variables as **topics** that define a subspace where the documents are projected. A generic document can now be defined as:

$$d_i = \sum_{j=1}^{k} g(d_i, t_k)$$

Furthermore, each topic becomes a linear combination of words. As the weight of many words is close to zero, we can decide to take only the top r words to define a topic; therefore, we get:

$$t_i \approx \sum_{j=1}^{r} h_{ji} w_j$$

Here, each h_{ji} is obtained after sorting the columns of M_{twk}. To better understand the process, let's show a complete example based on a subset of Brown corpus (500 documents from the `news` category):

```
from nltk.corpus import brown

>>> sentences = brown.sents(categories=['news'])[0:500]
>>> corpus = []

>>> for s in sentences:
>>>     corpus.append(' '.join(s))
```

After defining the corpus, we need to tokenize and vectorize using a tf-idf approach:

```
from sklearn.feature_extraction.text import TfidfVectorizer

>>> vectorizer = TfidfVectorizer(strip_accents='unicode',
stop_words='english', norm='12', sublinear_tf=True)
>>> Xc = vectorizer.fit_transform(corpus).todense()
```

Now it's possible to apply an SVD to the `Xc` matrix (remember that in SciPy, the `V` matrix is already transposed):

```
from scipy.linalg import svd

>>> U, s, V = svd(Xc, full_matrices=False)
```

As the corpus is not very small, it's useful to set the parameter `full_matrices=False` to save computational time. We assume we have two topics, so we can extract our sub-matrices:

```
import numpy as np

>>> rank = 2

>>> Uk = U[:, 0:rank]
>>> sk = np.diag(s)[0:rank, 0:rank]
>>> Vk = V[0:rank, :]
```

If we want to analyze the top 10 words per topic, we need to consider that:

$$M_{twk} = V_k$$

Therefore, we can obtain the most significant words per topic after sorting the matrix using the `get_feature_names()` method provided by the vectorizers:

```
>>> Mtwks = np.argsort(Vk, axis=1)[::-1]

>>> for t in range(rank):
>>>    print('\nTopic ' + str(t))
>>>        for i in range(10):
>>>            print(vectorizer.get_feature_names()[Mtwks[t, i]])

Topic 0
said
mr
city
hawksley
president
year
time
council
election
federal

Topic 1
plainfield
wasn
copy
released
absence
africa
clash
exacerbated
facing
difficulties
```

In this case, we're considering only non-negative values in the matrix `Vk`; however, as a topic is a mixture of words, the negative components should also be taken into account. In this case, we need to sort the absolute values of `Vk`:

```
>>> Mtwks = np.argsort(np.abs(Vk), axis=1)[::-1]
```

If we want to analyze how a document is represented in this sub-space, we must use:

$$M_{dtk} = U_k \Sigma_k$$

Let's consider, for example, the first document of our corpus:

```
>>> print(corpus[0])
The Fulton County Grand Jury said Friday an investigation of Atlanta's
recent primary election produced `` no evidence '' that any irregularities
took place .

>>> Mdtk = Uk.dot(sk)

>>> print('d0 = %.2f*t1 + %.2f*t2' % (Mdtk[0][0], Mdtk[0][1]))
d0 = 0.15*t1 + -0.12*t2
```

As we are working in a bidimensional space, it's interesting to plot all the points corresponding to each document:

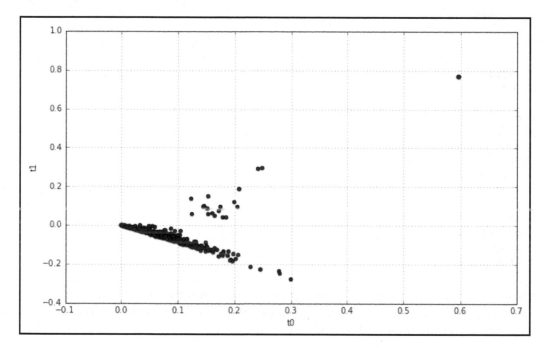

In the previous figure, we can see that many documents are correlated, with a small group of outliers. This is probably due to the fact that our choice of two topics is restrictive. If we repeat the same experiment using two Brown corpus categories (news and fiction), we observe a different behavior:

```
sentences = brown.sents(categories=['news', 'fiction'])
corpus = []

for s in sentences:
 corpus.append(' '.join(s))
```

I don't repeat the remaining calculations because they are similar. (The only difference is that our corpus is now quite bigger and this leads to a longer computational time. For this reason, we're going to discuss an alternative, which is much faster.) Plotting the points corresponding to the documents, we now get:

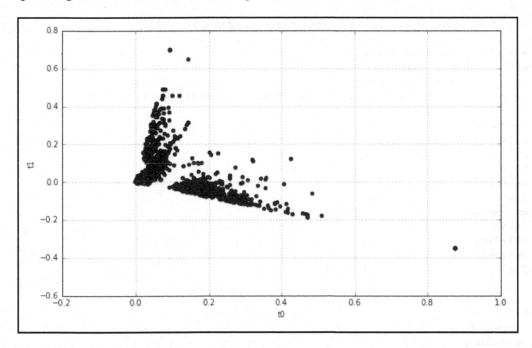

Now it's easier to distinguish two groups, which are almost orthogonal (meaning that many documents belong to only one category). I suggest repeating this experiment with different corpora and ranks. Unfortunately, it's impossible to plot more than three dimensions, but it's always possible to check whether the sub-space describes the underlying semantics correctly using only numerical computations.

As anticipated, the standard SciPy SVD implementation can be really slow when the occurrence matrix is huge; however, scikit-learn provides a truncated SVD implementation, `TruncatedSVD`, that works only with the sub-space. The result is much faster (it can directly manage sparse matrices too). Let's repeat the previous experiments (with a complete corpus) using this class:

```
from sklearn.decomposition import TruncatedSVD

>>> tsvd = TruncatedSVD(n_components=rank)
>>> Xt = tsvd.fit_transform(Xc)
```

Through the `n_components` parameter, it's possible to set the desired rank, discarding the remaining parts of the matrices. After fitting the model, we get the document-topic matrix M_{dtk} directly as the output of the method `fit_transform()`, while the topic-word matrix M_{twk} can be accessed using the instance variable `components_`:

```
>>> Mtws = np.argsort(tsvd.components_, axis=1)[::-1]

>>> for t in range(rank):
>>>     print('\nTopic ' + str(t))
>>>         for i in range(10):
>>>             print(vectorizer.get_feature_names()[Mwts[t, i]])

Topic 0
said
rector
hans
aloud
liston
nonsense
leave
whiskey
chicken
fat

Topic 1
bong
varnessa
schoolboy
kaboom
keeeerist
aggravated
jealous
hides
mayonnaise
fowl
```

The reader can verify how much faster this process can be; therefore, I suggest using a standard SVD implementation only when it's needed to have access to the full matrices. Unfortunately, as is also written in the documentation, this method is very sensitive to the algorithm and the random state. It also suffers from a phenomenon called **sign indeterminacy**, which means that the signs of all components can change if a different random seed is used. I suggest you declare:

```
import numpy as np

np.random.seed(1234)
```

Do this with a fixed seed at the beginning of every file (even Jupyter notebooks) to be sure that it's possible to repeat the calculations and always obtain the same result.

Moreover, I advise repeating this experiment using **non-negative matrix factorization**, as described in `Chapter 3`, *Feature Selection and Feature Engineering*.

Probabilistic latent semantic analysis

The previous model was based on a deterministic approach, but it's also possible to define a probabilistic model over the space determined by documents and words. In this case, we're not making any assumption about Apriori probabilities (this will be done in the next approach), and we're going to determine the parameters that maximize the log-likelihood of our model. In particular, consider the plate notation (if you want to know more about this technique, read `https://en.wikipedia.org/wiki/Plate_notation`) shown in the following figure:

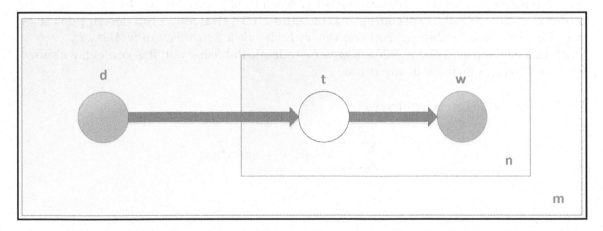

We assume we have a corpus of m documents and each of them is composed of n words (both elements are observed and therefore represented as gray circles); however, we also assume the presence of a limited set of k common latent factors (topics) that link a document with a group of words (as they are not observed, the circle is white). As already written, we cannot observe them directly, but we're allowed to assume their existence.

The joint probability to find a document with a particular word is:

$$P(d, w) = P(w|d)P(d)$$

Therefore, after introducing the latent factors, the conditional probability to find a word in a specific document can be written as:

$$P(w|d) = \sum_{i=1}^{k} P(w|t_i)\, P(t_i|d)$$

The initial joint probability $P(d, w)$ can be also expressed using the latent factors:

$$P(d, w) = \sum_{i=1}^{k} P(t_i)P(w|t_i)\, P(d|t_i)$$

This includes the prior probability $P(t)$. As we don't want to work with it, it's preferable to use the expression $P(w|d)$. To determine the two conditional probability distributions, a common approach is the **expectation-maximization (EM)** strategy. A full description can be found in Hofmann T., *Unsupervised Learning by Probabilistic Latent Semantic Analysis*, Machine Learning 42, 177-196, 2001, Kluwer Academic Publishers. In this context, we show only the final results without any proof.

The log-likelihood can be written as:

$$L = \sum_{d} \sum_{w} M_{dw}(d, w) \cdot logP(d, w)$$

Which becomes:

$$L = \sum_d \sum_w \left(M_{dw}(d,w) \cdot logP(d) + M_{dw}(d,w) \cdot log \sum_k P(t_k|d)P(w|t_k) \right)$$

M_{dw} is an occurrence matrix (normally obtained with a count vectorizer) and $M_{dw}(d, w)$ is the frequency of the word w in document d. For simplicity, we are going to approximate it by excluding the first term (which doesn't depend on t_k):

$$L \approx \sum_d \sum_w M_{dw}(d,w) \cdot log \sum_k P(t_k|d)P(w|t_k)$$

Moreover, it's useful to introduce the conditional probability $P(t|d,w)$, which is the probability of a topic given a document and a word. The EM algorithm maximizes the expected complete log-likelihood under the posterior probability $P(t|d,w)$:

$$E[L_c] = \sum_d \sum_w M_{dw}(d,w) \sum_k P(t|d,w) \cdot logP(t_k|d)P(w|t_k)$$

The **E** phase of the algorithm can be expressed as:

$$P(t|d,w) = \frac{P(t|d)P(w|t)}{\sum_k P(t_k|d)P(w|t_k)}$$

It must be extended to all topics, words, and documents and must be normalized with the sum per topic in order to always have consistent probabilities.

The **M** phase is split into two computations:

$$\begin{cases} P(w|t) = \dfrac{\sum_d M_{dw}(d,w) \cdot P(t|d,w)}{\sum_w \sum_d M_{dw}(d,w) \cdot P(t|d,w)} \\ P(t|d) = \dfrac{\sum_w M_{dw}(d,w) \cdot P(t|d,w)}{\sum_w M_{dw}(d,w)} \end{cases}$$

Also in this case, the calculations must be extended to all topics, words, and documents. But in the first case, we sum by document and normalize by summing by word and document, while in the second, we sum by word and normalize by the length of the document.

The algorithm must be iterated until the log-likelihood stops increasing its magnitude. Unfortunately, scikit-learn doesn't provide a PLSA implementation (maybe because the next strategy, LDA, is considered much more powerful and efficient), so we need to write some code from scratch. Let's start by defining a small subset of the Brown corpus, taking 10 sentences from the `editorial` category and 10 from the `fiction` one:

```
>>> sentences_1 = brown.sents(categories=['editorial'])[0:10]
>>> sentences_2 = brown.sents(categories=['fiction'])[0:10]
>>> corpus = []

>>> for s in sentences_1 + sentences_2:
>>>     corpus.append(' '.join(s))
```

Now we can vectorize using the `CountVectorizer` class:

```
import numpy as np

from sklearn.feature_extraction.text import CountVectorizer

>>> cv = CountVectorizer(strip_accents='unicode', stop_words='english')
>>> Xc = np.array(cv.fit_transform(corpus).todense())
```

At this point, we can define the rank (we choose 2 for simplicity), two constants that will be used later, and the matrices to hold the probabilities $P(t|d)$, $P(w|t)$, and $P(t|d,w)$:

```
>>> rank = 2
>>> alpha_1 = 1000.0
>>> alpha_2 = 10.0

>>> Ptd = np.random.uniform(0.0, 1.0, size=(len(corpus), rank))
>>> Pwt = np.random.uniform(0.0, 1.0, size=(rank, len(cv.vocabulary_)))
>>> Ptdw = np.zeros(shape=(len(cv.vocabulary_), len(corpus), rank))

>>> for d in range(len(corpus)):
>>>     nf = np.sum(Ptd[d, :])
>>>     for t in range(rank):
>>>         Ptd[d, t] /= nf

>>> for t in range(rank):
>>>     nf = np.sum(Pwt[t, :])
>>>     for w in range(len(cv.vocabulary_)):
>>>         Pwt[t, w] /= nf
```

The two matrices $P(t|d)$, $P(w|t)$ must be normalized so as to be coherent with the algorithm; the other one is initialized to zero. Now we can define the log-likelihood function:

```
>>> def log_likelihood():
>>>     value = 0.0
>>>
>>>     for d in range(len(corpus)):
>>>         for w in range(len(cv.vocabulary_)):
>>>             real_topic_value = 0.0
>>>
>>>             for t in range(rank):
>>>                 real_topic_value += Ptd[d, t] * Pwt[t, w]
>>>
>>>             if real_topic_value > 0.0:
>>>                 value += Xc[d, w] * np.log(real_topic_value)
>>>
>>>     return value
```

And finally the expectation-maximization functions:

```
>>> def expectation():
>>>     global Ptd, Pwt, Ptdw
>>>
>>>     for d in range(len(corpus)):
>>>         for w in range(len(cv.vocabulary_)):
>>>             nf = 0.0
>>>
>>>             for t in range(rank):
>>>                 Ptdw[w, d, t] = Ptd[d, t] * Pwt[t, w]
>>>                 nf += Ptdw[w, d, t]
>>>
>>>             Ptdw[w, d, :] = (Ptdw[w, d, :] / nf) if nf != 0.0 else 0.0
```

In the preceding function, when the normalization factor is 0, the probability $P(t|w, d)$ is set to 0.0 for each topic:

```
>>> def maximization():
>>>     global Ptd, Pwt, Ptdw
>>>
>>>     for t in range(rank):
>>>         nf = 0.0
>>>
>>>         for d in range(len(corpus)):
>>>             ps = 0.0
>>>
>>>             for w in range(len(cv.vocabulary_)):
>>>                 ps += Xc[d, w] * Ptdw[w, d, t]
>>>
```

```
>>>            Pwt[t, w] = ps
>>>            nf += Pwt[t, w]
>>>
>>>        Pwt[:, w] /= nf if nf != 0.0 else alpha_1
>>>
>>>    for d in range(len(corpus)):
>>>        for t in range(rank):
>>>            ps = 0.0
>>>            nf = 0.0
>>>
>>>            for w in range(len(cv.vocabulary_)):
>>>                ps += Xc[d, w] * Ptdw[w, d, t]
>>>                nf += Xc[d, w]
>>>
>>>            Ptd[d, t] = ps / (nf if nf != 0.0 else alpha_2)
```

The constants alpha_1 and alpha_2 are used when a normalization factor becomes 0. In that case, it can be useful to assign the probability a small value; therefore we divided the numerator for those constants. I suggest trying with different values so as to tune up the algorithm for different tasks.

At this point, we can try our algorithm with a limited number of iterations:

```
>>> print('Initial Log-Likelihood: %f' % log_likelihood())

>>> for i in range(50):
>>>     expectation()
>>>     maximization()
>>>     print('Step %d - Log-Likelihood: %f' % (i, log_likelihood()))

Initial Log-Likelihood: -1242.878549
Step 0 - Log-Likelihood: -1240.160748
Step 1 - Log-Likelihood: -1237.584194
Step 2 - Log-Likelihood: -1236.009227
Step 3 - Log-Likelihood: -1234.993974
Step 4 - Log-Likelihood: -1234.318545
Step 5 - Log-Likelihood: -1233.864516
Step 6 - Log-Likelihood: -1233.559474
Step 7 - Log-Likelihood: -1233.355097
Step 8 - Log-Likelihood: -1233.218306
Step 9 - Log-Likelihood: -1233.126583
Step 10 - Log-Likelihood: -1233.064804
Step 11 - Log-Likelihood: -1233.022915
Step 12 - Log-Likelihood: -1232.994274
Step 13 - Log-Likelihood: -1232.974501
Step 14 - Log-Likelihood: -1232.960704
Step 15 - Log-Likelihood: -1232.950965
...
```

It's possible to verify the convergence after the 30th step. At this point, we can check the top five words per topic considering the *P(w|t)* conditional distribution sorted in descending mode per topic weight:

```
>>> Pwts = np.argsort(Pwt, axis=1)[::-1]

>>> for t in range(rank):
>>>     print('\nTopic ' + str(t))
>>>         for i in range(5):
>>>             print(cv.get_feature_names()[Pwts[t, i]])

Topic 0
years
questions
south
reform
social

Topic 1
convened
maintenance
penal
year
legislators
```

Latent Dirichlet Allocation

In the previous method, we didn't make any assumptions about the topic prior to distribution and this can result in a limitation because the algorithm isn't driven by any real-world intuition. LDA, instead, is based on the idea that a topic is characterized by a small ensemble of important words and normally a document doesn't cover many topics. For this reason, the main assumption is that the prior topic distribution is a symmetric **Dirichlet** one. The probability density function is defined as:

$$f(\bar{x}; \alpha) = \frac{\Gamma(k\alpha)}{\Gamma(\alpha)^k} \prod_{i=1}^{k} x_i^{\alpha-1} \ where \ \bar{x} = (x_1, x_2, ..., x_k)$$

If the concentration parameter alpha is below 1.0, the distribution will be sparse as desired. This allows us to model topic-document and topic-word distributions, which will always be concentrated on a few values. In this way we can avoid the following:

- The topic mixture assigned to a document could becoming flat (many topics with similar weight)
- The structure of a topic considering the word ensemble could becoming similar to a background (in fact, only a limited number of words must be important; otherwise the semantic boundaries fade out).

Using the plate notation, we can represent the relationship among documents, topics, and words as shown in the following figure:

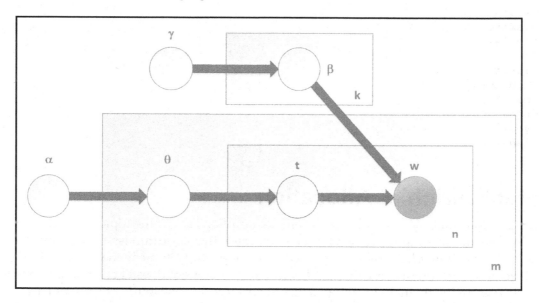

In the previous figure, alpha is the Dirichlet parameter for the topic-document distribution, while gamma has the same role for the topic-word distribution. Theta, instead, is the topic distribution for a specific document, while beta is the topic distribution for a specific word.

If we have a corpus of m documents and a vocabulary of n words (each document has n_i words) and we assume to have k different topics, the generative algorithm can be described with the following steps:

- For each document, draw a sample (a topic mixture) from the topic-document distribution:

$$\theta_i \sim Dir(\alpha) \ \forall \, i \in (1, m)$$

- For each topic, draw a sample from the from the topic-word distribution:

$$\beta_i \sim Dir(\gamma) \ \forall \, i \in (1, k)$$

Both parameters must be estimated. At this point, considering the occurrence matrix M_{dw} and the notation z_{mn} to define the topic assigned to the n-th word in the m-th document, we can iterate over documents (index d) and words (index w):

- A topic for document d and word w is chosen according to:

$$z_{dw} \sim Categorical(\theta_d)$$

- A word is chosen according to:

$$w_{wj} \sim Categorical(\beta_{z_{dw}})$$

In both cases, a categorical distribution is a one-trial multinomial one. A complete description of how the parameters are estimated is quite complex and it's beyond the scope of this book; however, the main problem is finding the distribution of latent variables:

$$p(\bar{z}, \theta, \beta | \bar{w}, \alpha, \gamma) = \frac{p(\bar{z}, \theta, \beta | \alpha, \gamma)}{p(\bar{w} | \alpha, \gamma)}$$

The reader can find a lot more information in Blei D., Ng A., Jordan M., *Latent Dirichlet Allocation*, Journal of Machine Learning Research, 3, (2003) 993-1022. However, a very important difference between LDA and PLSA is about the generative ability of LDA, which allows working with unseen documents. In fact, the PLSA training process finds the optimal parameters *p(t|d)* only for the corpus, while LDA adopts random variables. It's possible to understand this concept by defining the probability of theta (a topic mixture) as joint with a set of topics and a set of words, and conditioned to the model parameters:

$$p(\theta, \bar{z}, \bar{w} | \alpha, \gamma) = p(\theta | \alpha) \prod_i p(z_i | \theta) \, p(w_i | z_i, \gamma)$$

As shown in the previously mentioned paper, the probability of a document (a set of words) conditioned to the model parameters, can be obtained by integration:

$$p(\bar{w} | \alpha, \gamma) = \int p(\theta | \alpha) \left(\prod_i \sum_{z_i} p(z_i | \theta) p(w_i | z_i, \gamma) \right) d\theta$$

This expression shows the difference between PLSA and LDA. Once learned *p(t|d)*, PLSA cannot generalize, while LDA, sampling from the random variables, can always find a suitable topic mixture for an unseen document.

scikit-learn provides a full LDA implementation through the class `LatentDirichletAllocation`. We're going to use it with a bigger dataset (4,000 documents) built from a subset of the Brown corpus:

```
>>> sentences_1 = brown.sents(categories=['reviews'])[0:1000]
>>> sentences_2 = brown.sents(categories=['government'])[0:1000]
>>> sentences_3 = brown.sents(categories=['fiction'])[0:1000]
>>> sentences_4 = brown.sents(categories=['news'])[0:1000]
>>> corpus = []

>>> for s in sentences_1 + sentences_2 + sentences_3 + sentences_4:
>>>     corpus.append(' '.join(s))
```

Now we can vectorize, define, and train our LDA model by assuming that we have eight main topics:

```
from sklearn.decomposition import LatentDirichletAllocation

>>> cv = CountVectorizer(strip_accents='unicode', stop_words='english',
```

```
analyzer='word', token_pattern='[a-z]+')
>>> Xc = cv.fit_transform(corpus)

>>> lda = LatentDirichletAllocation(n_topics=8, learning_method='online',
max_iter=25)
>>> Xl = lda.fit_transform(Xc)
```

In `CountVectorizer`, we added a regular expression to filter the tokens through the parameter `token_pattern`. This is useful as we are not using a full tokenizer and, in the corpus, there are also many numbers that we want to filter out. The class `LatentDirichletAllocation` allows us to specify the learning method (through `learning_method`), which can be either batch or online. We have chosen online because it's faster; however, both methods adopt variational Bayes to learn the parameters. The former adopts the whole dataset, while the latter works with mini-batches. The online option will be removed in the 0.20 release; therefore, you can see a deprecation warning when using it now. Both theta and beta Dirichlet parameters can be specified through `doc_topic_prior` (theta) and `topic_word_prior` (beta). The default value (adopted by us too) is 1.0 / `n_topics` . It's important to keep both values small and, in particular, less than 1.0 in order to encourage sparseness. The maximum number of iterations (`max_iter`) and other learning-related parameters can be applied by reading the built-in documentation or visiting `http://scikit-learn.org/stable/modules/generated/sklearn.decomposition.LatentDirichletAllocation.html`.

Now we can test our model by extracting the top five keywords per topic. Just like `TruncatedSVD`, the topic-word distribution results are stored in the instance variable `components_`:

```
>>> Mwts_lda = np.argsort(lda.components_, axis=1)[::-1]

>>> for t in range(8):
>>>     print('\nTopic ' + str(t))
>>>         for i in range(5):
>>>             print(cv.get_feature_names()[Mwts_lda[t, i]])

Topic 0
code
cadenza
unlocks
ophthalmic
quo

Topic 1
countless
harnick
leni
```

addle
chivalry

Topic 2
evasive
errant
tum
rum
orations

Topic 3
grigory
tum
absurdity
tarantara
suitably

Topic 4
seventeenth
conant
chivalrous
janitsch
knight

Topic 5
hypocrites
errantry
adventures
knight
errant

Topic 6
counter
rogues
tum
lassus
wars

Topic 7
pitch
cards
cynicism
silences
shrewd

There are some repetitions, probably due to the composition of some topics, and the reader can try different prior parameters to observe the changes. It's possible to do an experiment to check whether the model works correctly.

Let's consider two documents:

```
>>> print(corpus[0])
It is not news that Nathan Milstein is a wizard of the violin .

>>> print(corpus[2500])
The children had nowhere to go and no place to play , not even sidewalks .
```

They are quite different and so are their topic distributions:

```
>>> print(Xl[0])
[ 0.85412134 0.02083335 0.02083335 0.02083335 0.02083335 0.02083677
  0.02087515 0.02083335]

>>> print(Xl[2500])
[ 0.22499749 0.02500001 0.22500135 0.02500221 0.025 0.02500219
  0.02500001 0.42499674]
```

We have a dominant topic ($0.85t_0$) for the first document and a mixture ($0.22t_0 + 0.22t_2 + 0.42t_7$) for the second one. Now let's consider the concatenation of both documents:

```
>>> test_doc = corpus[0] + ' ' + corpus[2500]
>>> y_test = lda.transform(cv.transform([test_doc]))

>>> print(y_test)
[[ 0.61242771 0.01250001 0.11251451 0.0125011 0.01250001 0.01250278
   0.01251778 0.21253611]]
```

In the resulting document, as expected, the mixture has changed: $0.61t_0 + 0.11t_2 + 0.21t_7$. In other words, the algorithm introduced the previously dominant topic 5 (which is now stronger) by weakening both topic 2 and topic 7. This is reasonable, because the length of the first document is less than the second one, and therefore topic 5 cannot completely cancel the other topics out.

Sentiment analysis

One the most widespread applications of NLP is sentiment analysis of short texts (tweets, posts, comments, reviews, and so on). From a marketing viewpoint, it's very important to understand the semantics of these pieces of information in terms of the sentiment expressed. As you can understand, this task can be very easy when the comment is precise and contains only a set of positive/negative words, but it becomes more complex when in the same sentence there are different propositions that can conflict with each other. For example, *I loved that hotel. It was a wonderful experience* is clearly a positive comment, while *The hotel is good, however, the restaurant was bad and, even if the waiters were kind, I had to fight with a receptionist to have another pillow*. In this case, the situation is more difficult to manage, because there are both positive and negative elements, resulting in a neutral review. For this reason, many applications aren't based on a binary decision but admit intermediate levels (at least one to express the neutrality).

These kind of problems are normally supervised (as we're going to do), but there are also cheaper and more complex solutions. The simplest way to evaluate the sentiment is to look for particular keywords. This dictionary-based approach is fast and, together with a good stemmer, can immediately mark positive and negative documents. On the flip side, it doesn't consider the relationship among terms and cannot learn how to weight the different components. For example, *Lovely day, bad mood* will result in a neutral (+1, -1), while with a supervised approach it's possible to make the model learn that *mood* is very important and *bad mood* will normally drive to a negative sentiment. Other approaches (much more complex) are based on topic modeling (you can now understand how to apply LSA or LDA to determine the underlying topics in terms of positivity or negativity); however, they need further steps to use topic-word and topic-document distributions. It can be helpful in the real semantics of a comment, where, for example, a positive adjective is normally used together with other similar components (like verbs). Say, *Lovely hotel, I'm surely coming back*. In this case (if the number of samples is big enough), a topic can emerge from the combination of words such as *lovely* or *amazing* and (positive) verbs such as *returning* or *coming back*.

An alternative is to consider the topic distribution of positive and negative documents and work with a supervised approach in the topic sub-space. Other approaches include deep-learning techniques (such as Word2Vec or Doc2Vec) and are based on the idea of generating a vectorial space where similar words are close to each other, in order to easily manage synonyms. For example, if the training set contains the sentence *Lovely hotel* but it doesn't contain *Wonderful hotel*, a Word2Vec model can learn from other examples that *lovely* and *wonderful* are very close; therefore the new document *Wonderful hotel* is immediately classified using the knowledge provided by the first comment. An introduction to this technique, together with some technical papers, can be found at `https`
`://code.google.com/archive/p/word2vec/`.

Let's now consider our example, which is based on a subset of the *Twitter Sentiment Analysis Training Corpus* dataset. In order to speed up the process, we have limited the experiment to 1,00,000 tweets. After downloading the file (see the box at the end of this paragraph), it's necessary to parse it (using the UTF-8 encoding):

```
>>> dataset = 'dataset.csv'

>>> corpus = []
>>> labels = []

>>> with open(dataset, 'r', encoding='utf-8') as df:
>>>     for i, line in enumerate(df):
>>>         if i == 0:
>>>             continue
>>>
>>>         parts = line.strip().split(',')
>>>         labels.append(float(parts[1].strip()))
>>>         corpus.append(parts[3].strip())
```

The `dataset` variable must contain the full path to the CSV file. This procedure reads all the lines skipping the first one (which is the header), and stores each tweet as a new list entry in the `corpus` variable, and the corresponding sentiment (which is binary, 0 or 1) in the `labels` variable. At this point, we proceed as usual, tokenizing, vectorizing, and preparing the training and test sets:

```
from nltk.tokenize import RegexpTokenizer
from nltk.corpus import stopwords
from nltk.stem.lancaster import LancasterStemmer

from sklearn.feature_extraction.text import TfidfVectorizer
from sklearn.model_selection import train_test_split

>>> rt = RegexpTokenizer('[a-zA-Z0-9\.]+')
>>> ls = LancasterStemmer()
```

```
>>> sw = set(stopwords.words('english'))

>>> def tokenizer(sentence):
>>>     tokens = rt.tokenize(sentence)
>>>     return [ls.stem(t.lower()) for t in tokens if t not in sw]

>>> tfv = TfidfVectorizer(tokenizer=tokenizer, sublinear_tf=True,
ngram_range=(1, 2), norm='12')
>>> X = tfv.fit_transform(corpus[0:100000])
>>> Y = np.array(labels[0:100000])

>>> X_train, X_test, Y_train, Y_test = train_test_split(X, Y,
test_size=0.1)
```

We have chosen to include dots together with letters and numbers in the `RegexpTokenizer` instance because they are useful for expressing particular emotions. Moreover, the n-gram range has been set to (1, 2), so we include bigrams (the reader can try with trigrams too). At this point, we can train a random forest:

```
from sklearn.ensemble import RandomForestClassifier

import multiprocessing

>>> rf = RandomForestClassifier(n_estimators=20,
n_jobs=multiprocessing.cpu_count())
>>> rf.fit(X_train, Y_train)
```

Now we can produce some metrics to evaluate the model:

```
from sklearn.metrics import precision_score, recall_score

>>> print('Precision: %.3f' % precision_score(Y_test, rf.predict(X_test)))
Precision: 0.720

>>> print('Recall: %.3f' % recall_score(Y_test, rf.predict(X_test)))
Recall: 0.784
```

The performances are not excellent (it's possible to achieve better accuracies using Word2Vec); however, they are acceptable for many tasks. In particular, a 78% recall means that the number of false negatives is about 20% and it can be useful when using sentiment analysis for an automatic processing task (in many cases, the risk threshold to auto-publish a negative review is quite a bit lower, and, therefore, a better solution must be employed). The performances can be also confirmed by the corresponding ROC curve:

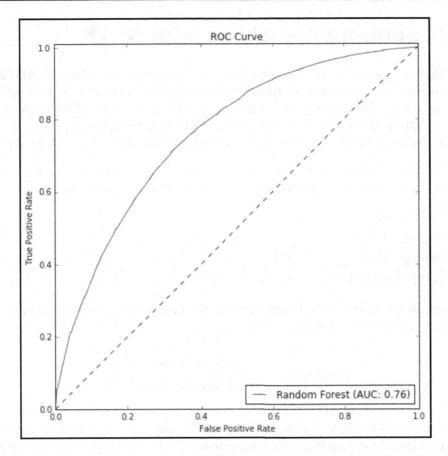

The *Twitter Sentiment Analysis Training Corpus* dataset (as a CSV file) used in the example can be downloaded from `http://thinknook.com/wp-content/uploads/2012/09/Sentiment-Analysis-Dataset.zip`. Considering the amount of data, the training process can be very long (even taking hours on slower machines).

VADER sentiment analysis with NLTK

For the English language, NLTK provides an already trained model called **VADER** (**Valence Aware Dictionary and sEntiment Reasoner**) that works in a slightly different way and adopts a rule engine together with a lexicon to infer the sentiment intensity of a piece of text. More information and details can be found in Hutto C.J., Gilbert E., *VADER: A Parsimonious Rule-based Model for Sentiment Analysis of Social Media Text*, AAAI, 2014.

The NLTK version uses the `SentimentIntensityAnalyzer` class and can immediately be used to have a polarity sentiment measure made up of four components:

- Positive factor
- Negative factor
- Neutral factor
- Compound factor

The first three don't need any explanation, while the last one is a particular measure (a normalized overall score), which is computed as:

$$Compound = \frac{\sum_i Sentiment\ (w_i)}{\sqrt{(\sum_i Sentiment\ (w_i))^2 + \alpha}}$$

Here, *Sentiment(w_i)* is the score valence of the word w_i and alpha is a normalization coefficient that should approximate the maximum expected value (the default value set in NLTK is 15). The usage of this class is immediate, as the following snippet can confirm:

```
from nltk.sentiment.vader import SentimentIntensityAnalyzer

>>> text = 'This is a very interesting and quite powerful sentiment
analyzer'

>>> vader = SentimentIntensityAnalyzer()
>>> print(vader.polarity_scores(text))
{'neg': 0.0, 'neu': 0.535, 'pos': 0.465, 'compound': 0.7258}
```

The NLTK Vader implementation uses the library Twython for some functionalities. Even though it's not necessary, in order to avoid a warning, it's possible to install it using pip (`pip install twython`).

References

- Hofmann T., *Unsupervised Learning by Probabilistic Latent Semantic Analysis*, Machine Learning 42, 177-196, 2001, Kluwer Academic Publishers.
- Blei D., Ng A., Jordan M., *Latent Dirichlet Allocation, Journal of Machine Learning Research*, 3, (2003) 993-1022.
- Hutto C.J., Gilbert E., *VADER: A Parsimonious Rule-based Model for Sentiment Analysis of Social Media Text*, AAAI, 2014.

Summary

In this chapter, we introduced topic modeling. We discussed latent semantic analysis based on truncated SVD, probabilistic latent semantic analysis (which aims to build a model without assumptions about latent factor prior probabilities), and latent Dirichlet allocation, which outperformed the previous method and is based on the assumption that the latent factor has a sparse prior Dirichlet distribution. This means that a document normally covers only a limited number of topics and a topic is characterized only by a few important words.

In the last section, we discussed sentiment analysis of documents, which is aimed at determining whether a piece of text expresses a positive or negative feeling. In order to show a feasible solution, we built a classifier based on an NLP pipeline and a random forest with average performances that can be used in many real-life situations.

In the next chapter, we're going to briefly introduce deep learning, together with the TensorFlow framework. As this topic alone requires a dedicated book, our goal is to define the main concepts with some practical examples. If the reader wants to have further information, at the end of the chapter, a complete reference list will be provided.

14
A Brief Introduction to Deep Learning and TensorFlow

In this chapter, we're going to briefly introduce deep learning with some examples based on TensorFlow. This topic is quite complex and needs dedicated books; however, our goal is to allow the reader to understand some basic concepts that can be useful before starting a complete course. In the first section, we're presenting the structure of artificial neural networks and how they can be transformed in a complex computational graph with several different layers. In the second one, instead, we're going to introduce the basic concepts concerning TensorFlow and we'll show some examples based on algorithms already discussed in previous chapters. In the last section, we briefly present Keras, a high-level deep learning framework and we build an example of image classification using a convolutional neural network.

Deep learning at a glance

Deep learning has become very famous in the last few decades, thanks to hundreds of applications that are changing the way we interact with many electronic (and non-electronic) systems. Speech, text, and image recognition; autonomous vehicles; and intelligent bots (just to name a few) are common applications normally based on deep learning models and have outperformed any previous classical approach.

To better understand what a deep architecture is (considering that this is only a brief introduction), we need to step back and talk about standard artificial neural networks.

Artificial neural networks

An **artificial neural network** (**ANN**) or simply neural network is a directed structure that connects an input layer with an output one. Normally, all operations are differentiable and the overall vectorial function can be easily written as:

$$\bar{y} = f(\bar{x})$$

Here:

$$\bar{x} = (x_1, x_2, \dots, x_n) \ and \ \bar{y} = (y_1, y_2, \dots, y_m)$$

The adjective "neural" comes from two important elements: the internal structure of a basic computational unit and the interconnections among them. Let's start with the former. In the following figure, there's a schematic representation of an artificial neuron:

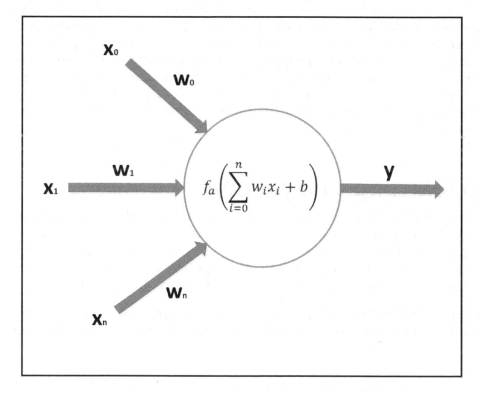

A neuron core is connected with n input channels, each of them characterized by a synaptic weight w_i. The input is split into its components and they are multiplied by the corresponding weight and summed. An optional bias can be added to this sum (it works like another weight connected to a unitary input). The resulting sum is filtered by an activation function f_a (for example a sigmoid, if you recall how a logistic regression works) and the output is therefore produced. In Chapter 5, *Logistic Regression*, we also discussed perceptrons (the first artificial neural networks), which correspond exactly to this architecture with a binary-step activation function. On the other hand, even a logistic regression can be represented as a single neuron neural network, where $f_a(x)$ is a sigmoid. The main problem with this architecture is that it's intrinsically linear because the output is always a function of the dot product between the input vector and the weight one. You already know all the limitations that such a system has; therefore it's necessary to step forward and create the first **Multi-layer Perceptron** (MLP). In the following figure, there's a schematic representation of an MLP with an n-dimensional input, p hidden neurons, and a k-dimensional output:

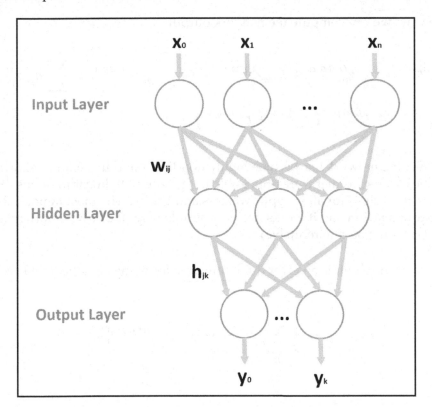

There are three layers (even though the number can be larger): the input layer, which receives the input vectors; a hidden layer; and the output one, which is responsible for producing the output. As you can see, every neuron is connected to all the neurons belonging the next layer and now we have two weight matrices, $W = (w_{ij})$ and $H = (h_{jk})$, using the convention that the first index is referred to the previous layer and the second to the following one.

Therefore, the net input to each hidden neuron and the corresponding output is:

$$\begin{cases} z_j^{Input} = w_{0j}x_0 + w_{1j}x_1 + \cdots + w_{nj}x_n = \sum_i w_{ij}x_i \\ z_j^{Output} = f_a^{Hidden}\left(z_j^{Input} + b_j^{Hidden}\right) \end{cases}$$

In the same way, we can compute the network output:

$$\begin{cases} y_k^{Input} = h_{0k}z_0^{Output} + h_{1k}z_1^{Output} + \cdots + h_{pk}z_p^{Output} = \sum_j h_{jk}z_j^{Output} \\ y_k^{Output} = f_a^{Output}\left(y_k^{Input} + b_k^{Output}\right) \end{cases}$$

As you can see, the network has become highly non-linear and this feature allows us to model complex scenarios that were impossible to manage with linear methods. But how can we determine the values for all synaptic weights and biases? The most famous algorithm is called **back-propagation** and it works in a very simple way (the only important assumption is that both $f_a(x)$ must be differentiable).

First of all, we need to define an error (loss) function; for many classification tasks, it can be the total squared error:

$$L = \frac{1}{2}\sum_n \left\| \bar{y}_n^{Predicted} - \bar{y}_n^{Target} \right\|^2$$

Here we have assumed to have N input samples. Expanding it, we obtain:

$$L = \frac{1}{2} \sum_n \sum_k \left(f_a^{Output} \left(\sum_j h_{jk} z_j^{Output} \right) - y_k^{Target} \right)^2 = \frac{1}{2} \sum_n \sum_k \delta_k^2$$

This function depends on all variables (weights and biases), but we can start from the bottom and consider first only h_{jk} (for simplicity I'm not considering the biases as normal weights); therefore we can compute the gradients and update the weights:

$$\frac{\partial L}{\partial h_{jk}} = \sum_n \delta_k \frac{\partial f_a^{Output}}{\partial y_k^{Input}} \frac{\partial y_k^{Input}}{\partial h_{jk}} = \sum_n \delta_k z_j^{Output} \frac{\partial f_a^{Output}}{\partial y_k^{Input}} = \sum_n \alpha_k z_j^{Output}$$

In the same way, we can derive the gradient with respect to w_{ij}:

$$\frac{\partial L}{\partial w_{ij}} = \sum_n \sum_k \delta_k \frac{\partial f_a^{Output}}{\partial y_k^{Input}} \frac{\partial y_k^{Input}}{\partial z_j^{Output}} \frac{\partial z_j^{Output}}{\partial z_j^{Input}} \frac{\partial z_j^{Input}}{\partial w_{ij}}$$

$$= \sum_n \sum_k \delta_k h_{jk} x_i \frac{\partial f_a^{Output}}{\partial y_k^{Input}} \frac{\partial z_j^{Output}}{\partial z_j^{Input}} = \sum_n \sum_k \alpha_k h_{jk} x_i \frac{\partial z_j^{Output}}{\partial z_j^{Input}}$$

As you can see, the term alpha (which is proportional to the error delta) is back-propagated from the output layer to the hidden one. If there are many hidden layers, this procedure should be repeated recursively until the first layer. The algorithm adopts the gradient descent method; therefore it updates the weights iteratively until convergence:

$$\begin{cases} h_{jk}^{(t+1)} = h_{jk}^{(t)} - \eta \dfrac{\partial L}{\partial h_{jk}} \\ w_{ij}^{(t+1)} = w_{ij}^{(t)} - \eta \dfrac{\partial L}{\partial w_{ij}} \end{cases}$$

Here, the parameter `eta` (Greek letter in the formula) is the learning rate.

In many real problems, the stochastic gradient descent method is adopted (read `https://en` `.wikipedia.org/wiki/Stochastic_gradient_descent`, for further information), which works with batches of input samples, instead of considering the entire dataset. Moreover, many optimizations can be employed to speed up the convergence, but they are beyond the scope of this book. In Goodfellow I., Bengio Y., Courville A., *Deep Learning*, MIT Press, the reader can find all the details about the majority of them. For our purposes, it's important to know that we can build a complex network and, after defining a global loss function, optimize all the weights with a standard procedure. In the section dedicated to TensorFlow, we're going to show an example of MLP, but we're not implementing the learning algorithm because, luckily, all optimizers have already been built and can be applied to every architecture.

Deep architectures

MLPs are powerful, but their expressiveness is limited by the number and the nature of the layers. Deep learning architectures, on the other side, are based on a sequence of heterogeneous layers which perform different operations organized in a computational graph. The output of a layer, correctly reshaped, is fed into the following one, until the output, which is normally associated with a loss function to optimize. The most interesting applications have been possible thanks to this stacking strategy, where the number of variable elements (weights and biases) can easily reach over 10 million; therefore, the ability to capture small details and generalize them exceeds any expectations. In the following section, I'm going to introduce briefly the most important layer types.

Fully connected layers

A fully connected (sometimes called dense) layer is made up of n neurons and each of them receives all the output values coming from the previous layer (like the hidden layer in a MLP). It can be characterized by a weight matrix, a bias vector, and an activation function:

$$\bar{y} = f(W\bar{x} + \bar{b})$$

They are normally used as intermediate or output layers, in particular when it's necessary to represent a probability distribution. For example, a deep architecture could be employed for an image classification with *m* output classes. In this case, the *softmax* activation function allows having an output vector where each element is the probability of a class (and the sum of all outputs is always normalized to 1.0). In this case, the argument is considered as a **logit** or the logarithm of a probability:

$$logit_i = W_i \bar{x} + b_i$$

W_i is the i-th row of W. The probability of a class y_i is obtained by applying the *softmax* function to each *logit*:

$$P(y_i) = Softmax(logit_i) = \frac{e^{logit_i}}{\sum_j e^{logit_j}}$$

This type of output can easily be trained using a cross-entropy loss function, as already discussed for logistic regression.

Convolutional layers

Convolutional layers are normally applied to bidimensional inputs (even though they can be used for vectors and 3D matrices) and they became particularly famous thanks to their extraordinary performance in image classification tasks. They are based on the discrete convolution of a small kernel *k* with a bidimensional input (which can be the output of another convolutional layer):

$$(k * Y) = Z(i,j) = \sum_m \sum_n k(m,n)Y(i-m,j-n)$$

A layer is normally made up of n fixed-size kernels, and their values are considered as weights to learn using a back-propagation algorithm. A convolutional architecture, in most cases, starts with layers with few larger kernels (for example, 16 (8 x 8) matrices) and feeds their output to other layers with a higher number of smaller kernels (32 (5 x 5), 128 (4 x 4), and 256 (3 x 3)). In this way, the first layers should learn to capture more generic features (such as orientation), while the following ones will be trained to capture smaller and smaller elements (such as the position of eyes, nose, and mouth in a face). The output of the last convolutional layer is normally flattened (transformed into a 1D vector) and used as input for one or more fully connected layers.

In the following figure, there's a schematic representation of a convolution over a picture:

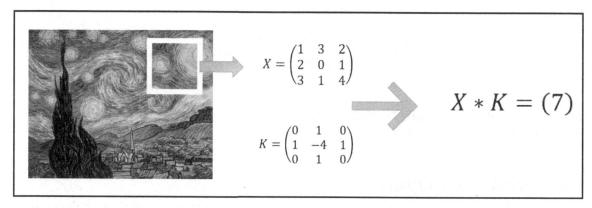

Each square set of 3 x 3 pixels is convoluted with a Laplacian kernel and transformed into a single value, which corresponds to the sum of upper, lower, left, and right pixels (considering the centre) minus four times the central one. We're going to see a complete example using this kernel in the following section.

To reduce the complexity when the number of convolutions is very high, one or more **pooling layers** can be employed. Their task is to transform each group of input points (pixels in an image) into a single value using a predefined strategy. The most common pooling layers are:

- **Max pooling**: Every bidimensional group of (m x n) pixels is transformed into a single pixel whose value is the greatest in the group.
- **Average pooling**: Every bidimensional group of (m x n) pixels is transformed into a single pixel whose value is the average of the group.

In this way, the dimensionality of the original matrix can be reduced with a loss of information, but that can often be discarded (in particular in the first layers where the granularity of the features is coarse). Another important category of layers are the **zero-padding** ones. They work by adding null values (0) before and after the input (1D) or at the left, right, top and bottom side of 2D input.

Dropout layers

A dropout layer is used to prevent overfitting of the network by randomly setting a fixed number of input elements to 0. This layer is adopted during the training phase, but it's normally deactivated during test, validation, and production phases. Dropout networks can exploit higher learning rates, moving in different directions on the loss surface (setting to zero a few random input values in the hidden layers is equivalent to training different sub-models) and excluding all the error-surface areas that don't lead to a consistent optimization. Dropout is very useful in very big models, where it increases the overall performance and reduces the risk of freezing some weights and overfitting the model.

Recurrent neural networks

A recurrent layer is made up of particular neurons that present recurrent connections so as to bind the state at time t to its previous values (in general, only one). This category of computational cells is particularly useful when it's necessary to capture the temporal dynamics of an input sequence. In many situations, in fact, we expect an output value that must be correlated with the history of the corresponding inputs. But an MLP, as well as the other models that we've discussed, are stateless. Therefore, their output is determined only by the current input. RNNs overcome this problem by providing an internal memory which can capture short-term and long-term dependencies.

The most common cells are **Long Short-Term Memory** (**LSTM**) and **Gated Recurrent Unit** (**GRU**) and they can both be trained using a standard back-propagation approach. As this is only an introduction, I cannot go deeper (RNN mathematical complexity is non-trivial); however, it's useful to remember that whenever a temporal dimension must be included in a deep model, RNNs offer stable and powerful support.

A brief introduction to TensorFlow

TensorFlow is a computational framework created by Google and has become one of the most diffused deep-learning toolkits. It can work with both CPUs and GPUs and already implements most of the operations and structures required to build and train a complex model. TensorFlow can be installed as a Python package on Linux, Mac, and Windows (with or without GPU support); however, I suggest you follow the instructions provided on the website (the link can be found in the infobox at the end of this chapter) to avoid common mistakes.

The main concept behind TensorFlow is the computational graph, or a set of subsequent operations that transform an input batch into the desired output. In the following figure, there's a schematic representation of a graph:

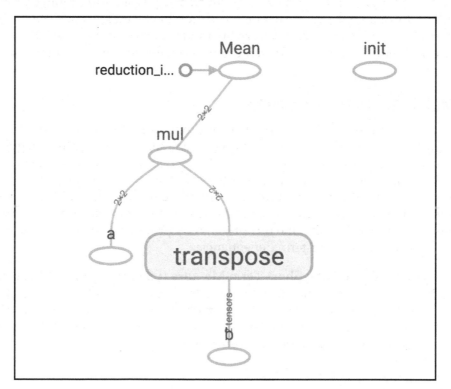

Starting from the bottom, we have two input nodes (**a** and **b**), a transpose operation (that works on **b**), a matrix multiplication and a mean reduction. The **init** block is a separate operation, which is formally part of the graph, but it's not directly connected to any other node; therefore it's autonomous (indeed, it's a global initializer).

As this one is only a brief introduction, it's useful to list all of the most important strategic elements needed to work with TensorFlow so as to be able to build a few simple examples that can show the enormous potential of this framework:

- **Graph**: This represents the computational structure that connects a generic input batch with the output tensors through a directed network made of operations. It's defined as a `tf.Graph()` instance and normally used with a Python context manager.
- **Placeholder**: This is a reference to an external variable, which must be explicitly supplied when it's requested for the output of an operation that uses it directly or indirectly. For example, a placeholder can represent a variable x, which is first transformed into its squared value and then summed to a constant value. The output is then x^2+c, which is materialized by passing a concrete value for x. It's defined as a `tf.placeholder()` instance.
- **Variable**: An internal variable used to store values which are updated by the algorithm. For example, a variable can be a vector containing the weights of a logistic regression. It's normally initialized before a training process and automatically modified by the built-in optimizers. It's defined as a `tf.Variable()` instance. A variable can also be used to store elements which must not be considered during training processes; in this case, it must be declared with the parameter `trainable=False`.
- **Constant**: A constant value defined as a `tf.constant()` instance.
- **Operation**: A mathematical operation that can work with placeholders, variables, and constants. For example, the multiplication of two matrices is an operation defined as `tf.matmul(A, B)`. Among all operations, gradient calculation is one of the most important. TensorFlow allows determining the gradients starting from a determined point in the computational graph, until the origin or another point that must be logically before it. We're going to see an example of this operation.

- **Session**: This is a sort of wrapper-interface between TensorFlow and our working environment (for example, Python or C++). When the evaluation of a graph is needed, this macro-operation will be managed by a session, which must be fed with all placeholder values and will produce the required outputs using the requested devices. For our purposes, it's not necessary to go deeper into this concept; however, I invite the reader to retrieve further information from the website or from one of the resources listed at the end of this chapter. It's declared as an instance of `tf.Session()` or, as we're going to do, an instance of `tf.InteractiveSession()`. This type of session is particularly useful when working with notebooks or shell commands, because it places itself automatically as the default one.
- **Device**: A physical computational device, such as a CPU or a GPU. It's declared explicitly through an instance of the class `tf.device()` and used with a context manager. When the architecture contains more computational devices, it's possible to split the jobs so as to parallelize many operations. If no device is specified, TensorFlow will use the default one (which is the main CPU or a suitable GPU if all the necessary components are installed).

We can now analyze some simple examples using these concepts.

Computing gradients

The option to compute the gradients of all output tensors with respect to any connected input or node is one of the most interesting features of TensorFlow, because it allows us to create learning algorithms without worrying about the complexity of all transformations. In this example, we first define a linear dataset representing the function $f(x) = x$ in the range (-100, 100):

```
import numpy as np

>>> nb_points = 100
>>> X = np.linspace(-nb_points, nb_points, 200, dtype=np.float32)
```

The corresponding plot is shown in the following figure:

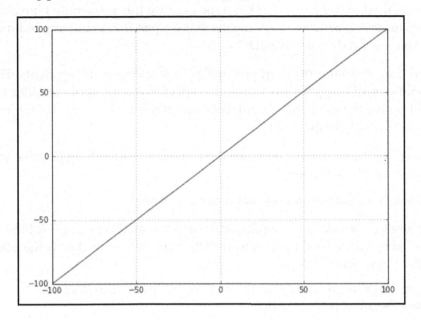

Now we want to use TensorFlow to compute:

$$\begin{cases} g(x) = x^3 \\ \dfrac{\partial g}{\partial x} \\ \dfrac{\partial^2 g}{\partial x^2} \end{cases}$$

The first step is defining a graph:

```
import tensorflow as tf

>>> graph = tf.Graph()
```

Within the context of this graph, we can define our input placeholder and other operations:

```
>>> with graph.as_default():
>>>     Xt = tf.placeholder(tf.float32, shape=(None, 1), name='x')
>>>     Y = tf.pow(Xt, 3.0, name='x_3')
>>>     Yd = tf.gradients(Y, Xt, name='dx')
>>>     Yd2 = tf.gradients(Yd, Xt, name='d2x')
```

A placeholder is generally defined with a type (first parameter), a shape, and an optional name. We've decided to use a `tf.float32` type because this is the only type also supported by GPUs. Selecting `shape=(None, 1)` means that it's possible to use any bidimensional vectors with the second dimension equal to 1.

The first operation computes the third power if `Xt` is working on all elements. The second operation computes all the gradients of `Y` with respect to the input placeholder `Xt`. The last operation will repeat the gradient computation, but in this case, it uses `Yd`, which is the output of the first gradient operation.

We can now pass some concrete data to see the results. The first thing to do is create a session connected with this graph:

```
>>> session = tf.InteractiveSession(graph=graph)
```

By using this session, we ask any computation using the method `run()`. All the input parameters must be supplied through a feed-dictionary, where the key is the placeholder, while the value is the actual array:

```
>>> X2, dX, d2X = session.run([Y, Yd, Yd2], feed_dict={Xt:
X.reshape((nb_points*2, 1))})
```

We needed to reshape our array to be compliant with the placeholder. The first argument of `run()` is a list of tensors that we want to be computed. In this case, we need all operation outputs. The plot of each of them is shown in the following figure:

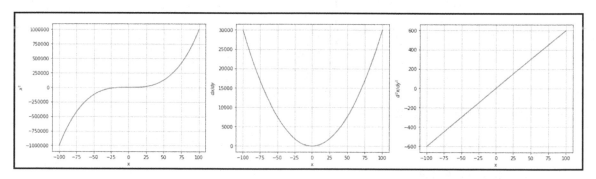

As expected, they represent respectively: x^3, $3x^2$, and $6x$.

Logistic regression

Now we can try a more complex example implementing a logistic regression algorithm. The first step, as usual, is creating a dummy dataset:

```
from sklearn.datasets import make_classification

>>> nb_samples = 500
>>> X, Y = make_classification(n_samples=nb_samples, n_features=2,
n_redundant=0, n_classes=2)
```

The dataset is shown in the following figure:

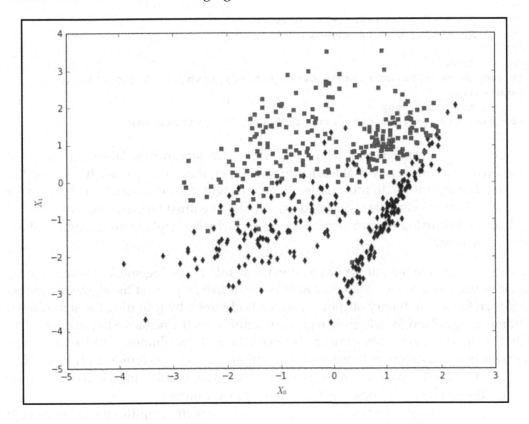

At this point, we can create the graph and all placeholders, variables, and operations:

```
import tensorflow as tf

>>> graph = tf.Graph()

>>> with graph.as_default():
>>>     Xt = tf.placeholder(tf.float32, shape=(None, 2), name='points')
>>>     Yt = tf.placeholder(tf.float32, shape=(None, 1), name='classes')
>>>
>>>     W = tf.Variable(tf.zeros((2, 1)), name='weights')
>>>     bias = tf.Variable(tf.zeros((1, 1)), name='bias')
>>>
>>>     Ye = tf.matmul(Xt, W) + bias
>>>     Yc = tf.round(tf.sigmoid(Ye))
>>>
>>>     loss =
tf.reduce_mean(tf.nn.sigmoid_cross_entropy_with_logits(logits=Ye,
labels=Yt))
>>>     training_step =
tf.train.GradientDescentOptimizer(0.025).minimize(loss)
```

The placeholder `Xt` is needed for the points, while `Yt` represents the labels. At this point, we need to involve a couple of variables: if you remember, they store values that are updated by the training algorithm. In this case, we need a weight vector `W` (with two elements) and a single `bias`. When a variable is declared, its initial value must be provided; we've decided to set both to zero using the function `tf.zeros()`, which accepts as argument the shape of the desired tensor.

Now we can compute the output (if you don't remember how logistic regression works, please step back to `Chapter 5`, *Logistic Regression*) in two steps: first the sigmoid exponent `Ye` and then the actual binary output `Yc`, which is obtained by rounding the sigmoid value. The training algorithm for a logistic regression minimizes the negative log-likelihood, which corresponds to the cross-entropy between the real distribution `Y` and `Yc`. It's easy to implement this loss function; however, the function `tf.log()` is numerically unstable (when its value becomes close to zero, it tends to negative infinity and yields a `NaN` value); therefore, TensorFlow has implemented a more robust function, `tf.nn.sigmoid_cross_entropy_with_logits()`, which computes the cross-entropy assuming the output is produced by a sigmoid. It takes two parameters, the `logits` (which corresponds to the exponent `Ye`) and the target `labels`, that are stored in `Yt`.

Now we can work with one of the most powerful TensorFlow features: the training optimizers. After defining a loss function, it will be dependent on placeholders, constants, and variables. A training optimizer (such as `tf.train.GradientDescentOptimizer()`), through its method `minimize()`, accepts the loss function to optimize. Internally, according to every specific algorithm, it will compute the gradients of the loss function with respect to all trainable variables and will apply the corresponding corrections to the values. The parameter passed to the optimizer is the learning rate.

Therefore, we have defined an extra operation called `training_step`, which corresponds to a single stateful update step. It doesn't matter how complex the graph is; all trainable variables involved in a loss function will be optimized with a single instruction.

Now it's time to train our logistic regression. The first thing to do is to ask TensorFlow to initialize all variables so that they are ready when the operations have to work with them:

```
>>> session = tf.InteractiveSession(graph=graph)
>>> tf.global_variables_initializer().run()
```

At this point, we can create a simple training loop (it should be stopped when the loss stops decreasing; however, we have a fixed number of iterations):

```
>>> feed_dict = {
>>>     Xt: X,
>>>     Yt: Y.reshape((nb_samples, 1))
>>> }

>>> for i in range(5000):
>>>     loss_value, _ = session.run([loss, training_step],
feed_dict=feed_dict)
>>>     if i % 100 == 0:
>>>     print('Step %d, Loss: %.3f' % (i, loss_value))
Step 0, Loss: 0.269
Step 100, Loss: 0.267
Step 200, Loss: 0.265
Step 300, Loss: 0.264
Step 400, Loss: 0.263
Step 500, Loss: 0.262
Step 600, Loss: 0.261
Step 700, Loss: 0.260
Step 800, Loss: 0.260
Step 900, Loss: 0.259
...
```

As you can see, at each iteration we ask TensorFlow to compute the loss function and a training step, and we always pass the same dictionary containing X and Y. At the end of this loop, the loss function is stable and we can check the quality of this logistic regression by plotting the separating hyperplane:

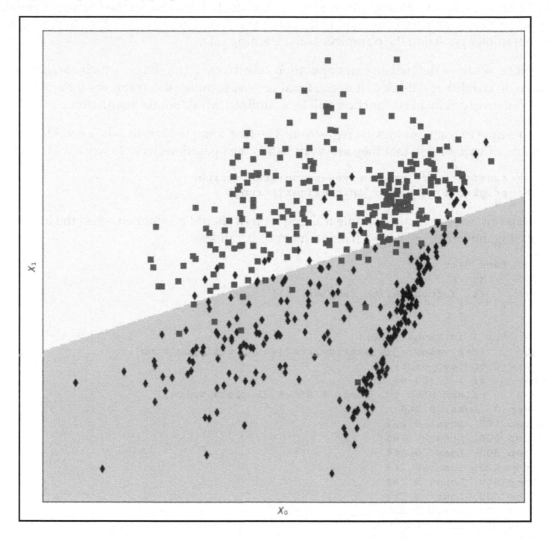

The result is approximately equivalent to the one obtained with the scikit-learn implementation. If we want to know the values of both coefficients (weights) and intercept (bias), we can ask TensorFlow to retrieve them by calling the method `eval()` on each variable:

```
>>> Wc, Wb = W.eval(), bias.eval()

>>> print(Wc)
[[-1.16501403]
 [ 3.10014033]]

>>> print(Wb)
[[-0.12583369]]
```

Classification with a multi-layer perceptron

We can now build an architecture with two dense layers and train a classifier for a more complex dataset. Let's start by creating it:

```
from sklearn.datasets import make_classification

>>> nb_samples = 1000
>>> nb_features = 3

>>> X, Y = make_classification(n_samples=nb_samples,
n_features=nb_features,
>>> n_informative=3, n_redundant=0, n_classes=2, n_clusters_per_class=3)
```

Even if we have only two classes, the dataset has three features and three clusters per class; therefore it's almost impossible that a linear classifier can separate it with very high accuracy. A plot of the dataset is shown in the following figure:

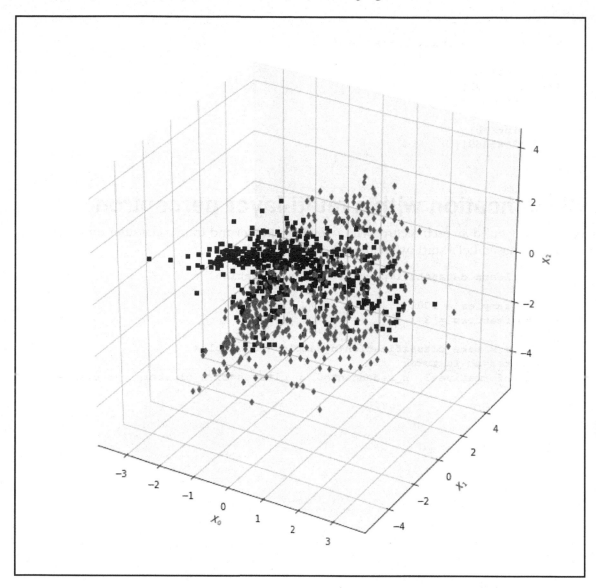

For benchmarking purposes, it's useful to test a logistic regression:

```
from sklearn.model_selection import train_test_split
from sklearn.linear_model import LogisticRegression

>>> X_train, X_test, Y_train, Y_test = train_test_split(X, Y,
test_size=0.2)

>>> lr = LogisticRegression()
>>> lr.fit(X_train, Y_train)
>>> print('Score: %.3f' % lr.score(X_test, Y_test))
Score: 0.715
```

The score computed on the test set is about 71%, which is not really bad but below an acceptable threshold. Let's try with an MLP with 50 hidden neurons (with hyperbolic tangent activation) and 1 sigmoid output neuron. The hyperbolic tangent is:

$$\tanh(x) = \frac{e^x - e^{-x}}{e^x + e^{-x}}$$

And it's bounded asymptotically between -1.0 and 1.0.

We are not going to implement each layer manually, but we're using the built-in class `tf.contrib.layers.fully_connected()`. It accepts the input tensor or placeholder as the first argument and the number of layer-output neurons as the second one. The activation function can be specified using the attribute `activation_fn`:

```
import tensorflow as tf
import tensorflow.contrib.layers as tfl

>>> graph = tf.Graph()

>>> with graph.as_default():
>>>     Xt = tf.placeholder(tf.float32, shape=(None, nb_features), name='X')
>>>     Yt = tf.placeholder(tf.float32, shape=(None, 1), name='Y')
>>>
>>>     layer_1 = tfl.fully_connected(Xt, num_outputs=50,
activation_fn=tf.tanh)
>>>     layer_2 = tfl.fully_connected(layer_1, num_outputs=1,
>>>                                   activation_fn=tf.sigmoid)
>>>
>>>     Yo = tf.round(layer_2)
>>>
```

```
>>>     loss = tf.nn.l2_loss(layer_2 - Yt)
>>>     training_step =
tf.train.GradientDescentOptimizer(0.025).minimize(loss)
```

As in the previous example, we have defined two placeholders, `Xt` and `Yt`, and two fully connected layers. The first one accepts as input `Xt` and has 50 output neurons (with `tanh` activation), while the second accepts as input the output of the previous layer (`layer_1`) and has only one sigmoid neuron, representing the class. The rounded output is provided by `Yo`, while the loss function is the total squared error, and it's implemented using the function `tf.nn.l2_loss()` computed on the difference between the output of the network (`layer_2`) and the target class placeholder `Yt`. The training step is implemented using a standard gradient descent optimizer, as for the logistic regression example.

We can now implement a training loop, splitting our dataset into a fixed number of batches (the number of samples is defined in the variable `batch_size`) and repeating a complete cycle for `nb_epochs` epochs:

```
>>> session = tf.InteractiveSession(graph=graph)
>>> tf.global_variables_initializer().run()

>>> nb_epochs = 200
>>> batch_size = 50

>>> for e in range(nb_epochs):
>>>     total_loss = 0.0
>>>     Xb = np.ndarray(shape=(batch_size, nb_features), dtype=np.float32)
>>>     Yb = np.ndarray(shape=(batch_size, 1), dtype=np.float32)
>>>
>>>     for i in range(0, X_train.shape[0]-batch_size, batch_size):
>>>         Xb[:, :] = X_train[i:i+batch_size, :]
>>>         Yb[:, 0] = Y_train[i:i+batch_size]
>>>
>>>         loss_value, _ = session.run([loss, training_step],
>>>                                     feed_dict={Xt: Xb, Yt: Yb})
>>>         total_loss += loss_value
>>>
>>>         Y_predicted = session.run([Yo],
>>>             feed_dict={Xt: X_test.reshape((X_test.shape[0],
nb_features))})
>>>         accuracy = 1.0 -
>>>             (np.sum(np.abs(np.array(Y_predicted[0]).squeeze(axis=1) -
Y_test)) /
>>>             float(Y_test.shape[0]))
>>>
>>>         print('Epoch %d) Total loss: %.2f - Accuracy: %.2f' %
>>>             (e, total_loss, accuracy))
```

```
Epoch 0)  Total loss:  78.19 - Accuracy:  0.66
Epoch 1)  Total loss:  75.02 - Accuracy:  0.67
Epoch 2)  Total loss:  72.28 - Accuracy:  0.68
Epoch 3)  Total loss:  68.52 - Accuracy:  0.71
Epoch 4)  Total loss:  63.50 - Accuracy:  0.79
Epoch 5)  Total loss:  57.51 - Accuracy:  0.84

. . .
Epoch 195)  Total loss:  15.34 - Accuracy:  0.94
Epoch 196)  Total loss:  15.32 - Accuracy:  0.94
Epoch 197)  Total loss:  15.31 - Accuracy:  0.94
Epoch 198)  Total loss:  15.29 - Accuracy:  0.94
Epoch 199)  Total loss:  15.28 - Accuracy:  0.94
```

As it's possible to see, without particular attention to all details, the accuracy computed on the test set is 94%. This is an acceptable value, considering the structure of the dataset. In Goodfellow I., Bengio Y., Courville A., *Deep Learning*, MIT Press, the reader will find details of many important concepts that can still improve the performance and speed up the convergence process.

Image convolution

Even if we're not building a complete deep learning model, we can test how convolution works with a simple example. The input image we're using is already provided by SciPy:

```
from scipy.misc import face

>>> img = face(gray=True)
```

The original picture is shown here:

We're going to apply a Laplacian filter, which emphasizes the boundary of each shape:

```
import numpy as np

>>> kernel = np.array(
>>>     [[0, 1, 0],
>>>      [1, -4, 0],
>>>      [0, 1, 0]],
>>>     dtype=np.float32)

>>> cfilter = np.zeros((3, 3, 1, 1), dtype=np.float32)
>>> cfilter[:, :, 0, 0] = kernel
```

The kernel must be repeated twice because the TensorFlow convolution function `tf.nn.conv2d` expects an input and an output filter. We can now build the graph and test it:

```
import tensorflow as tf

>>> graph = tf.Graph()

>>> with graph.as_default():
>>>     x = tf.placeholder(tf.float32, shape=(None, 768, 1024, 1),
name='image')
>>>     f = tf.constant(cfilter)
```

```
>>>     y = tf.nn.conv2d(x, f, strides=[1, 1, 1, 1], padding='SAME')

>>> session = tf.InteractiveSession(graph=graph)

>>> c_img = session.run([y], feed_dict={x: img.reshape((1, 768, 1024, 1))})
>>> n_img = np.array(c_img).reshape((768, 1024))
```

The parameters `strides` is a four-dimensional vector (each value corresponds to the input dimensions, so the first is the batch and the last one is the number of channels) that specifies how many pixels the sliding window must shift. In this case, we want to cover all the image shifting pixel to pixel. The parameter `padding` determines how the new dimensions must be computed and whether it's necessary to apply a zero padding. In our case, we're using the value `SAME`, which computes the dimensions by rounding off to the next integer the original dimensions divided by the corresponding strides value (as the latter are both 1.0, the resulting image size will be exactly like the original one).

The output image is shown here:

 The installation instructions for every operating system can be found on h ttps://www.tensorflow.org/install/.

A quick glimpse inside Keras

Keras (`https://keras.io`) is a high-level deep learning framework that works seamlessly with low-level backends like TensorFlow, Theano or CNTK. In Keras a model is like a sequence of layers where each output is fed into the following computational block until the final layer is reached. The generic structure of a model is:

```
from keras.models import Sequential

>>> model = Sequential()

>>> model.add(...)
>>> model.add(...)
...
>>> model.add(...)
```

The class `Sequential` defines a generic empty model, that already implements all the methods needed to `add` layers, `compile` the model according to the underlying framework, to `fit` and `evaluate` the model and to `predict` the output given an input. All the most common layers are already implemented, including:

- Dense, Dropout and Flattening layers
- Convolutional (1D, 2D and 3D) layers
- Pooling layers
- Zero padding layers
- RNN layers

A model can be compiled using several loss functions (like MSE or cross-entropy) and all the most diffused Stochastic Gradient Descent optimization algorithms (like RMSProp or Adam). For further details about the mathematical foundation of these methods, please refer to Goodfellow I., Bengio Y., Courville A., *Deep Learning*, MIT Press. As it's impossible to discuss all important elements in such a short space, I prefer to create a complete example of image classification based on a convolutional network. The dataset we're going to use is the CIFAR-10 (`https://www.cs.toronto.edu/~kriz/cifar.html`) which is made up of 60000 small RGB images (32 x 32) belonging to 10 different categories (airplane, automobile, bird, cat, deer, dog, frog, horse, ship, truck). In the following figure, a subset of images is shown:

Since the last release, Keras allows us to download this dataset using a built-in function; therefore, no further actions are required to use it.

The first step is loading the dataset and splitting it into training and test subsets:

```
from keras.datasets import cifar10

>>> (X_train, Y_train), (X_test, Y_test) = cifar10.load_data()
```

The training dataset contains 50000 images, while the test set 10000. Now it's possible to build the model. We want to use a few convolutional layers to capture the specific elements of each category. As explained in the previous section, these particular layers can learn to identify specific geometric properties and generalize in an excellent way. In our small architecture, we start with a (5 x 5) filter size to capture all the low-level features (like the orientation) and proceed by increasing the number of filters and reducing their size. In this way, the high-level features (like the shape of a wheel or the relative position of eyes, nose, and mouth) can also be captured.

```
from keras.models import Sequential
from keras.layers.convolutional import Conv2D, ZeroPadding2D
from keras.layers.pooling import MaxPooling2D

>>> model = Sequential()

>>> model.add(Conv2D(32, kernel_size=(5, 5), activation='relu',
input_shape=(32 ,32, 3)))
>>> model.add(MaxPooling2D(pool_size=(2, 2)))

>>> model.add(Conv2D(64, kernel_size=(4, 4), activation='relu'))
>>> model.add(ZeroPadding2D((1, 1)))

>>> model.add(Conv2D(128, kernel_size=(3, 3), activation='relu'))
>>> model.add(MaxPooling2D(pool_size=(2, 2)))
>>> model.add(ZeroPadding2D((1, 1)))
```

The first instruction creates a new empty model. At this point, we can all the layers we want to include in the computational graph. The most common parameters of a convolutional layer are:

- **The number of filters**
- **Kernel size** (as tuple)
- **Strides** (the default value is [1, 1]). This parameter specifies how many pixels the sliding window must consider when shifting on the image. [1, 1] means that no pixels are discarded. [2, 2] means that every horizontal and vertical shift will have a width of 2 pixels and so forth.
- **Activation** (the default value is None, meaning that the identity function will be used)
- **Input shape** (only for the first layer is this parameter mandatory)

Our first layer has 32 (5 x 5) filters with a **ReLU (Rectified Linear Unit)** activation. This function is defined as:

$$f_{ReLU}(x) = \max(0, x)$$

The second layer reduces the dimensionality with a max pooling considering (2 x 2) blocks. Then we apply another convolution with 64 (4 x 4) filters followed by a zero padding (1 pixel at the top, bottom, left and right side of the input) and finally, we have the third convolutional layer with 128 (3 x 3) filters followed by a max pooling and a zero padding.

At this point, we need to flatten the output of the last layer, so to work like in a MLP:

```
from keras.layers.core import Dense, Dropout, Flatten

>>> model.add(Dropout(0.2))
>>> model.add(Flatten())
>>> model.add(Dense(128, activation='relu'))
>>> model.add(Dropout(0.2))
>>> model.add(Dense(10, activation='softmax'))
```

A dropout (with a probability of 0.2) is applied to the output of the last zero-padding layer; then this multidimensional value is flattened and transformed in a vector. This value is fed into a fully-connected layer with 128 neurons and ReLU activation. Another dropout is applied to the output (to prevent the overfitting) and, finally, this vector is fed into another fully connected layer with 10 neurons with a *softmax* activation:

$$f_{Softmax}(x) = \frac{e^x}{\sum_i e^{x_i}}$$

In this way, the output of the model represents a discrete probability distribution (each value is the probability of the corresponding class).

The last step before training the model is compiling it:

```
>>> model.compile(loss='categorical_crossentropy', optimizer='adam',
metrics=['accuracy'])
```

Keras will transform the high-level description into low-level operations (like the ones we have discussed in the previous section) with a categorical cross-entropy loss function (see the example of TensorFlow logistic regression) and the Adam optimizer. Moreover, it will apply an accuracy metric to dynamically evaluate the performance.

At this point, the model can be trained. We need only two preliminary operations:

- Normalizing the images so they have values between 0 and 1
- Applying the one-hot encoding to the integer label

The first operation can be simply performed by dividing the dataset by 255, while the second can be easily carried out using the built-in function `to_categorical()`:

```
from keras.utils import to_categorical

>>> model.fit(X_train / 255.0, to_categorical(Y_train), batch_size=32,
epochs=15)
```

We want to train with batches made up of 32 images and for a period of 15 epochs. The reader is free to change all these values to compare the results. The output provided by Keras shows the progress in the learning phase:

```
Epoch 1/15
50000/50000 [==============================] - 25s - loss: 1.5845 - acc:
0.4199
Epoch 2/15
50000/50000 [==============================] - 24s - loss: 1.2368 - acc:
0.5602
Epoch 3/15
50000/50000 [==============================] - 26s - loss: 1.0678 - acc:
0.6247
Epoch 4/15
50000/50000 [==============================] - 25s - loss: 0.9495 - acc:
0.6658
Epoch 5/15
50000/50000 [==============================] - 26s - loss: 0.8598 - acc:
0.6963
Epoch 6/15
50000/50000 [==============================] - 26s - loss: 0.7829 - acc:
0.7220
Epoch 7/15
50000/50000 [==============================] - 26s - loss: 0.7204 - acc:
0.7452
Epoch 8/15
50000/50000 [==============================] - 26s - loss: 0.6712 - acc:
0.7629
Epoch 9/15
50000/50000 [==============================] - 27s - loss: 0.6286 - acc:
0.7779
Epoch 10/15
50000/50000 [==============================] - 27s - loss: 0.5753 - acc:
0.7952
```

```
Epoch 11/15
50000/50000 [==============================] - 27s - loss: 0.5433 - acc:
0.8049
Epoch 12/15
50000/50000 [==============================] - 27s - loss: 0.5112 - acc:
0.8170
Epoch 13/15
50000/50000 [==============================] - 27s - loss: 0.4806 - acc:
0.8293
Epoch 14/15
50000/50000 [==============================] - 28s - loss: 0.4551 - acc:
0.8365
Epoch 15/15
50000/50000 [==============================] - 28s - loss: 0.4342 - acc:
0.8444
```

At the end of the 15th epoch, the accuracy on the training set is about 84% (a very good result). The final operation is evaluating the model with the test set:

```
>>> scores = model.evaluate(X_test / 255.0, to_categorical(Y_test))
>>> print('Loss: %.3f' % scores[0])
>>> print('Accuracy: %.3f' % scores[1])
Loss: 0.972
Accuracy: 0.719
```

The final validation accuracy is lower (about 72%) than the one achieved during the training phase. This is a normal behavior for deep models, therefore, when optimizing the algorithm, it's always a good practice to use the cross validation or a well-defined test set (with the same distribution of the training set and 25-30% of total samples).

Of course, we have presented a very simple architecture, but the reader can go deeper into these topics and create more complex models (Keras also contains some very famous pre-trained architectures like VGG16/19 and Inception V3 that can also be used to perform image classifications with 1000 categories).

 All the information needed to install Keras with different backends, and the official documentation can be found on the website: https://keras.io

References

- Goodfellow I., Bengio Y., Courville A., *Deep Learning*, MIT Press
- Abrahams S., Hafner D., *TensorFlow for Machine Intelligence: A Hands-On Introduction to Learning Algorithms*, Bleeding Edge Press
- Bonaccorso G., *Neural Artistic Style Transfer with Keras,* `https://github.com/giu seppebonaccorso/Neural_Artistic_Style_Transfer`
- Krizhevsky A, Learning Multiple Layers of Features from Tiny Images, 2009 (`https://www.cs.toronto.edu/~kriz/learning-features-2009-TR.pdf`)

Summary

In this chapter, we have briefly discussed some basic deep learning concepts, and the reader should now understand what a computational graph is and how it can be modeled using TensorFlow. A deep architecture, in fact, can be seen as a sequence of layers connected to each other. They can have different characteristics and purposes, but the overall graph is always a directed structure that associates input values with a final output layer. Therefore, it's possible to derive a global loss function that will be optimized by a training algorithm. We also saw how TensorFlow computes the gradients of an output tensor with respect to any previous connected layer and therefore how it's possible to implement the standard back-propagation strategy seamlessly to deep architectures. We did not discuss actual deep learning problems and methods because they require much more space; however, the reader can easily find many valid resources to continue his/her exploration in this fascinating field.

In the next chapter, we're going to summarize many of the concepts previously discussed in order to create complex machine learning architectures.

15
Creating a Machine Learning Architecture

In this chapter, we're going to summarize many of the concepts discussed in the book with the purpose of defining a complete machine learning architecture that is able to preprocess the input data, decompose/augment it, classify/cluster it, and eventually, show the results using graphical tools. We're also going to show how scikit-learn manages complex pipelines and how it's possible to fit them, and search for the optimal parameters in the global context of a complete architecture.

Machine learning architectures

Until now we have discussed single methods that could be employed to solve specific problems. However, in real contexts, it's very unlikely to have well-defined datasets that can be immediately fed into a standard classifier or clustering algorithm. A machine learning engineer often has to design a full architecture that a non-expert could consider like a black-box where the raw data enters and the outcomes are automatically produced. All the steps necessary to achieve the final goal must be correctly organized and seamlessly joined together in a processing chain similar to a computational graph (indeed, it's very often a direct acyclic graph). Unfortunately, this is a non-standard process, as every real-life problem has its own peculiarities. However, there are some common steps which are normally included in almost any ML pipeline.

In the following picture, there's a schematic representation of this process:

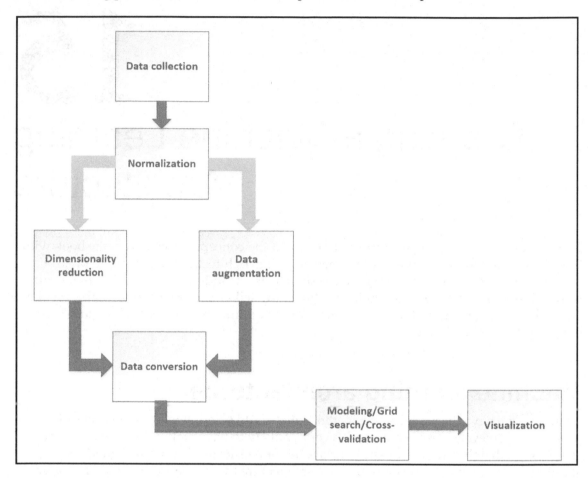

Now we will briefly explain the details of each phase with some possible solutions.

Data collection

The first step is always the most generic because it depends on each single context. However, before working with any data, it's necessary to collect it from all the sources where it's stored. The ideal situation is to have a **comma separated values (CSV)** (or another suitable format) dump that can be immediately loaded, but more often, the engineer has to look for all the database tables, define the right SQL query to collect all the pieces of information, and manage data type conversion and encoding. We're not going to discuss this topic, but it's important not to under-evaluate this stage because it can be much more difficult than expected. I suggest, whenever possible, to extract flattened tables, where all the fields are placed on the same row, because it's easier to manipulate a large amount of data using a DBMS or a big data tool, but it can be very time and memory consuming if done on a normal PC directly with Python tools. Moreover, it's important to use a standard character encoding for all text fields. The most common choice is UTF-8, but it's also possible to find DB tables encoded with other charsets and normally it's a good practice to convert all the documents before starting with the other operations. A very famous and powerful Python library for data manipulation is pandas (part of SciPy). It's based on the concept of DataFrame (an abstraction of SQL table) and implements many methods that allow the selection, joining, grouping, and statistical processing of datasets that can fit in memory. In *Heydt M., Learning pandas - Python Data Discovery and Analysis Made Easy*, Packt, the reader can find all the information needed to use this library to solve many real-life problems. A common problem that must be managed during this phase, is imputing the missing features. In `Chapter 3`, *Feature Selection and Feature Engineering*, we discussed some practical methods that can be employed automatically before starting with the following steps.

Normalization

Normalizing a numeric dataset is one of the most important steps, particularly when different features have different scales. In Chapter 3, *Feature Selection and Feature Engineering*, we discussed several methods that can be employed to solve this problem. Very often, it's enough to use a StandardScaler to whiten the data, but sometimes it's better to consider the impact of noisy features on the global trend and use a RobustScaler to filter them out without the risk of conditioning the remaining features. The reader can easily verify the different performances of the same classifier (in particular, SVMs and neural networks) when working with normalized and unnormalized datasets. As we're going to see in the next section, it's possible to include the normalization step in the processing pipeline as one of the first actions and include the C parameter in grid search in order to impose an *L1/L2* weight normalization during the training phase (see the importance of regularization in Chapter 4, *Linear Regression*, when discussing about Ridge, Lasso and ElasticNet).

Dimensionality reduction

This step is not always mandatory, but, in many cases, it can be a good solution to memory leaks or long computational times. When the dataset has many features, the probability of some hidden correlation is relatively high. For example, the final price of a product is directly influenced by the price of all materials and, if we remove one secondary element, the value changes slightly (more generally speaking, we can say that the total variance is almost preserved). If you remember how PCA works, you know that this process decorrelates the input data too. Therefore, it's useful to check whether a PCA or a Kernel PCA (for non-linear datasets) can remove some components while keeping the explained variance close to 100 percent (this is equivalent to compressing the data with minimum information loss). There are also other methods discussed in Chapter 3, *Feature Selection and Feature Engineering* (like NMF or SelectKBest), that can be useful for selecting only the best features according to various criteria (like ANOVA or chi-squared). Testing the impact of each factor during the initial phases of the project can save time that can be useful when it's necessary to evaluate slower and more complex algorithms.

Data augmentation

Sometimes the original dataset has only a few non-linear features and it's quite difficult for a standard classifier to capture the dynamics. Moreover, forcing an algorithm on a complex dataset can result in overfitting the model because all the capacity is exhausted in trying to minimize the error considering only the training set, and without taking into account the generalization ability. For this reason, it's sometimes useful to enrich the dataset with derived features that are obtained through functions of the existing ones.
`PolynomialFeatures` is an example of data augmentation that can really improve the performances of standard algorithms and avoid overfitting. In other cases, it can be useful to introduce trigonometric functions (like $sin(x)$ or $cos(x)$) or correlating features (like $x_1 x_2$). The former allows a simpler management of radial datasets, while the latter can provide the classifier with information about the cross-correlation between two features. In general, data augmentation can be employed before trying a more complex algorithm; for example, a logistic regression (that is a linear method) can be successfully applied to augmented non-linear datasets (we saw a similar situation in `Chapter 4`, *Linear Regression*, when we had discussed the polynomial regression). The choice to employ a more complex (with higher capacity) model or to try to augment the dataset is up to the engineer and must be considered carefully, taking into account both the pros and the cons. In many cases, for example, it's preferable not to modify the original dataset (which could be quite large), but to create a scikit-learn interface to augment the data in real time. In other cases, a neural model can provide faster and more accurate results without the need for data augmentation. Together with parameter selection, this is more of an art than a real science, and the experiments are the only way to gather useful knowledge.

Data conversion

This step is probably the simplest and, at the same time, the most important when handling categorical data. We have discussed several methods to encode labels using numerical vectors and it's not necessary to repeat the concepts already explained. A general rule concerns the usage of integer or binary values (one-hot encoding). The latter is probably the best choice when the output of the classifier is the value itself, because, as discussed in `Chapter 3`, *Feature Selection and Feature Engineering*, it's much more robust to noise and prediction errors. On the other hand, one-hot encoding is quite memory-consuming. Therefore, whenever it's necessary to work with probability distributions (like in NLP), an integer label (representing a dictionary entry or a frequency/count value) can be much more efficient.

Modeling/Grid search/Cross-validation

Modeling implies the choice of the classification/clustering algorithm that best suits every specific task. We have discussed different methods and the reader should be able to understand when a set of algorithms is a reasonable candidate, and when it's better to look for another strategy. However, the success of a machine learning technique often depends on the right choice of each parameter involved in the model as well. As already discussed, when talking about data augmentation, it's very difficult to find a precise method to determine the optimal values to assign, and the best approach is always based on a grid search. scikit-learn provides a very flexible mechanism to investigate the performance of a model with different parameter combinations, together with cross-validation (that allows a robust validation without reducing the number of training samples), and this is indeed a more reasonable approach, even for experts engineers. Moreover, when performing different transformations, the effect of a choice can impact the whole pipeline, and, therefore, (we're going to see a few examples in the next section) I always suggest for application of the grid search to all components at the same time, to be able to evaluate the cross-influence of each possible choice.

Visualization

Sometimes, it's useful/necessary to visualize the results of intermediate and final steps. In this book, we have always shown plots and diagrams using matplotlib, which is part of SciPy and provides a flexible and powerful graphics infrastructure. Even if it's not part of the book, the reader can easily modify the code in order to get different results; for a deeper understanding, refer to Mcgreggor D., *Mastering matplotlib*, Packt. As this is an evolving sector, many new projects are being developed, offering new and more stylish plotting functions. One of them is Bokeh (`http://bokeh.pydata.org`), that works using some JavaScript code to create interactive graphs that can be embedded into web pages too.

scikit-learn tools for machine learning architectures

Now we're going to present two very important scikit-learn classes that can help the machine learning engineer to create complex processing structures including all the steps needed to generate the desired outcomes from the raw datasets.

Pipelines

scikit-learn provides a flexible mechanism for creating pipelines made up of subsequent processing steps. This is possible thanks to a standard interface implemented by the majority of classes therefore most of the components (both data processors/transformers and classifiers/clustering tools) can be exchanged seamlessly. The class `Pipeline` accepts a single parameter `steps`, which is a list of tuples in the form (name of the component—instance), and creates a complex object with the standard fit/transform interface. For example, if we need to apply a PCA, a standard scaling, and then we want to classify using a SVM, we could create a pipeline in the following way:

```
from sklearn.decomposition import PCA
from sklearn.pipeline import Pipeline
from sklearn.preprocessing import StandardScaler
from sklearn.svm import SVC

>>> pca = PCA(n_components=10)
>>> scaler = StandardScaler()
>>> svc = SVC(kernel='poly', gamma=3)

>>> steps = [
>>>     ('pca', pca),
>>>     ('scaler', scaler),
>>>     ('classifier', svc)
>>> ]

>>> pipeline = Pipeline(steps)
```

At this point, the pipeline can be fitted like a single classifier (using the standard methods `fit()` and `fit_transform()`), even if the the input samples are first passed to the `PCA` instance, the reduced dataset is normalized by the `StandardScaler` instance, and finally, the resulting samples are passed to the classifier.

A pipeline is also very useful together with `GridSearchCV`, to evaluate different combinations of parameters, not limited to a single step but considering the whole process. Considering the previous example, we can create a dummy dataset and try to find the optimal parameters:

```
from sklearn.datasets import make_classification

>>> nb_samples = 500
>>> X, Y = make_classification(n_samples=nb_samples, n_informative=15,
n_redundant=5, n_classes=2)
```

The dataset is quite redundant. Therefore, we need to find the optimal number of components for PCA and the best kernel for the SVM. When working with a pipeline, the name of the parameter must be specified using the component ID followed by a double underscore and then the actual name, for example, `classifier__kernel` (if you want to check all the acceptable parameters with the right name, it's enough to execute: `print(pipeline.get_params().keys())`). Therefore, we can perform a grid search with the following parameter dictionary:

```
from sklearn.model_selection import GridSearchCV

>>> param_grid = {
>>>     'pca__n_components': [5, 10, 12, 15, 18, 20],
>>>     'classifier__kernel': ['rbf', 'poly'],
>>>     'classifier__gamma': [0.05, 0.1, 0.2, 0.5],
>>>     'classifier__degree': [2, 3, 5]
>>> }

>>> gs = GridSearchCV(pipeline, param_grid)
>>> gs.fit(X, Y)
```

As expected, the best estimator (which is a complete pipeline) has 15 principal components (that means they are uncorrelated) and a radial-basis function SVM with a relatively high `gamma` value (0.2):

```
>>> print(gs.best_estimator_)
Pipeline(steps=[('pca', PCA(copy=True, iterated_power='auto',
n_components=15, random_state=None,
  svd_solver='auto', tol=0.0, whiten=False)), ('scaler',
StandardScaler(copy=True, with_mean=True, with_std=True)), ('classifier',
SVC(C=1.0, cache_size=200, class_weight=None, coef0=0.0,
  decision_function_shape=None, degree=2, gamma=0.2, kernel='rbf',
  max_iter=-1, probability=False, random_state=None, shrinking=True,
  tol=0.001, verbose=False))])
```

The corresponding score is:

```
>>> print(gs.best_score_)
0.96
```

It's also possible to use a `Pipeline` together with `GridSearchCV` to evaluate different combinations. For example, it can be useful to compare some decomposition methods, mixed with various classifiers:

```
from sklearn.datasets import load_digits
from sklearn.decomposition import NMF
from sklearn.feature_selection import SelectKBest, f_classif
from sklearn.linear_model import LogisticRegression

>>> digits = load_digits()

>>> pca = PCA()
>>> nmf = NMF()
>>> kbest = SelectKBest(f_classif)
>>> lr = LogisticRegression()

>>> pipeline_steps = [
>>>     ('dimensionality_reduction', pca),
>>>     ('normalization', scaler),
>>>     ('classification', lr)
>>> ]

>>> pipeline = Pipeline(pipeline_steps)
```

We want to compare **principal component analysis (PCA)**, **non-negative matrix factorization (NMF)**, and k-best feature selection based on the ANOVA criterion, together with logistic regression and kernelized SVM:

```
>>> pca_nmf_components = [10, 20, 30]

>>> param_grid = [
>>>     {
>>>         'dimensionality_reduction': [pca],
>>>         'dimensionality_reduction__n_components': pca_nmf_components,
>>>         'classification': [lr],
>>>         'classification__C': [1, 5, 10, 20]
>>>     },
>>>     {
>>>         'dimensionality_reduction': [pca],
>>>         'dimensionality_reduction__n_components': pca_nmf_components,
>>>         'classification': [svc],
>>>         'classification__kernel': ['rbf', 'poly'],
>>>         'classification__gamma': [0.05, 0.1, 0.2, 0.5, 1.0],
>>>         'classification__degree': [2, 3, 5],
>>>         'classification__C': [1, 5, 10, 20]
>>>     },
>>>     {
```

```
>>>          'dimensionality_reduction': [nmf],
>>>          'dimensionality_reduction__n_components': pca_nmf_components,
>>>          'classification': [lr],
>>>          'classification__C': [1, 5, 10, 20]
>>>      },
>>>      {
>>>          'dimensionality_reduction': [nmf],
>>>          'dimensionality_reduction__n_components': pca_nmf_components,
>>>          'classification': [svc],
>>>          'classification__kernel': ['rbf', 'poly'],
>>>          'classification__gamma': [0.05, 0.1, 0.2, 0.5, 1.0],
>>>          'classification__degree': [2, 3, 5],
>>>          'classification__C': [1, 5, 10, 20]
>>>      },
>>>      {
>>>          'dimensionality_reduction': [kbest],
>>>          'classification': [svc],
>>>          'classification__kernel': ['rbf', 'poly'],
>>>          'classification__gamma': [0.05, 0.1, 0.2, 0.5, 1.0],
>>>          'classification__degree': [2, 3, 5],
>>>          'classification__C': [1, 5, 10, 20]
>>>      },
>>> ]

>>> gs = GridSearchCV(pipeline, param_grid)
>>> gs.fit(digits.data, digits.target)
```

Performing a grid search, we get the pipeline made up of PCA with 20 components (the original dataset 64 features) and an RBF SVM with a very small gamma value (0.05) and a medium (5.0) *L2* penalty parameter C :

```
>>> print(gs.best_estimator_)
Pipeline(steps=[('dimensionality_reduction', PCA(copy=True,
iterated_power='auto', n_components=20, random_state=None,
  svd_solver='auto', tol=0.0, whiten=False)), ('normalization',
StandardScaler(copy=True, with_mean=True, with_std=True)),
('classification', SVC(C=5.0, cache_size=200, class_weight=None, coef0=0.0,
  decision_function_shape=None, degree=2, gamma=0.05, kernel='rbf',
  max_iter=-1, probability=False, random_state=None, shrinking=True,
  tol=0.001, verbose=False))])
```

Considering the need to capture small details in the digit representations, these values are an optimal choice. The score for this pipeline is indeed very high:

```
>>> print(gs.best_score_)
0.968836950473
```

Feature unions

Another interesting class provided by scikit-learn is FeatureUnion, which allows concatenating different feature transformations into a single output matrix. The main difference with a pipeline (which can also include a feature union) is that the pipeline selects from alternative scenarios, while a feature union creates a unified dataset where different preprocessing outcomes are joined together. For example, considering the previous results, we could try to optimize our dataset by performing a PCA with 10 components joined with the selection of the best 5 features chosen according to the ANOVA metric. In this way, the dimensionality is reduced to 15 instead of 20:

```
from sklearn.pipeline import FeatureUnion

>>> steps_fu = [
>>>     ('pca', PCA(n_components=10)),
>>>     ('kbest', SelectKBest(f_classif, k=5)),
>>> ]

>>> fu = FeatureUnion(steps_fu)

>>> svc = SVC(kernel='rbf', C=5.0, gamma=0.05)

>>> pipeline_steps = [
>>>     ('fu', fu),
>>>     ('scaler', scaler),
>>>     ('classifier', svc)
>>> ]

>>> pipeline = Pipeline(pipeline_steps)
```

We already know that a RBF SVM is a good choice, and, therefore, we keep the remaining part of the architecture without modifications. Performing a cross-validation, we get:

```
from sklearn.model_selection import cross_val_score

>>> print(cross_val_score(pipeline, digits.data, digits.target,
cv=10).mean())
0.965464333604
```

The score is slightly lower than before (< 0.002) but the number of features has been considerably reduced and therefore also the computational time. Joining the outputs of different data preprocessors is a form of data augmentation and it must always be taken into account when the original number of features is too high or redundant/noisy and a single decomposition method doesn't succeed in capturing all the dynamics.

References

- Mcgreggor D., *Mastering matplotlib*, Packt
- Heydt M., *Learning pandas - Python Data Discovery and Analysis Made Easy*, Packt

Summary

In this final chapter, we discussed the main elements of machine learning architecture, considering some common scenarios and the procedures that are normally employed to prevent issues and improve the global performance. None of these steps should be discarded without a careful evaluation because the success of a model is determined by the joint action of many parameter, and hyperparameters, and finding the optimal final configuration starts with considering all possible preprocessing steps.

We saw that a grid search is a powerful investigation tool and that it's often a good idea to use it together with a complete set of alternative pipelines (with or without feature unions), so as to find the best solution in the context of a global scenario. Modern personal computers are fast enough to test hundreds of combinations in a few hours, and when the datasets are too large, it's possible to provision a cloud server using one of the existing providers.

Finally, I'd like to repeat that till now (also considering the research in the deep learning field), creating an up-and-running machine learning architecture needs a continuous analysis of alternative solutions and configurations, and there's no silver bullet for any but the simplest cases. This is a science that still keeps an artistic heart!

Index

CPSIA information can be obtained
at www.ICGtesting.com
Printed in the USA
LVOW04s2327110318
569504LV00003B/68/P